The VELVETEEN RABBIT at 100

Portrait of Margery Williams Bianco by James Bolivar Manson, 1911.
Courtesy of National Portrait Gallery, Smithsonian Institution.

Children's Literature Association Series

The VELVETEEN RABBIT at 100

Edited by Lisa Rowe Fraustino

University Press of Mississippi / Jackson

The University Press of Mississippi is the scholarly publishing agency of
the Mississippi Institutions of Higher Learning: Alcorn State University,
Delta State University, Jackson State University, Mississippi State University,
Mississippi University for Women, Mississippi Valley State University,
University of Mississippi, and University of Southern Mississippi.

www.upress.state.ms.us

The University Press of Mississippi is a member
of the Association of University Presses.

Copyright © 2023 by University Press of Mississippi
All rights reserved

First printing 2023

∞

Library of Congress Cataloging-in-Publication Data

Names: Fraustino, Lisa Rowe, editor.
Title: The Velveteen Rabbit at 100 / Lisa Rowe Fraustino.
Other titles: Children's Literature Association series.
Description: Jackson : University Press of Mississippi, 2023. | Series:
Children's literature association series | Includes bibliographical
references and index.
Identifiers: LCCN 2023003141 (print) | LCCN 2023003142 (ebook) | ISBN
9781496845993 (hardback) | ISBN 9781496846006 (trade paperback) | ISBN
9781496846013 (epub) | ISBN 9781496846020 (epub) | ISBN 9781496846037
(pdf) | ISBN 9781496846044 (pdf)
Subjects: LCSH: Bianco, Margery Williams, 1881–1944. Velveteen rabbit. |
Children's literature—History and criticism. | Fantasy
literature—History and criticism. | Fantasy fiction—History and
criticism. | Philosophy in literature. | Children—Books and reading.
Classification: LCC PS3503.I193 Z93 2023 (print) | LCC PS3503.I193
(ebook) | DDC 813/.52—dc23/eng/20230222
LC record available at https://lccn.loc.gov/2023003141
LC ebook record available at https://lccn.loc.gov/2023003142

British Library Cataloging-in-Publication Data available

*To Dan Deloria, my wonderful husband
who shows sincere interest in my work,
and our dog, Cholla,
who has an undying interest
in rabbits both plush and real.*

Contents

ix   Acknowledgments

3   Introduction. *The Velveteen Rabbit* at 100
        —Lisa Rowe Fraustino

23   Chapter 1. Virtual Realities: Animation and Simulacrum in
        The Velveteen Rabbit's Tradition and Legacy
        —Holly Blackford Humes

38   Chapter 2. Visualizing Velveteen: Original Illustrations and
        Subsequent Adaptations
        —Kelly Blewett and Alisa Clapp-Itnyre

62   Chapter 3. Plush, Plastic, and Plato: Purpose and Being in
        The Velveteen Rabbit and *Toy Story*
        —Melanie Hurley

78   Chapter 4. Personhood and Love: Interrogating "Realness" in
        The Velveteen Rabbit
        —Claudia Mills

90   Chapter 5. Becoming Real through Matter That Matters:
        An Onto-Epistemological Analysis of *The Velveteen Rabbit*
        —Adrianna Zabrzewska

103   Chapter 6. "Real" Stuffed Animals: Rabbit Tales in the Anthropocene
        —Jiwon Rim

114   Chapter 7. Illustrations and the Eco-Reality of *The Velveteen Rabbit*
        —Wenduo Zhang

130	Chapter 8. *The Velveteen Rabbit* in Italy —Claudia Camicia and Elena Paruolo
156	Chapter 9. Boy Caretaking and Authority in a Twenty-First-Century Fairy Tale —Paige Sammartino
166	Chapter 10. Born-Again Bunnies: The Velveteen Rabbit, Edward Tulane, and Redemptive Love —Maleeha Malik, Elisabeth Graves, and Lisa Rowe Fraustino
181	Chapter 11. "For Nursery Magic Is Very Strange and Wonderful": The Queer Space of the Nursery in *The Velveteen Rabbit* —Karlie Herndon
197	Chapter 12. Metamorphosis: The Disabled Toy Made "Real" as an Eternally Abled Rabbit —Scott T. Pollard and Kara K. Keeling
211	Chapter 13. Whiteness and the Selective Tradition in *The Velveteen Rabbit* —KaaVonia Hinton
229	About the Contributors
235	Index

Acknowledgments

First, I must thank the contributors of these thirteen fine essays, created in the depths of a pandemic in the midst of political turmoil. Despite difficulties in obtaining research materials during lockdown, despite the weights of fears, anxieties, losses, and COVID brain fog that we all lived through even if we didn't contract the virus, these scholars kept at the work. They refined their arguments through multiple drafts and placed their scholarship in conversation with one another in ways that I hope readers will find interesting and useful.

Marilla MacGregor, the Hollins graduate student who served as the editorial intern on this volume, made invaluable contributions. Her questions and suggestions helped to make all the essays stronger. She deserves many thanks.

My own scholarly interest in *The Velveteen Rabbit* grew from my teaching while focusing on rabbit stories as a case study on critical approaches to anthropomorphism and animal studies in children's literature and culture. Thus, I must thank the hundreds of students in my classes over the years who have contributed to my evolving thoughts on animal stories in general and *The Velveteen Rabbit* in particular.

I especially want to thank Maleeha Malik, who in a Hollins University graduate seminar on anthropomorphism made the stunning connection between *The Velveteen Rabbit* and Kate DiCamillo's *The Miraculous Journey of Edward Tulane* that led to our collaboration on our chapter in this volume. To broaden my understanding of the text, I assigned *Edward Tulane* to an undergraduate class at Eastern Connecticut State University, where Elisabeth Graves completed her final project on *Edward* as a religious allegory—and the collaboration became a trinity.

Finally, I thank the anonymous readers of the draft manuscript whose careful review and thoughtful commentary made the volume so much better.

—Lisa Rowe Fraustino

The VELVETEEN RABBIT at 100

Introduction

The Velveteen Rabbit at 100

—Lisa Rowe Fraustino

> The rabbit finds the idea melancholy: he wants the prize of life without the decline that goes with it. But, like all of us, there is nothing that he can do.
> —Margaret Blount, *Animal Land* (189)

In the midst of my editing this volume during the novel coronavirus pandemic, Jared Misner contributed an essay to the Modern Love section of the *New York Times* titled "My Best Friend Is Gone, and Nothing Feels Right" with the subtitle "If Grief Is the Price of Love, I Am Unable to Pay." Misner's heartfelt requiem to his best friend, Alison, who died of COVID-19 at age twenty-nine, ends with an allusion to a passage from *The Velveteen Rabbit* (1922) that Alison had read at his wedding two years earlier:

> The rabbit asks if becoming real hurts. The skin horse tells him yes, sometimes, it does. Sometimes your eyes will get rubbed off in the process and you'll lose some of your shine. But that's how you know you're real. Nothing real can remain untouched.
> The whole time they're talking about love, of course.

Misner leaves us with these words: "Alison made me real. Alison ruined me. And I am better because of it."

Across disciplines with vastly different methods, purposes, and audiences, *The Velveteen Rabbit* after one hundred years in print continues to enrich popular, critical, and creative discourse around its famous question, "What is REAL?" (Williams 3, emphasis original). First published in 1922 and immediately popular, this classic by Margery Williams has never been out of print.[1] Besides the multiple editions and international translations issued with different illustrators—increasingly since 1983, after the text came out of copyright, *The Velveteen Rabbit* has been adapted for film, television, and theater, in a range of mediums, including animation, Claymation, live action, musical, and dance. Countless fans of *The Velveteen Rabbit* use its famous quotable lines not only in nursery wall décor but also in epigraphs and extended metaphors for philosophical life lessons in their writings. The well-known story has also engendered contemporary self-help books, such as *The Velveteen Principles: A Guide to Becoming Real. Hidden Wisdom from a Children's Classic* (Raiten-D'Antonio) and *The Velveteen Woman: Becoming Real through God's Transforming Love* (Waggone). In 1971, *The Velveteen Rabbit* won the Lewis Carroll Shelf Award that the University of Wisconsin used to give books it deemed worthy of sitting next to Alice, and in 2007, a poll of the National Education Association ranked it in the "Teachers' Top 100 Books for Children." Not surprisingly, research on *The Velveteen Rabbit* turns up numerous pedagogical approaches and not just in reading and language arts as the story's central themes have been applied to urban school reform, autism and literacy, and the teaching of history.

Literary scholars have most commonly read the rabbit-turned-Real as a parable of child development or metaphoric myth, often through philosophical, psychoanalytic, and sociological lenses. Meanwhile, multidisciplinary thinkers have used the story to explore metaphysics, questions of attachment and separation, the meaning and dignity of becoming older, death and renewal, love and personal relationships, and even such esoteric topics as developing professionalism among pharmacy students or understanding the swimming reflex. Clearly, a century after the debut of what its acquiring editor, Sidney Powell, at Heinemann believed would be a classic (Moore 8), *The Velveteen Rabbit* is still relevant—and perhaps, judging from the results of a recent web search, even more relevant than ever to nostalgic adult readers if not to a young audience. Frequently, the book inspires the kind of sentimental, often nostalgic response stirred up by *The Giving Tree* (1964), *Love You Forever* (1986), or *The Rainbow Fish* (1992)—and, it must be said, a corresponding dismissive response from many in the literati.

Given that the story starts with the Rabbit as a stocking-stuffer gift, it makes sense that Faith McNulty includes it in her 1982 *New Yorker* roundup column "Children's Books for Christmas." However, her message is more of the what-not-to-give variety. Her review includes a colorful description of *The Velveteen Rabbit* as a "blatant tearjerker" by a "sly author" who "manipulates her naïve readers" (McNulty 179) and "plucks at a child's deepest fears and longings" (80). This might be acceptable to McNulty if not for the unforgivable "sin" of "its sad, sleazy message"; that is, "The book gives no hint that there is any way to meet the tragedy of lost love and betrayal other than letting the heart break" (180). This betrayal comes from the Boy who, despite making the toy Real through love, doesn't give further thought to the old Rabbit, or even to the splendid new replacement toy rabbit, because he's so eager to go to the seaside after his recovery from scarlet fever. Magical transformation into a happily-ever-after rabbit with legs doesn't mend the toy's heartbreak for McNulty.

Similarly, Meaghan Russell claims in a 2012 mini-essay for the *Minnesota Review*: "Too often, animals have been mere devices, slaughtered for the sake of pathos.... Novelists keep this cheap trick under their hats. And when they need a reliable show stopper to really affect us, out comes the rabbit. The Velveteen Rabbit. I'll just stop there" (43). Brynn Downing, in a 2017 creative nonfiction essay, "Rabbitdom," published in the *Prairie Schooner*, lyrically expresses a similar concern: "The crux of *The Velveteen Rabbit* is a creature's wish to be more than stuffing and velvet nose—to be made Real by love. He is told by the Skin Horse it will hurt. The story always disturbed me, how quickly the rabbit is cast off, how easily he changes form" (57). Of course, the old Rabbit has been cast off on doctor's orders because what he sees is not a "Real" sentient being but an easily replaced object, "a mass of scarlet fever germs" that "must be burnt" along with "the old picture-books" that the Boy looked at during his illness (Williams 14). Given that scarlet fever was a leading cause of death in children in the early twentieth century, it may be unfair to view the discard as a "betrayal" by the Boy even if all he can think of is going to the seaside rather than pining over the loss of a beloved toy. This, after all, is the way of children, so "innocent and heartless," to quote J. M. Barrie's last words in *Peter Pan in Kensington Gardens and Peter and Wendy* (226).

The Sly Author

Margery Williams was born in London on July 22, 1881, and died September 4, 1944, in New York City. Though she published twenty-seven books, including five translations of works from French and Norwegian, and though she won the John Newbery Honor Medal for her novel *Winterbound* (1936) in 1937, she is primarily known today as the author of *The Velveteen Rabbit*.

While biographers make no mention of her mother that I have been able to find, it is frequently noted that Williams's father, Robert Williams, was a warm and encouraging influence. A fellow of the classics at Oxford as well as a barrister and an opinion writer for periodicals, he held liberal views of education, prescient of today's unschooling movement. Williams was taught to read early and then allowed to explore her interests freely, without instruction and largely alone because her only sister was six years older. Anne Carroll Moore, who knew Williams well, quotes her as saying, "My favorite book in my father's library was Wood's *Natural History* in three big green volumes, and I knew every reptile, bird and beast in those volumes before I knew the multiplication table" (13). Her father's death, when Williams was seven years old, was a deeply saddening formative experience that would shape her artistic vision.

Williams spent the rest of her childhood back and forth between the United States and England. After two happy years at the Convent School in rural Pennsylvania, ending at age seventeen, she knew she wanted to become an author. At nineteen, she returned to London hoping to publish. That she did and more. Peggy Whalen-Levitt sums up Williams's next few years: "By 1906, when she was twenty-five, she had published four adult novels;[2] married Francesco Bianco, a dealer in rare books; and given birth to two children" (63). Williams's attentions turned away from writing to care for Cecco (born August 15, 1905) and Pamela (born December 31, 1906). They lived in Paris and then Turin while Captain Bianco served in the Italian Army during World War I and returned to London before the family permanently relocated to the United States.

They moved in 1921 to support the artistic development of Pamela, a child prodigy in drawing and painting. After the twelve-year-old's 1919 solo exhibition at the Leicester Galleries in London, Gertrude Vanderbilt took Pamela under her patronage and arranged an exhibition at the Anderson Galleries in New York. Upon viewing Pamela's artistic works, which were inspired by the works of Walter de la Mare—a well-known poet whose writing for children Williams greatly admired, de la Mare himself was inspired to write an ekphrastic collection of poems. Heinemann published their recursive collaboration in a 1919 volume, *Flora: A Book of Drawings with Illustrative Poems*. According to the prefatory note about Pamela Bianco, "Her remarkable talent for decorative invention, and her poetic imagery drew crowds to the exhibition, and obtained the enthusiastic praise of the entire press" (Bianco and de la Mare). Today, it may surprise most children's literature scholars to learn that, during their lifetimes, Pamela Bianco was actually far more famous than her mother.[3]

Inspired by de la Mare, with her children now in adolescence, Williams resumed writing, turning her hand to "stories she had told them [her children] when they were small, stories about their toys" (Bechtel 148) as well as "those she herself had loved as a child" (Whalen-Levitt 63). The first of these was based on her "almost forgotten Tubby who was the rabbit, and old Dobbin the Skin Horse" (Williams qtd. in Moore 15) and published by *Harper's Bazaar* in 1921 "as a vehicle for original illustrations by Pamela" (Chu). We now know this story, "The Velveteen Rabbit," as her first children's book. In it, Harry E. Eiss writes, Williams "discovered the wonder and sense of the miraculous invoked by the works of de la Mare and expressed it through a simplicity and directness matching a child's worldview" (47). Moore first encountered *The Velveteen Rabbit* when its American publisher, George H. Doran Co.,[4] sent her the prepublication pages and asked her opinion on how the book would sell. She found the themes stunningly poignant because she had recently spent time in France and England where she had formed "vivid first-hand impressions of children whose toys and pets and books had been destroyed" (Moore 8). A century later, readers may not be aware of this postwar context for young readers who had suffered deprivation and loss.

A number of successful children's books followed *The Velveteen Rabbit* in rapid succession, now under the name Margery Williams Bianco.[5] Two were illustrated by Pamela Bianco, including *The Little Wooden Doll* (1925) and *The Skin Horse* (1927), the latter a subject of brief discussion by Scott T. Pollard and Kara K. Keeling in this volume. In "A Tribute to Margery Bianco," Williams's contemporary and friend of the family Louise Seaman Bechtel describes the reason for the author's success: "This kind of imagination, playing not upon fairies but upon the real things a child knows, his toys and his pets, struck a note . . . to which children will always answer" (148). She singles out Williams's "touch of the true artist that keeps the most important thing predominant in a dramatic simplification. The Velveteen Rabbit belongs to a Boy—we do not know his name, or what his home looked like, or exactly how many people were in his family, because it doesn't matter to the rabbit's story" (Bechtel 148). Williams shared her philosophy of "Writing Books for Boys and Girls" in a speech to the National Council of Teachers of English in 1936, the year her Newbery Honor Book *Winterbound* was published. "In writing a real life story I think it should be real life, as far as one can present it," she said (Bianco 163). "Things shouldn't be made any easier than they actually are" because it's unfair to readers when "each difficulty is promptly surmounted and something always turns up in time to save a situation." She believed: "Children know much better. They know that things don't happen just that way, and that if you really want to accomplish anything at all—no matter how small—you generally have to work pretty darn hard over it, and go through a lot of misgivings and discouragement along the way" (Bianco 163). This philosophy, from someone who drew on her own and her children's real-life toy stories and who had also lost her father at an early age, perhaps explains the Rabbit's suffering and that tear of despair from which the nursery magic fairy springs. Williams would likely have appreciated Misner's words I quoted earlier: "Alison made me real. Alison ruined me. And I am better because of it."

Margaret Blount quips, in *Animal Land: The Creatures of Children's Fiction*, "The path of every toy is always downwards" because while we give them human attributes, breakable and disposable toys they remain (189). She asks, "When such creatures are given thoughts and emotions, how can they be other than tragic?" Blount answers her question with *The Velveteen Rabbit*:

> The only way out of the difficulty is to turn toys into cheerful ageless beings such as Larry the Lamb or Winnie the Pooh, neither of whom lives in the real world at all, but in some place where a small boy and his bear will always be playing. But the fairy-tale satisfaction of this short, perfect allegory would not be valid if the rabbit

were not part of the child's real life. The allegory is about human love and human childhood. (189)⁶

While the magical ending isn't realism, it's realistic in its aims: to show the spiritual rewards of loving through a lot of misgivings and discouragement. Williams aimed to create what she called "imaginative literature as an interpretation" (Moore 11), something she admired in Dhan Gopal Mukerji's writing about his mother, "the extraordinary gentle wisdom with which she used legend and stories to interpret the spiritual problems of life" (Moore 12).

Many early shapers of children's literature in the United States found Williams to be not only a talented writer but also an insightful critic whose ideas influenced the direction of the field. Bertha Mahony Miller found her "a rarely able critic" (vi) and valued her advice on manuscripts submitted for publication in *The Horn Book* (xi). Moore also lauded Williams's "rare quality of criticism" (3). After the author's death in 1944, Moore and Miller collaborated to edit *Writing and Criticism: A Book for Margery Bianco* (Horn Book, 1951), in which they recount why they were "impressed with the quality and variety of Mrs. Bianco's interests, her skill as a writer and translator, the reliability and richness of her background, and, above all, by the wisdom, the humor, the spiritual integrity she brought to the field of children's books after World War I" (Moore 3). Intended "to make something of Margery Williams Bianco's life and work known to later generations" (Moore 3), this book, ironically and unfortunately, is now rare and found primarily in special collections. Despite the efforts of her contemporaries who themselves have become legends, most of Williams's contributions to the field of children's literature are in danger of being lost to history. Perhaps this has happened because, in the words of Eiss, "Her writing is a product of a time when children's literature presented an ethos that many children and critics find unrealistic today, an ethos combining love, beauty, health, nature, God, family, truth, and the natural goodness of the child's worldview" (49). Perhaps a pandemic ethos during a time of global climate change and alternative facts, dovetailed with the hundredth anniversary of *The Velveteen Rabbit*, will ignite renewed interest in the author's life and collective works.

The Scholarship

Academic scholars have, like bloggers and the literati, also weighed in on the pathos of *The Velveteen Rabbit*, some finding it troubling and others, touching. According to Eiss in a brief article in the series Dictionary of Literary Biography, "The story's poignancy, and its fairy tale quality, often compared to work by Hans Christian Andersen, keep *The Velveteen Rabbit* from becoming overly sentimental"

(47). In a 1988 *Children's Literature in Education* article about "the toy as child," Geraldine DeLuca admits that "the maudlin nature" of *The Velveteen Rabbit* "always disturbed me" (211) because of "a confusing message": "What happens, I can't help wondering, to the toys in the nursery in *The Velveteen Rabbit* that don't get to sleep next to the little boy, that don't get loved? Do they go to heaven or do they stay in some nursery limbo, like unbaptized souls?" (212). In her early years as a scholar, Ellen Handler Spitz was so "dismayed" by *The Velveteen Rabbit* that she "avoided it when selecting books to read aloud to [her] own children at bedtime" (585). The passivity and "abject submission" of the protagonist left her "aghast" (Spitz 587). It "seemed a betrayal of heroic virtues—enterprise, ambition, self-assertion, and perseverance" (Spitz 588). Then, in 2009, after attending a dramatic adaptation of the story performed by the Enchantment Theatre of Philadelphia, she reconsidered. The producers had imagined and staged the playtime between the Boy and Rabbit, giving the passive toy heroic agency. "In this interpolated moment of play," writes Spitz, "Enchantment Theatre confers upon its protagonist the active role that is never explicitly vouchsafed him/it in the original text. We are made to see that the love between the Rabbit and the boy [sic] is, at least temporarily, mutual" (588). Spitz ends her essay about *The Velveteen Rabbit* "not one whit less harrowed by its unacknowledged grief and by its tragic loss of love," but "less cautious about reading it aloud to children, less wary of its manifest submissiveness, more open to its latent substance" (590). Perhaps when reading the words on the page, Spitz had never before thought to imagine all the "splendid games together, in whispers" that the Boy and Rabbit have together in the nursery (Williams 6).

Marina Warner does clearly understand the mutuality of their relationship when, writing in the same year as Spitz's reconsideration, she calls *The Velveteen Rabbit* "that most tender and thoughtful of children's stories" and theorizes on the soul of toys: "The question of the real haunts the psychology of play and through play, the theory of fantasy: Is the state of animation that the power of thought can conjure sufficient to make reality present?" (5). Regarding the famous lines of the Skin Horse about becoming real, Warner states: "The inner journey of a playing child takes shape in relation to the things that her games animate, and sensory qualities of every kind—appealing to smell, touch, hearing, even taste, as well as sight—enhance the potential of becoming Real like the Skin Horse" (6). It seems that dismay over the story arises from cynical adult literalism while delight stems from remembering the young child's real experience of make-believe.

The early advocate of children's literature as a scholarly discipline Francelia Butler did include *The Velveteen Rabbit* in her 1977 anthology *Sharing Literature with Children*, acknowledging that "the sentimentality of this book is distasteful to many adults" and redirecting the reader's attention to the child's "simple, creative play-world of stuffed animals and blocks" (23). For children, beloved toys do come to life, and Butler viewed *The Velveteen Rabbit* as "a gentle and sensitive rendering of this theme" (23). Butler was not alone in defending the classic among those who discussed what books to celebrate and recommend in the early days of the Children's Literature Association. In a 1980 Readers' Choice survey that Perry Nodelman conducted for the *ChLA Quarterly*, *The Velveteen Rabbit* made it to the rankings of "storybooks for younger children most admired" (3) in a ten-way tie for fourth place (along with *The Tale of Peter Rabbit* [1902]—and missing from the Readers' Choice list was "that other classic story about a bunny in a nursery," *Goodnight Moon* [1947]) (Pereira 169). While the methodology and accuracy of Nodelman's survey was contested, the result did show that *The Velveteen Rabbit* was widely admired.

It is surprising, then, despite its longevity and its 2,450,000 hits on a Google search in January of 2022, that *The Velveteen Rabbit* has inspired a relatively thin dossier of serious literary scholarship and scant engagement in extended dialogue between existing arguments—a gap that this volume seeks to correct. The first to apply a psychoanalytic reading of the text was Steven V. Daniels in the 1990 issue of *Children's Literature*. His essay, "*The Velveteen Rabbit*: A Kleinian Perspective," applies Melanie Klein's post-Freudian ideas about splitting parental figures into good and bad as a way to cope with the ambivalence of separation in early childhood development, thus explaining the anxieties represented in and triggered by *The Velveteen Rabbit*. Daniels concludes that "the story regresses to persecutory fears and the solace available only through idealization," which explains both the "oddities and suppressions in the text" (26) and the responses of critics like McNulty.

In his 1993 essay "Death and Renewal in *The Velveteen Rabbit*: A Sociological Reading," Allan Kellehear stands up for the story in debate with Daniels, arguing: "Although the Rabbit was discarded by the Boy's guardians and not, it should be well noted, by the Boy himself, the love between them continues on in both their subsequent lives and memories. Therefore the story's theme is not about the 'ambivalence of separation' (Daniels, 1990) but rather the robust ability of love to transcend separation, even in death" (46). Of the scholarly literature published before the current volume, Kellehear's sociological reading of the "near-death imagery" and the "imaginative support for the story's final message, that real love continues even when the beloved is taken away" (47) perhaps does the most to help us understand why quotations from *The Velveteen Rabbit* so often appear in sermons, eulogies, and titles of essays about far-flung topics one hundred years after its original publication.

Lois Rostow Kuznets likely had not seen Kellehear's article before her 1994 monograph *When Toys Come Alive: Narratives of Animation, Metamorphosis, and Development* went into production, as she does not engage his ideas in her brief discussion of *The Velveteen Rabbit*. Given the story's continuing popularity and prominence in toy literature, I find it surprising that Kuznets gives the text only three pages of attention, especially given a dominant motif identified in her introduction: "Toys, when they are shown as inanimate objects developing into live beings, embody human anxiety about what it means to be 'real'—an independent subject or self rather than an object or other submitting to the gaze of more powerfully real and potentially rejecting live beings" (2). One might expect to see an endnote crediting Williams.

Kuznets does recap central arguments in Daniels, including the failure of the fairy-magic ending to repair separation anxieties. She wittily concludes, "Although Daniels does not say so, I speculate that Rabbit himself needs a transitional object to carry out such a reparation" (Kuznets 62). This is a line that Mitzi Myers quotes in her review of the monograph, also commenting on *The Velveteen Rabbit* as "the work that an amazing number of my students wax lyrical over, rather to my puzzlement" (184). Kuznets's own critique is that the Rabbit's acquisition of an immortal natural body—"the ability to live 'for ever and ever' in the midst of mortal rabbits"—"is a violation of the mythic metamorphic tradition" (61). Of course, those who read through a Christian worldview have no problem with this biological materialist contradiction. Metaphorically, if the Rabbit is a stand-in for a human child, Rabbit-land becomes the afterlife for someone born again. This is pointed out quite clearly in "Love and Immortality in *The Velveteen Rabbit* and *The Little Mermaid*," a chapter in Vigen Guroian's 1998 book *Tending the Heart of Virtue: How Classic Stories Awaken a Child's Moral Imagination*.[7] Guroian might have helped Myers better understand her students' lyrical waxing as he reports that in his religion classes they "have not hesitated to conclude that Williams has written an allegory not only of love but of immortality" (69). Though he refers to Jack Zipes in his discussion of *The Little Mermaid*, Guroian cites no literary critics of *The Velveteen Rabbit*, only the child psychologist Robert Coles and philosopher Martin Buber.

Mary Galbraith, in the 1999 *ChLA Quarterly* article "'Goodnight Nobody' Revisited: Using an Attachment Perspective to Study Picture Books about Bedtime," briefly positions *The Velveteen Rabbit* with *Where the Wild Things Are* as a bedtime story of the "hostile type": "The child is depicted in solitary confinement in his child-space, enduring the abandonment or rejection of other humans by fantasizing attachments with toys or dream-figures" (174). She mentions Kuznets in a note discussing transitional objects but, strangely, not Daniels. Susan Honeyman also quotes Kuznets—in fact, referring to the same primary motif I included above—in her 2006 *ChLA Quarterly* essay "Manufactured Agency and the Playthings Who Dream It for Us." In her discussion of *The Velveteen Rabbit*, Honeyman agrees with Daniels that the rabbit wants to be "really Real," not just loved but also alive—which is "a lose-lose situation" given that living always leads to dying (118). But what Honeyman finds disturbing "is that in all this sentimentalizing on the value of love, the audience (targeted, at least, as children) is encouraged to embrace an object position—not to love better but to better please those by whom they wish to be loved" (119). This reading strains the conceptual metaphor of anthropomorphism by presupposing that child readers identify with the plush rabbit as a mirror of their human selves rather than as a literal toy that they love and make Real only in fantasy. The child, being human, *has* to face the mortality—like the Boy ill with deadly scarlet fever—that the "real" (not "real Real") toy never will.[8]

In her 2007 essay "PC Pinocchios: Parents, Children, and the Metamorphosis Tradition in Science Fiction," Holly Blackford [Humes] also waves to Kuznets and includes *The Velveteen Rabbit* as an example of "narrative elements [that] are common to folk-based stories of child development" in which "toys are simultaneously child characters and more than children. They stand for children when they embark on journeys to understand their relationship to their creators and develop their own sense of consciousness and agency; characters undergo metamorphosis when they have explored and mastered what it means to be human" (76). Blackford Humes sees the Rabbit as representing developmental concerns for both children and parents as a quest for human value, and she finds the deus ex machina ending true to the folk tradition. (And I am delighted that Blackford Humes has expanded her insightful reading of *The Velveteen Rabbit* for inclusion in the current volume.)

Most recently, Kirsten Jacobson added a philosopher's voice to the slowly growing critical dossier with "Heidegger, Winnicott, and *The Velveteen Rabbit*: Anxiety, Toys, and the Drama of Metaphysics," the first chapter in Peter R. Costello's edited volume *Philosophy in Children's Literature* (2011). Jacobson does not include a literature survey of previous scholarship on her primary text but rather reads the depiction of reality in *The Velveteen Rabbit* through insights from Aristotle, Simone de Beauvoir, Jacques Derrida, Georg Wilhelm Friedrich Hegel, Martin Heidegger, and other philosophers as well as psychologists such as Eva-Maria Simms, J. H. van den Berg, and D. W. Winnicott. She looks at the Boy and his toy as "being both a subject and an object of views and values" (Jacobson 16) in ways that could resolve what prior critics see as inconsistencies, violations, or disturbing oddities.

When doing research for my proposal to edit this volume, I was both disappointed and excited to find the lack of abundance in previous scholarship. Obviously, we learn and grow in our understanding when we can build from the foundations established by other thinkers over time. At the same time, the gaps leave us plenty of spaces to explore and burrow into the meanings that have kept *The Velveteen Rabbit* alive and Real in the imaginations of readers for a century.

Thirteen Ways of Looking at a Rabbit

While each essay in this volume can stand alone, and all could be read in any order a reader might wish, I have placed the chapters in a sequence designed to flow with coherence from beginning to end, showing connections between readings from a wide array of critical approaches. Along the way, readers will find useful examples of how we might look at other classic storybooks, not just *The Velveteen Rabbit*, in new ways that combine hindsight with evolving sensibilities about representation.

The volume opens with a chapter by Blackford Humes that places *The Velveteen Rabbit* in a wide context of nonhuman characters who become sentient and experience the virtual game of testing the boundaries of reality. Using theory of puppetry, animation, simulacrum, and virtual reality, Blackford Humes traverses the unstable boundaries of the real—and who defines it. By applying the simulacra theory of Jean Baudrillard, who tracks the ascendency of the model or simulation of the real throughout the twentieth century, particularly with shifting media and media theory, the chapter seeks to understand how the intertwined concepts of "modernity" and "simulacra" are deeply at issue throughout the story. The confusion of meaning in *The Velveteen Rabbit* is a tragic mirror of the century's breakdown in distinctions between representations and referents, as the century transformed its experience by grasping for the real through images, models, and simulations of reality. By analyzing the rabbit's inability to sort and separate models and originals, which are dependent on one another for recognition in a culture of commodities, media, and images, Blackford Humes argues that Rabbit's status as simulacrum moves him from puppet to avatar, contingent upon virtual communities. Rather than interpreting *The Velveteen Rabbit* as a failure or deus ex machina, she points out that it is precisely the irresolvable nature of the existential dilemma that we appreciate most.

In chapter 2, Kelly Blewett and Alisa Clapp-Itnyre focus on the role of illustrations in *The Velveteen Rabbit*. They begin by taking a close look at the illustrations of William Nicholson, arguing that the artist's framing and coloration of the original 1922 illustrations, though likely constrained by financial considerations, underscore the text's deeper psychological themes in ways that later adaptations resist and reinterpret. Of the book's seven original illustrations, five feature portrait-style presentations of the Rabbit and none feature human actors (the Boy, Nana, or the doctor). Stylistic elements of the illustrations reflect the state of mind of the Rabbit as he negotiates two transformations (new toy to loved toy; loved toy to real rabbit). Nicholson's attention to the psychology of the Rabbit reflects the then-current Freudian focus on the psyche and anticipates later criticism. A significant resurgence of interest in the 1980s through the present has resulted in illustrated editions that tend to displace the Rabbit as the central figure in favor of emphasizing the Boy, as the 1980s focus on childhood, child-psychology, and resistance to gender stereotypes now held sway. In all, this chapter provides a case study of how illustrators across time have used rich visual language to support competing interpretations of a classic children's story. Ultimately, Blewett and Clapp-Itnyre suggest that the illustrations, with their flexibility to reflect current trends, have helped the story to endure.

Despite the seventy-three years between the publication of *The Velveteen Rabbit* and the release of Pixar's first film in their *Toy Story* franchise in 1995, Melanie Hurley argues, in chapter 3, that these two toy narratives share four key motifs that develop sophisticated, but markedly different, philosophical perspectives. Both *The Velveteen Rabbit* and the *Toy Story* films feature sentient toys questioning who and what they are; an intense bond between a child and a toy (or toys); the toy(s) becoming trash; and the toy's (or toys') seemingly imminent but finally avoided destruction. Through these motifs, Williams's classic picture book employs a model of reality and knowledge similar to that which Plato constructs across his *Republic*, *Symposium*, and *Phaedo*, while the *Toy Story* films take a position that is similar to, yet distinct from, Albert Camus's position in "The Myth of Sisyphus." Furthermore, Pixar's existential commentary is not limited to the *Toy Story* franchise, with *WALL-E* (2008) showing that humans must struggle against hostile forces, most notably our trash, if we are to maintain life on earth. Both *The Velveteen Rabbit* and the *Toy Story* films are deeply philosophical, but it is *Toy Story*, in abandoning idealist philosophy and idealistic storytelling, that takes the toy narrative in its necessary direction for the 1990s, 2000s, and beyond.

Claudia Mills, in chapter 4, reads *The Velveteen Rabbit* as a story about a toy rabbit's yearning for the moral status of "personhood." In seeking to become "Real," the Rabbit seeks the moral standing of a "person," a being who has value in *itself*, value for its *own* sake. We may thus gain insight into this beloved text by examining the philosophical concept of "personhood": that which gives an entity moral standing, investing it with moral significance. Proposed criteria for personhood include rationality, the capacity for self-reflection, and the capacity to care for others. Less demanding standards for moral standing take mere sentience as key: that is, the ability to feel pleasure and pain. When the Velveteen Rabbit asks the Skin Horse, "Does [being Real] hurt?" the Skin Horse replies, "Sometimes." By the sentience view, the ability to be hurt is not a possible consequence of being "Real" but absolutely central to it. So, the Velveteen Rabbit actually already possesses all these criteria for personhood: he can reason, reflect, care for others, and feel deeply. An ongoing question in the philosophy of love is whether we love another in recognition of his value or whether we confer value upon him through loving him. The Velveteen Rabbit achieves reality not as the passive object of another's love, but rather as an active, loving agent himself—not by being loved, but by loving. Examining the story through an ethical lens, moreover, it seems preferable to encourage young readers, rather than merely hoping someday to be loved, to themselves undertake the risks of loving.

Inspired by the works of philosopher Karen Barad, chapter 5 by Adrianna Zabrzewska applies the categories of materiality and realness to investigate the Velveteen Rabbit's onto-epistemological status and the relationship with his human companion. The first part of Williams's book shows us that to be a distinct, embodied self—and to be loved as that self by someone else—is an active, gradual, and potentially hurtful process of becoming that invites interdependence and vulnerability. It is a material-discursive process rooted in the experience of being a flawed, finite, and fragile body. The Velveteen Rabbit's understanding of himself arises in a perpetually moving, changing knot of human and nonhuman matter and meaning, as he goes on to acquire the privilege of becoming Real in the eyes of the Boy. However, when the Rabbit leaves the limited existence of a toy and embraces the elevated ideal of a real flesh rabbit, his relationship with the Boy is rendered meaningless. In the second part of the book, the Velveteen Rabbit transcends from a beloved toy into a redeemed soul. Once the story reveals itself to be a fable of redemption and eternal life, love and materiality have no more place in it. As such, *The Velveteen Rabbit* illustrates both the principles of Barad's philosophy and the order that this philosophy seeks to battle.

Through a brief history of stuffed rabbits, Jiwon Rim, in chapter 6, places both the wild rabbits and the toy rabbit of *The Velveteen Rabbit* within a history of technological domination and the violent molding of animal bodies into natural and unnatural shapes. The stuffed toy rabbit is not a fake animal that has nothing to do with the real animal. Rather, it is one of the animal products of the all-encompassing system of animal commodification. Walter Potter's stuffed rabbits, the taxidermic outcome of once-living, historically real animals that do not look natural but instead resemble the rabbits of Beatrix Potter's illustrations, point to the common origin of the image of the authentic wild animal and the denaturalized bodies of toy animals. In B. Potter's work, Peter of *The Tale of Peter Rabbit* (1901) looks disturbingly like he is modeled from real, captured rabbits, a testament to the uncomfortable historical origin of now-familiar toy rabbits. If the two Potters' works show both the natural animal and the unnatural animal in construction via the technique of animal stuffing, *The Velveteen Rabbit* takes us to a world populated with denaturalized animals and haunted by the vision of the authentic natural animal. *The Velveteen Rabbit* puts life into the plight of the thingified animal incorporated in the fully-fledged system of industrial capitalism, bringing readers uncomfortably close to the ethical problem of manufactured and commodified animals in the form of "a real tear" that trickles down the "little shabby velvet nose" of the disposable toy rabbit (Williams 16). *The Velveteen Rabbit* is thus an animal tale of the Anthropocene in which all animals are "insignificant and commonplace" things made in the system of industrial capitalism, while nonmade animals can hardly be said to exist.

In chapter 7, Wenduo Zhang looks into the Japanese edition of *The Velveteen Rabbit*, adapted and illustrated by Komako Sakai, as a miniature ecosystem of words and pictures that interact with each other and create meaning through counterpoints. The chapter also focuses on the depictions of nature and how illustrating techniques contribute to our understanding of the story. Light and color distinguish real animals from inanimate objects and nature from built environments. Sakai's illustrations of the Skin Horse emphasize the texture of animal skin and sewing lines, reminding readers of the real animals that existed before the toy animal. With detailed and colorful illustrations of nature, the pictures amplify a love of nature that the words do not explicitly mention. Pictures can show power structure through the use of size and position of characters. The change of size celebrates the Rabbit's growth as it becomes alive, implying real animals are preferable despite the Boy's affection for the toy. Sakai creates distance through the separation of the Rabbit from the Boy in the latter half of the story and multiple frames on the last page. The separation creates a sense of loneliness and independence that complicates the story. The last image simultaneously suggests the separation of humans from nature and a longing of reunion, inviting us to read the story as an environmental text and to reflect on our relationship with nature in real life.

Chapter 8, by Claudia Camicia and Elena Paruolo, presents a detailed survey of *The Velveteen Rabbit*'s dissemination and reception in Italy over the past thirty years. It draws comparisons between the English original and the Italian translations/adaptations/reductions focusing on artistic, stylistic, and linguistic choices and shows how *The Velveteen Rabbit*'s popularity rate rose beginning in 2007, as testified not only by its various media versions but also by several reviews, appreciations, and uses of the story by educators, therapists, and staff-training personnel. The chapter draws parallels between Williams's story, Carlo Collodi's *The Adventures of Pinocchio* (1881–83), and Gianni Rodari's *La freccia azzurra* (1964) (*The Befana's Toyshop*, 1970), where toys long to cast off their inanimate condition and come to life. This similarity suggests that *Pinocchio* may have been a possible influence on *The Velveteen Rabbit*, and Rodari might also have read *The Velveteen Rabbit*. Finally, this research provides an exhaustive overview of *The Velveteen Rabbit* in the Italian editorial market by highlighting how the story represents the aims of education and healing and how it gains importance as a sort of "manifesto" for children's rights in making the audience understand that everybody has the right to learn, to be respected as children, to be appreciated for what they are, to have protection and friendship, to fulfill their dreams, to love and to be loved, and to rejoice in life.

Though *The Velveteen Rabbit* and *The Little Prince* transport readers to fantastic worlds where a toy rabbit can come to life and a little boy can travel the universe,

Paige Sammartino, in chapter 9, shows that the books share a humble truth in their narratives: that which is loved, no matter how small, holds great meaning and significance. For the Little Prince, the time he's spent caring for his rose on his tiny asteroid has endeared her to him and made her unique even among the thousands of roses he discovers in an ordinary garden on earth. For the Velveteen Rabbit, the time he's spent in the arms and imagination of his Boy has made him Real and transformed him from toy to living animal. Sammartino places these two classic texts in conversation to discuss how their fairy-tale styles foster the message of how that which is loved has value as well as to consider the role of the child character (and reader) in this dynamic. The chapter discusses the Boy and the Little Prince as child—and, more specifically, boy—caretakers of the Rabbit and rose respectively and considers the complementary experience of reading the books together, as one narrative follows the perspective of the child caretaker while the other follows the perspective of the subject of a child's care.

In chapter 10, Maleeha Malik, Elisabeth Graves, and Lisa Rowe Fraustino examine the many similarities of detail suggesting that Kate DiCamillo's *The Miraculous Journey of Edward Tulane* is an intertextual rewrite of *The Velveteen Rabbit*. Both are illustrated storybooks that begin with physical descriptions of splendid toy rabbits given to privileged, upper-class children as gifts. Children in both stories love their rabbits and consider them real. In fact, both stories build to their climactic turning points through the loss of their children, and thus their love, to illness or death. Both playthings experience physical wear and tear on their way to figurative rebirth. However, while an underlying question of both stories remains—"What does it mean to become real?" and the answer concerns being loved, DiCamillo provides a more nuanced and child-centric resolution through the developmental growth and change of Edward. He comes across less as a toy and more as an anthropomorphized stand-in for a human child reader than his velveteen counterpart, who identifies with living rabbits. In the end he is saved from eternal suffering by learning to love, accept loss, and open his broken heart to hope. With multiple biblical allusions woven throughout the text and illustrations, both explicit and subtle, *The Miraculous Journey of Edward Tulane* can thus be read as an allegorical rewrite of *The Velveteen Rabbit* to replace becoming Real through "nursery magic" with the redeeming power of Christian love.

Karlie Herndon, in chapter 11, reads the Boy's nursery as a queer space. The late Victorian nursery was unique in terms of space: it was a child-centered space where the young could learn and play without much adult interference, and it was a place in which children could test the boundaries of adult-sanctioned rules, including the rules of gender and sexuality. The nursery space allows for the Boy—a nameless stand-in for all boys—to play in whatever way he likes, particularly in bed. The nursery magic has its strongest effects in the sickbed, where the Rabbit is made Real, and his healing love brings the Boy back from a deadly fever. However, the medicalization of nonnormative sexuality plays out here in the removal of the Rabbit from the nursery. Even so, the Boy and Rabbit's love runs so deeply that the Rabbit is not only rewarded by becoming even more real through the reward of a living body but also by entering into a sort of rabbit heaven, where he can play with other real rabbits forever. This chapter continues the recovery work of queer theory, celebrating a space in which the rules of heteronormative adult gender and sexuality, particularly pleasurable activities, are transgressed to such an extent that the most loved toy is saved from the fire that seeks to eradicate the Boy's "unhealthy" bed-play. In this instance, the child's intense love for the Rabbit queers the adult heteronormative notions of pleasure through rewarding the Rabbit with a real body, with which he can seek out his own flesh-and-blood pleasures.

In chapter 12, Scott T. Pollard and Kara K. Keeling read *The Velveteen Rabbit* through the lens of disability studies. At first glance, *The Velveteen Rabbit* seems to pursue a conventionally ableist view of disability. Williams writes what all "normate" narratives do, using a term coined by Rosemarie Garland-Thomson (28): she would erase disability from the Boy's and toy's present and future, so that readers no longer have to worry because now the future is full of promise. But there is another interpretation of *The Velveteen Rabbit*—worth pursuing as a counternarrative to ableist closure—that opens the book up to a disabling reading, what Nancy Mairs characterizes in *Carnal Acts* (1990) as living with "ambivalences" without searching for a cure (or death or tragedy), a resolution, or a way out of or around the experience of disability (15). The toy becomes real once it is no longer pristine, ideal, or normate. Love makes disability real, makes the disabled body visible (and not repugnant). At the end of the book, the recovered Boy witnesses the visible traces of his beloved toy in the magically metamorphosed rabbit, made real twice over and thus preserving the trace of the disabled body. On the one hand, in *The Velveteen Rabbit*, Williams pursues a conventional ableist narrative, but on the other, the book remains a receptacle "capable of being in uncertainties" (to echo John Keats [49–50]), open to the possibility—as Teresa Michals and Claire McTiernan define disability studies— "that a life that includes impairment can also include positive change over time. It can include growth."

To end the volume, KaaVonia Hinton examines the ideology of whiteness in *The Velveteen Rabbit*. Over one hundred years ago, *The Brownies' Book*, one of the first magazines for Black children, was created to oppose the selective tradition of children's literature, a tradition designed to portray the images, values, and beliefs of Whites, including "racial intolerance, institutionalized discrimination, and social inequity" (Harris 192). In *The Velveteen Rabbit*, Williams appears to write a largely colorblind or neutral story in which she avoids explicitly attaching racial identity to characters. Yet, colorblindness is rooted in whiteness, particularly White ideas of what is natural, normal, and acceptable. Although whiteness is situated as an implied, subtle norm, White racial identity, and how it intersects with gender and class, is actually prominent throughout the storybook, especially in the representation of the pretty, powerful Fairy. Hinton's chapter reveals articulations of whiteness in the original 1922 version of *The Velveteen Rabbit* illustrated by Nicholson and four picture-book adaptations that maintain the selective tradition *The Brownies' Book* sought to challenge.

In chapters that discuss multiple editions or translations of *The Velveteen Rabbit* (i.e., chapters 2, 7, 8, and 13), we have organized the bibliography to include a separate Williams subsection. In the text, we have differentiated these citations by publication year.

Collectively, the essays in this volume more than double the amount of serious scholarship on *The Velveteen Rabbit*, both extending dialogue begun in previous decades and beginning fresh conversations in light of new media and virtual reality. Different illustrations, translations, adaptations, and comparisons give a rich range of perspectives on the underlying themes shared by every version of the story. Classical and contemporary philosophies lead us to consider the meaning of love and reality in ways both timeless and temporal. The Velveteen Rabbit is an Anthropocene Rabbit constructed in the selective tradition. He is also disabled. Here a traditional exegetical reading sits alongside queering the text. We offer thirteen ways of looking at this rabbit that Williams gave us.

Notes

1. *The Velveteen Rabbit*, her fifth book, was published like her first four under her given name, Margery Williams. Subsequent books were published under her married name, Margery Williams Bianco. Her fourth book, *The Thing in the Woods*, published in the US under the pen name Harper Williams in 1924, was republished in 2014.

2. While Williams did publish four adult novels before *The Velveteen Rabbit*, only three came out by the time she was twenty-five: *The Late Returning* in 1902, *The Price of Youth* in 1904, and *The Bar* in 1906. The fourth, *The Thing in the Woods*, first published in England, actually came out in 1914.

3. In the endnotes of her historical novel *The Velveteen Daughter*, based on the relationship of Margery and Pamela Bianco, Laurel Davis Huber reflects: "It continues to amaze me that this story has not come to light before now. To my knowledge, no biography of Margery Bianco has been published, and Pamela Bianco has been forgotten almost entirely" (381).

4. The George H. Doran Company, Williams's American publisher, was a powerhouse from 1908–1927 with a long list of notable authors, among them Arthur Conan Doyle, O. Henry, Virginia Wolf, and Sinclair Lewis. The company merged with Doubleday, Page & Company in 1927. The Doran name was dropped in 1946, at which time Doubleday was the largest publisher in the US. Today, after more mergers, Doubleday is part of the Knopf Doubleday Publishing Group.

5. For the sake of consistency and clarity (to distinguish her from Pamela), I will continue to refer to the author as Williams, though biographers and critics often choose to refer to her as Bianco even when writing about *The Velveteen Rabbit*.

6. Like many women of her time, Blount has left almost no trace of her biography in the public record. *Animal Land* includes *The Velveteen Rabbit* on its list of fourteen characters to whom the book is dedicated, "wherever they are" (Blount 5). Blount shows a wide-ranging knowledge of literature and shares her keen insights in vivid prose but is rarely quoted, perhaps because she did not have a PhD and published with a trade rather than academic press.

7. I have chosen not to discuss an article that would appear to be a religious reading of our primary text, "God's Velveteen Rabbit" (2009) by Paul Weithman, because it is not what it appears. Rather than interpreting Williams's story, Weithman uses an epigraph from *The Velveteen Rabbit* as a jumping off point for discussion of Nicholas Wolterstorff's *Justice: Rights and Wrongs* (2008).

8. For a thorough discussion of how conceptual metaphor operates in anthropomorphism, see Fraustino (153–59).

Works Cited

Barrie, J. M. *Peter Pan in Kensington Gardens and Peter and Wendy*. Oxford UP, 1991.

Bechtel, Louise Seaman. "A Tribute to Margery Bianco." *The Elementary English Review*, vol. 12, no. 6, 1935, pp. 147–49, 165. *JSTOR*, https://www.jstor.org/stable/41381851. Accessed 26 Jan. 2021.

Bianco, Margery. "Writing Books for Boys and Girls." *The Elementary English Review*, vol. 14, no. 5, 1937, pp. 161–64. *JSTOR*, https://www.jstor.org/stable/41381019. Accessed 26 Jan. 2021.

Bianco, Pamela, and Walter de la Mare. *Flora: A Book of Drawings with Illustrative Poems by Walter de la Mare*. Heinemann, 1919. *Internet Archive*, https://archive.org/details/florafloobianrich/page/n57/mode/2up. Accessed 26 Jan. 2021.

Blackford [Humes], Holly. "PC Pinocchios: Parents, Children, and the Metamorphosis Tradition in Science Fiction." *Folklore/Cinema: Popular Film as Vernacular Culture*, edited by Sharon R. Sherman and Mikel J. Koven, Utah State UP, 2007, pp. 74–92. *JSTOR*, https://www.jstor.org/stable/j.ctt4cgnbm.7. Accessed 13 May 2020.

Blount, Margaret. *Animal Land: The Creatures of Children's Fiction*. 1974. William Morrow, 1975.

Butler, Francelia. *Sharing Literature with Children*. David McKay Co., 1977.

Chu, Andrea Long. "The Velveteen Rabbit Was Always More Than a Children's Book." *Vulture*, 8 Nov. 2022, https://www.vulture.com/2022/11/velveteen-rabbit-margery-williams-bianco-book.html. Accessed 12 Dec. 2022.

Daniels, Steven V. "The Velveteen Rabbit: A Kleinian Perspective." *Children's Literature*, vol. 18, 1990, pp. 17–30. *Project Muse*, https://doi.org/10.1353/chl.0.0661.

DeLuca, Geraldine. "'A Condition of Complete Simplicity': The Toy as Child in *The Mouse and His Child*." *Children's Literature in Education*, vol. 19, no. 44, 1988, pp. 211–21.

Downing, Brynn. "Rabbitdom." *Prairie Schooner*, vol. 91, no. 2, summer 2017, pp. 52–58.

Eiss, Harry E. "Margery Williams Bianco (22 July 1881–4 September 1944)." *British Children's Writers, 1914–1960*, edited by Donald R. Hettinga and Gary D. Schmidt, Gale, 1996, pp. 45–49. Dictionary of Literary Biography.

Fraustino, Lisa Rowe. "The Rights and Wrongs of Anthropomorphism in Picture Books." *Ethics and Children's Literature*, edited by Claudia Mills, Routledge, 2014, pp. 145–62.

Galbraith, Mary. "'Goodnight Nobody' Revisited: Using an Attachment Perspective to Study Picture Books about Bedtime." *Children's Literature Association Quarterly*, vol. 23, no. 4, 1998–99, pp. 172–79.

Garland-Thomson, Rosemarie. "Eugenic World Building and Disability: The Strange World of Kazuo Ishiguro's *Never Let Me Go*." *Journal of Medical Humanities*, vol. 38, 2017, pp. 133–45, https://doi.org/10.1007/s10912-015-9368-y.

Guroian, Vigen. *Tending the Heart of Virtue: How Classic Stories Awaken a Child's Moral Imagination*. Oxford UP, 1998. *ProQuest*, http://ebookcentral.proquest.com/lib/uaz/detail.action?d. Accessed 26 Jan. 2021.

Harris, Violet J. "Race Consciousness, Refinement, and Radicalism: Socialization in *The Brownies' Book*." *Children's Literature Association Quarterly*, vol. 14, no. 4, 1989, pp. 192–96.

Honeyman, Susan. "Manufactured Agency and the Playthings Who Dream It for Us." *Children's Literature Association Quarterly*, vol. 31, no. 2, 2006, pp. 109–31. *Project Muse*, https://doi.org/10.1353/chq.2006.0038. Accessed 12 Feb. 2020.

Huber, Laurel Davis. *The Velveteen Daughter: A Novel*. She Writes Press, 2017.

Jacobson, Kirsten. "Heidegger, Winnicott, and *The Velveteen Rabbit*: Anxiety, Toys, and the Drama of Metaphysics." *Philosophy in Children's Literature*, edited by Peter R. Costello, Lexington Books, 2012, pp. 1–20.

Keats, John. *Letters*. U of Virginia P, 1901.

Kellehear, Allan. "Death and Renewal in *The Velveteen Rabbit*: A Sociological Reading." *Journal of Near-Death Studies*, vol. 12, no. 1, 1993, pp. 35–51.

Kuznets, Lois Rostow. *When Toys Come Alive: Narratives of Animation, Metamorphosis, and Development*. Yale UP, 1994.

McNulty, Faith. "Children's Books for Christmas." *New Yorker*, 6 Dec. 1982, pp. 176–82.

Michals, Teresa, and Claire McTiernan. "'Oh, Why Can't You Remain like This Forever!': Children's Literature, Growth, and Disability." *Disability Studies Quarterly*, vol. 38, no. 2, 2018, https://doi.org/10.18061/dsq.v38i2.6107.

Miller, Bertha Mahony. "Introduction." Moore and Miller, pp. iii–xii.

Misner, Jared. "My Best Friend Is Gone, and Nothing Feels Right." *New York Times*, 9 Oct. 2020, https://nyti.ms/34HgR1M. Accessed 9 Oct. 2020.

Moore, Anne Carroll. "Margery Williams Bianco." Moore and Miller, pp. 3–18.

Moore, Anne Carroll, and Bertha E. Mahony Miller, editors. *Writing and Criticism: A Book for Margery Bianco*. Horn Book, 1951.

Myers, Mitzi. "When Criticism Comes Alive: R Toys Us?" Review of *When Toys Come Alive: Narratives of Animation, Metamorphosis, and Development*, by Lois Rostow Kuznets. *Children's Literature*, vol. 24, 1996, pp. 181–87.

Nodelman, Perry. "Readers' Choice: ChLA Survey." *Children's Literature Association Quarterly*, vol. 4, no. 4, winter 1980, pp. 3–34.

Pereira, Daniel. "Bedtime Books, the Bedtime Story Ritual, and *Goodnight Moon*." *Children's Literature Association Quarterly*, vol. 44, no. 2, summer 2019, pp. 156–72.

Raiten-D'Antonio, Toni. *The Velveteen Principles: A Guide to Becoming Real. Hidden Wisdom from a Children's Classic*. Health Communications/Simon & Schuster, 2004.

Russell, Meaghan. "*The Minnesota Review* Loves: Literary Animal Advocacy." *The Minnesota Review*, no. 78, summer 2012, p. 43.

Spitz, Ellen Handler. "Reality by Enchantment." *American Imago*, vol. 65, no. 4, winter 2008, pp. 585–91.

Waggone, Brenda. *The Velveteen Woman: Becoming Real through God's Transforming Love*. 1999. iUniverse, 2009.

Warner, Marina. "Out of an Old Toy Chest." *Journal of Aesthetic Education*, vol. 43, no. 2, summer 2009, pp. 3–18.
Weithman, Paul. "God's Velveteen Rabbit." *Journal of Religious Ethics*, vol. 37, no. 2, 2009, pp. 243–60. *JSTOR*, https://www.jstor.org/stable/40378044. Accessed 15 Oct. 2019.
Whalen-Levitt, Peggy. "Margery Williams Bianco 1881–1944." *Writers for Children: Critical Studies of Major Authors Since the Seventeenth Century*, edited by Jane M. Bingham, Charles Scribner's Sons, 1988, pp. 63–67. *Gale eBooks*, GALEICX1380000018. Accessed 25 Jan. 2021.
Williams, Margery. *The Velveteen Rabbit: Or How Toys Become Real*. Heinemann, 1922. *Internet Archive*, https://archive.org/details/velveteenrabbitooobian. Accessed 15 Apr. 2020.

Chapter 1

Virtual Realities: Animation and Simulacrum in *The Velveteen Rabbit*'s Tradition and Legacy

—Holly Blackford Humes

> The Rabbit could not claim to be a model of anything, for he didn't know that real rabbits existed; he thought they were all stuffed with sawdust like himself.
> —Margery Williams, *The Velveteen Rabbit* (3)

In *When Toys Come Alive* (1994), Lois Rostow Kuznets observes that the deus ex machina of the Velveteen Rabbit's final transformation to being "Real" is problematic (61). It reveals the irresolvable conflict of the text's varying definitions of reality. The rabbit is first told the love of a child makes you "Real"; it seems that this requires much sacrifice and wear and tear (Williams 3–4). As discussed by Melanie Hurley and Claudia Mills in this volume, "Real" can be understood philosophically, spiritually, or materially, but my approach equates Williams's Real with an animating force or process conferred by relationship. The definition changes when the Rabbit meets a more "adolescent" or "peer" community of biological rabbits, who inadvertently define "Real" as mobility, independence, flesh, and conformity to the community of "hyperreal" wild rabbits. By extension of this faith in the a priori order of nature, pet rabbits who are flesh but domesticated are not Real either. The definitions become tangled when the first definition does not work out incredibly well for the rabbit, as it rarely does for characters who define themselves exclusively through the recognition of others.

Early in *The Velveteen Rabbit* (1922), we are told that the titular character lacks knowledge that he is a model for anything, which distinguishes him from the modern toys who seem to have the consciousness of simulation. The text then voices anxiety—"He longed to become Real, to know what it felt like"

(Williams 4–5)—about how much he can grow to bear the soul of the Boy (the puppet master) and how much he is a commodity, a simulacrum who veils the uncertain existence, or loss, of natural animal form. Knowing the flesh rabbits are "rabbits like himself" (8) betrays an imagined point of origin, an original behind the simulacrum, that will take shape and haunt him throughout the story. The question of whether there are Real rabbits or not is not initially asked, and this avoidance skirts the fundamental question of whether flesh rabbits are actually more Real or authentic than a loved toy. If we apply the simulacra theory of Jean Baudrillard, who tracks the ascendency of the model or simulation over the Real throughout the twentieth century, particularly with shifting media and media theory, we can understand how the intertwined concepts of "modernity" and "simulacra" are deeply at issue throughout the story. The confusion of meaning in *The Velveteen Rabbit* is a tragic mirror of the century's breakdown in distinctions between representations and referents, as the century transformed its experience by grasping for the Real through images, models, and simulations of reality.

If we place *The Velveteen Rabbit* in a very wide context of nonhuman characters who become sentient and experience the virtual game of testing the boundaries of reality, we find that no definition of authentic reality is definitive. Using theories of puppetry, animation, simulacrum, and virtual reality, I press the unstable boundaries of the Real—and who defines it—by analyzing the rabbit's inability to sort and separate models and originals, dependent on one another for recognition in a culture of commodities, media, and images. Tropes of child development permeate toy stories, as discourses of childhood and development are mapped onto nonhuman figures to simulate our ideals of childhood, rebellion, and self-actualization, while also veiling our paradoxical ideas of what it means to be human—and whether being human is a good thing. The endings of Carlo Collodi's *The Adventures of Pinocchio* (1883) and Steven Spielberg's *A.I.* (2001)—in which the child-toy and a pleasure model bot are linked together as fetishes of adults—convey reality as degradation rather than self-actualization, which suggests the question of reality is simply unanswerable and therefore destabilizes our very ideas of what it means to move from childhood to adulthood in a culture of images, commodities, and digital codes more perfect than us. Rather than interpreting *The Velveteen Rabbit* as a failure or deus ex machina, I argue it is precisely the irresolvable nature of the existential dilemma that we appreciate most. In fact, the Rabbit's organization of virtual communities for recognition moves him into the realm of the avatar.

Animating the Puppet

These questions are pressing in our age of simulacrum, digital culture, and virtual realities, but we can trace them through time since the early nineteenth century when Heinrich von Kleist wrote "On the Marionette Theatre" (1810), positing the puppet as absolute perfection because it—like a god—lacks human consciousness. Puppetry is a relevant theory for Rabbit because, presumably, the theory of how being Real is a matter of being loved by a child means also being played with and therefore becoming a puppet or vessel for a higher soul—akin to divine, animating love. To von Kleist, puppets are pure grace with their own center of gravity and perfection of movement—whereas humans are deeply flawed. The fact that the marionette is a vessel without consciousness makes it the perfect vehicle to bear the puppeteer's soul. This is deeply ironic since the primary role of the puppet as metaphor and as performer has always been, in European traditions, to parrot or plagiarize live-action theater (Shershow 43–49). However, as Victoria Nelson argues in *The Secret Life of Puppets* (2001), puppets and puppetry have always been paradoxically godlike and wondrous yet lower on the social hierarchy, identified with itinerancy, irreverence, street theater, parody, plagiarism, working classes, subversion, carnival, and cheap "magic" tricks of stagecraft compared to creative, illusive reality. Puppets bear the vexed status of children—are they a lesser form of human or closer to the divine?

The idea of the puppet brought to life and therefore animated by the artist's soul took root in romantic theory; for example, E. T. A. Hoffmann posited that dolls and automata were uncanny mechanical degradations simulating human life, whereas in his *Nutcracker and Mouse King* (1816), the children reject the mechanical castle given to them by Drosselmeier; and Marie, in particular, breathes her soul into the simpler, malleable toy. In Hoffmann's "Automatons" (1814) the main character, Lewis, longs for his childhood nutcracker, who seemed "really alive," in contrast to the mechanical Turk or the simulated humans programmed to play mechanical music. To a child, the lines between Real and not Real are fluid and "transitional," whereas to adults, as Sigmund Freud argues, the line produces the uncanny because it speaks to our discomfort with boundaries between life and death. The Velveteen Rabbit's story emphasizes both our postmodern uncertainty about boundaries between the Real and virtual and our modernist nostalgia for originals behind simulacra, which gesture to divine meaning. A culture of simulation, cinema, television, advertising, and endless images embodies "a precession of the model," whereas "facts no longer have a specific trajectory, [but] are born at the intersection of models" (Baudrillard 16). The flesh rabbits are hyperreal in the sense that they gesture to a totality of meaning or faith in a transcendent reality, quickly slipping away with the precession of simulacra in the twentieth century.

Theater theorists reacted to the German romantics and swiftly began a debate about whether puppets are better actors than humans because they more perfectly execute the will of the artist, as controversially argued in 1977 by Fyodor Sologub and Daniel Gerould in "The Theatre of One Will." Puppet theory paved the way for early twentieth-century animation development. Early animated shorts, as

Donald Crafton argues, continually emphasize the relationship of the creator's hand to the animated character, often conveying a genesis theme as the creator brings the inanimate to sentience and thereby breathes life or soul into the artwork (12). The figure of Pinocchio, whose story was written in late nineteenth-century Italy, has become an undercurrent in early animation films created by Walt Disney as he, too, sought to make animation a real, respected form for the middle class. Similarly, a pioneering stop-motion film *The Mascot* (1933) by Ladislas Starewicz used early film tricks to explore in feature length a stuffed animal coming to life and loving a child, animated by the relationship. He comes to life from the human mother's tear, shed over her sick child, and this tear—much as the Velveteen Rabbit's tear will animate a fairy to grant hyperreality—falls into the stuffed dog's heart and brings him to life. This parent-child genesis paradigm continues to influence films in which various dolls (*A.I.*), computers (*2001: Space Odyssey*, *War Games*, *Her*, etc.), cyborgs (*Ex Machina*), robots (*Bladerunner*), etc. play out the "toy story" of asking whether imperfections, relationships, self-awareness, bodies, or communities (often prosthetic) constitute reality.

Early in *The Velveteen Rabbit*, the Skin Horse explains to Rabbit that being Real is not a matter of how you are made. This suggests that being Real is not a matter of design. Yet Rabbit's scrunchy, pincushion-like backside and lack of gears, mobility, and sharpness make him the perfect shape for the Boy to put places and pose him. Steve Tillis notes that three elements create the illusion of reality with puppets—motion, voice, and design (119–57). Thus, the matter of design is actually crucial, as von Kleist romanticized. The design of a marionette defines the center of gravity, the axes around which all movement gracefully and consistently, even organically, rotates. Design determines movement and pantomime. Merely an open mouth combined with subtle forehead shifts express in pantomime the exaggerated gesture the puppeteer wants to reflect.

Neither puppeteer nor puppet nor technologies control the process, and "the aesthetics of puppetry" clarify that it is our perception of the simultaneous existence of object and performance that defines our response. According to Tillis, "We would call the process [of seeing puppets perform] double-vision, for, in the course of the performance, the audience sees the puppet, through perception and through imagination, as an object and as a life; that is, it sees the puppet in two ways at once" (64). Tillis adds that this double vision created by the puppet generates constant tension, standing in for our own predicament in being both objects and subjects alive in the world. Rabbit's tension is particularly sharp because he harbors the trace of a mythic "Real" animal and is, in fact, a commodity as much as a puppet.

It is Rabbit's predicament that the responses of others define whom he feels himself to be at any given moment. Although he has speech and an expressive "fat and bunchy" (Williams 1) design that the Boy can posture in particularly loving and playful ways, his motion is entirely determined by the Boy. Therefore his "commonplace" and nonmechanical design simulates the ideal Hoffmann defined in the nutcracker, which renders the Skin Horse's declaration a bit untenable, as untenable as his thesis that you do not mind being hurt when you are Real. If Spielberg's *A.I.* furthers any clear idea in its mess of Freudian fixations, it is that *mecha* (the Japanese word for "robots") before David do not plea for their lives and do not recoil at pain; David is more Real because he does, and it is unlikely that a sentient being feeling Real does not mind pain. In fact, this is contradicted in the story, when the pain of being disposed of creates a despairing outburst and a tear. The Velveteen Rabbit is actually perfectly designed to be a vessel for the Boy's soul, and therefore to be Real in terms of puppetry. A bunchy and squooshy body is precisely the means for him to conform to postures of sitting for picnics, for being smooshed into the pillow, and for the outdoor play they initiate.

The early scene with the other modern nursery toys in *The Velveteen Rabbit* embodies conditions of capitalism and the value of objects based on price and modern capacities for mechanical movement. When the toys mock Rabbit for not having modern elements, we are already aware of how reality (or value or authenticity) is always contingent on community values and a denial of simulacra's reality. The mechanical toys "pretend [to be] real" because they know of the originals of which they are models, but Rabbit cannot "claim to be a model of anything" (Williams 2), which would somehow make him more Real because, presumably, an original behind a simulacrum solidifies a transcendent reality or Platonic ideal. Yet he has "real thread whiskers" (1) and real questions about the process of living. As Steven V. Daniels notes, his passivity is poignant, which gives some readers pause; the theory that he has to be loved to become Real defines reality based on circumstances out of one's control—based on a consumer's desire, if you will (17). In fact, the Boy has no desire for Rabbit but is arbitrarily matched with him by Nana when his first toy is lost. Thus, it is not unexpected that the Boy will replace him later, not unlike the fickle adults who toss around toys based on whims. And Fairy, after all, grows from Rabbit's real tear, suggesting an ever-present reality acquired from pain and death.

If Rabbit evokes the problem of the precession of the model and the interaction of commodities that need consumers for purposes of animating desire, he also evokes early twentieth-century media when puppets and toys were spurring technological and theoretical developments in stop-motion animation. The earliest animation shorts often featured toys and other objects magically moving, promoting the illusion of life in cinema (Harryhausen and Dalton 36–50). Likewise, puppets increasingly found complexity and narrative representation in cinema, just as they found a secure place in experimental modern drama (Segel 34–75). Developments in model animation with toy dinosaurs were carried forth by Ray Harryhausen throughout the 1920s (Harryhausen and Dalton 50–51). Lines of the possible were quickly blurring through technology and artistry. Starewicz, after failed efforts to film beetle battles for a museum, began creating animated shorts of puppets crafted from dead insects in the 1910s, and many audiences believed actual bugs were trained as performing artists. The period in which Williams wrote *The Velveteen Rabbit* is likewise the period in which cinema would be slowly transforming media reception of animated beings, somewhere in between awareness of cinema puppetry and faith in the real or original animal behind the performing object.

Puppets have always been imitative and lower on the social hierarchy of dramatic arts (Shershow 56–89). The story of a commonplace Rabbit humbly trying to find his place taps into the history of model animation itself, not fully accepted into major cinema until the 1930s (Harryhausen and Dalton 54). A neighboring text that seems relevant to the story of the Velveteen Rabbit is Starewicz's *The Mascot*, the first feature-length tale of a stuffed dog coming to life to save an ill child. Not only does a tear animate the dog's heart, gesturing to a desire to heal the rupture between simulacrum and human reality that we see in *The Velveteen Rabbit*, but also Duffy's long quest to get an orange for the child who owns him establishes the purpose of the toy story. A long adventure ensues in which the dog falls into various mishaps with other toys, who are both grotesque and independent. These threatening toys are sequenced in the famous "Satan's Ball," where skeletons and glassware threaten the domesticated stuffed toy. In other words, we recognize the domestic toy as acceptable stop-motion because independently animated toys are actually threatening.

Toy communities represent the hostilities and realities of class culture, in which all animals are equal, but some are more equal than others. The boundary between Real and unreal seems more to do with the boundary between the domestic and wild. In the same way that the wild rabbits threaten the "owned" and therefore "real" identity of Rabbit, the toys of Sid's room in *Toy Story* seem independently animated and therefore embody the contrast between the "wild" or grotesque underside of the domestic and the tame toys caring for a child in Andy's room. Rabbit's body becomes more and more grotesque outside the house, where, as Scott T. Pollard and Kara K. Keeling argue in this volume, structures of ableism suddenly define Rabbit as disabled. The garden functions as a space where scenes of abjection occur—where Rabbit questions his body, likely due to the liminality of being between the domestic and independent.

Early cinema used toys and objects to play with scale and technology, often contrasting toys lovingly brought to life and properly domesticated with independent toy communities that could threaten and take action; for example, in the short "Revolt of the Toys" (1946), toys unite against a Nazi. This convention of "wild" toys underscores Kuznets's analysis that toy stories convey the terror of independence (4), for which Rabbit is not ready but which seems to entrance him when he sees the biological rabbits. Before he sees the "wild" flesh rabbits, all he wishes is to be loved by the Boy. Since he does not know the originals that he models, his wish articulates the deep irony of the simulacrum's contingent status. Rabbit is parallel to Buzz Lightyear of *Toy Story*. The puppet who is ignorant of his status as a puppet creates both an innocence and a pathos. Buzz, too, evinces the type of depressive anxiety Daniels equates with the Velveteen Rabbit (18) after seeing evidence of his mass production in media.

Being a toy or child's plaything taps into a long Western discourse of using puppetry as a symbol for someone lacking power or plagiarizing others. Puppets have also long been associated with women, lower classes, street theater, and itinerancy (Shershow 93), therefore situating Rabbit and Buzz in the position of the feminine despite male pronouns, individuals who cannot self-actualize because their job is to serve children—to be domesticated rather than wild. Further, the role of Skin Horse in explaining Rabbit's insufficiency and need parallels the role of media in *Toy Story*. It is the television that shows Buzz his status as a mass-produced commodity. Therefore, Skin Horse functions as a sort of outside medium introducing false ego ideals, standing for a screen that advertises all-consuming, monogamous love as the supreme goal of humanity, here named "reality." A false ideal becomes a real ideal when an influencer, like Skin Horse, broadcasts it as such, but a mediated ideal hardly embodies a realistically achievable goal that satisfies a quest for authenticity.

Virtualizing Reality

Although he promotes actualization through private relationship, Skin Horse most helpfully undercuts his own premise by noting that only through a gradual process do you "*become*" (Williams 4; emphasis added). It is obvious Rabbit does not heed this because he so suddenly believes and boasts that the Boy's pronouncement of his reality makes it so. Reality is a process that is perpetual—a dynamic and shifting process of perpetual uncertainty about communal validation (Jacobson 12). Rabbit already breathes, cries, feels, and asks questions, but the nursery community refuses to validate his reality. However, the Boy introduces the idea of real rabbits by making burrows and explaining they are like the ones real rabbits use. In this play space, therefore, a consciousness is born, and from the transitional play Rabbit learns three things: he gains some sort of awareness or idea of an original that he models; he learns there is another world beyond self; and he discovers that play is a space of simultaneously modeling and masking the Real. Their play is in some sense virtual, a simulated environment wherein social exchanges occur that mean one thing to Rabbit (his status as the Boy's real love object) and another thing to the Boy (reaching out to the world of real rabbits), as parent-child rituals often do (Clark 13–20). They play at night after Nana has left them, constructing a secret world where real and model, in fact, collide. This is important because in a child's transitional space, defined by D. W. Winnicott, the object or commodity and personal meaning fuse (Jacobson 10–15).

Again, the Boy makes burrows for Rabbit outside in the flower bed, suggesting the Boy is Rabbit's threshold guide to the sense of an expanding world, one in which a broader communal affirmation may await. Real is not just acceptance and communal validation, but also it is the deeper sense that one's very reality is understood and acknowledged. Diverse marginalized people find every day that their realities, histories, and needs are not authenticated in a world designed for and by people with greater power. Fascinatingly, the final community of hyperreal rabbits into which the Velveteen Rabbit is initiated is already being played and pantomimed in the relationship between Boy and Rabbit. The Boy has shown him, however unclearly, that a broader community of rabbits exists, and that Rabbit is a model for them, but that the real rabbits are models for how they play together. In play, the Velveteen Rabbit moves from toy to puppet, expressive of the Boy's understanding and creation of a real world of organic animals. In other words, the Boy's love (if we accept the Boy's behavior as love) generates the impulse for knowledge of more than a child's love. Their play sets in motion the dynamic "becoming" that will result in a hint of dissatisfaction with monogamy and dependence on one person for feeling real. This is ironic but also poignant, since the ways we act with wider communities are probably rooted in our familial relationships.

If we read the story closely, after Rabbit sees flesh rabbits, he has a secret desire to be with other bunnies, after which the Boy gets sick. In symbolic logic, argues Daniels, it is this desire, unspoken and unacknowledged (as a betrayal), that motivates the uncomfortable shift in how the bunny is first cherished and then finds himself tossed in a sack behind the shed (Williams 23). Daniels calls his thoughts of pointlessness depressive anxiety, which is not answered but altered altogether by the Fairy in her role as the deus ex machina. But does, as Daniels argues, the bunny desire to be more than a child's toy? Is this the unspoken secret of the text? Is there an unspoken acknowledgment that the Boy's articulation of the bunny's reality is insufficient, which then sheds critical light on the Skin Horse's insufficient thesis of being loved by a child as the epitome of reality? Are we always already aware in one relationship that there are others into which we might shift and therefore become something else? Even at the end, Rabbit and Boy have a brief recognition, an encounter that although both have moved on, a residue of the past "original" always haunts the relationship organized around simulacra.

The Boy's love might have made Rabbit Real, in terms of bearing the soul of puppetry, but it did not make him *alive*. Not only does the Boy introduce the idea of a hyperreality through play, and in one key scene of separation the Rabbit is viewed as dirty from his burrowing, but also the Boy names him "REAL" in performative protest to Nana, who calls Rabbit "a toy" (Williams 7, emphasis original). Rabbit does not actually feel real on his own, and his passive receipt of this news stunningly reifies his lack of agency and autonomy. It is at this moment he feels love in his heart, which is different from being loved; in other words, it is not for the Boy but for Rabbit's own desired reality that his heart feels love.

When Rabbit sees two real bunnies in the woods, he evinces no conscious awareness that they are not models of puppets that happen to be exceptionally well designed. Real *is* a matter of design, it turns out, and design fuels Rabbit's subjective perception of them as animated models, who mysteriously "changed shape" from "fat and bunchy" like him to "long and thin" as they move. As if love for his own nominal reality summoned them, his acceptance into the community of the Boy and even Nana (who looks at him differently) seems to have set in place a readiness to objectify monogamy and see there might be more to it: "Rabbit stared hard to see which side the clockwork stuck out, for he knew that people who jump generally have something to wind them up. But he couldn't see it. They were evidently a new kind of rabbit altogether" (9). Rabbit views the two new figures in the terms of puppetry, as simultaneously objects and lives. The three axes of design, motion, and speech come into focus. When Rabbit later talks to the rabbits, his protesting speech and denials of their taunts directly echo the Boy's to Nana in a prior scene, gesturing to the voice of the puppeteer at odds with the newly acquired lens on these two other "puppets." The Rabbit, ironically, gestures to the history of automata by looking for clockwork motion, for early automata ran on clockwork (Standage 2–11). To him, the real rabbits replay the history of mechanical simulacra; further, he views them as models of himself in the fact that sometimes they are fat and bunchy like him, and their seams and coats are measured in comparison to his own body. For Rabbit, in the twentieth-century industrial context, a simulacrum is real, and the original is lost and puzzling. The hyperreal rabbits bear traces of his own scrunchy body, rather than vice versa. The entire question of reality in *The Velveteen Rabbit* is anchored to confusion between simulacra culture and hyperreality; Rabbit sees them as improved models, and indeed, when he becomes one, he and the Boy recognize himself as an improved model in the evolutionary chain of simulation.

Although the theme of what Rabbit sees in the flesh bunnies is change, the dynamism that theorizes life as perpetual becoming, he processes seeing them entirely through his own reality, thinking he is the real thing and they are very good imitations or improved models. In a culture of endless images and parodies, for which the puppet always stands, everything is a simulation of everything else, and no original exists or can be understood without models. By now, the bunny should know he is understood as a model, which has been an implicit instruction in play space. After all, he sees them as "rabbits like himself" (Williams 8), acknowledging a common ancestor. The fact that he does not bring this assumption into consciousness sets up a paradox—we know models by originals, but we only know originals by models of them. Even language works this way, as Jacques Derrida suggests in his myriad writings on language and difference; we only learn the category of "cow" by the few we see. Therefore, we cannot learn any precise meaning of "cow" but learn a binary category of "not-cow," which helps us discern "cow." Rabbit can only view the two organic rabbits through the lens of simulation.

In fact, layers of simulation permeate gazes in the work. At the end, the Boy sees in the organic rabbit traces or simulations of the velveteen toy he once had; one always haunts the other. Similarly in life, we cannot tell whether simulated human beings (cyborgs, robots, androids, avatars) are models *of* us or whether they are ideals and we are the models of approximate ideals. Those who argue that perfect images of women in advertising hurt real women by making them feel inauthentic and less perfect are ironically pointing out that our "models" become gods to whom we, as lesser models, cannot measure up. Our seams always show when we have more perfect simulacra as ego ideals.

Various texts define reality for performing objects in various ways. If Rabbit's lack of mobility, autonomy, and communal validation inform his crisis of being inorganic, or the sudden consciousness of it, for other toys, like Pinocchio, autonomy is precisely the problem, and reality only comes with putting others first. If *The Velveteen Rabbit* offers the idea that love makes you become Real—and here we have confusion over loving and being loved—texts like *The Iron Giant* (1999) situate choice and free will as more important. By that standard, Rabbit fails. Whereas the Rabbit's tear and therefore innate sense of reality creates the Fairy, or the basis for entering the new organic community of peers, tears threaten characters like the Tin Man, who literally becomes paralyzed from fluids. What toys and puppet-like beings suggest is that reality shifts with community and market.

It seems to me that *The Velveteen Rabbit* replays the paradox of being human and especially being a child: experiencing constant change of communities and, consequently, mixed messages about which realities are valid. Varying environments have varying expectations, and what is expected from parents is not synonymous with what is expected at school or in sports or by peers and at parties. The expectation that a child can move between adult-governed worlds gracefully is exploded in toy stories, where radical entries into new communities shake the core meaning of the self. Pinocchio is a case in point. Each environment radically shifts his behavior and values. He cannot learn an abstract principle, like not to lie, because when he confesses that he has money to the Cat and Fox, they attack him; hiding the truth from Fairy makes perfect sense after learning that revealing too much to ill-motivated strangers is a terrible idea. Truth is often antithetical to social conventions and even politeness. The child who reveals on the phone that her mother is in the bathroom might be reprimanded for revealing too much truth. The child who tells her grandmother she does not like her present is scolded for impoliteness. Yet the lying Pinocchio is pecked by birds. Without any consistency in various communal realities, the lesson to learn is what Mikhail Bakhtin termed "heteroglossia." The real game in Alice's looking glass and other works about pawns is that social nuances in different communities trump consistencies.

However, it is not until Rabbit sees the flesh bunnies that he feels longing: "But all the while he was longing to dance, for a funny new tickly feeling ran through him, and he felt he would give anything in the world to be able to jump about like these rabbits did" (Williams 10–11). Rabbit has no experience of the jumping and dancing the rabbits are doing, and his voice takes on an emotional bravado when he denies his body's limitations. In fact, biological instinct prevails, as it does later when he does not realize his body has changed until he feels the instinct to twitch and itch, mechanical impulses rooted in a new organic design. Bunny's insistence that he is Real because the Boy said so means being Real is not a state one can ever really own. He feels most alone when the rabbits run off, wishing they would stay and hoping they return. This is the onset of desire, even paralleling sexuality with the focus on "a funny new tickly feeling" and the need for a working lower half of the body. The fact that he sees two bunnies suggests mating, for which rabbits are quite known. Their critique of his nonambulatory state is inherently castrating and at odds with his new tingles, much akin to Buzz's disintegration when he is told by mass media that he is not a flying toy.

Daniels and Kuznets both argue that the Boy's illness registers the guilt of abandonment because Rabbit develops desires beyond the Boy, which he cannot consciously utter or acknowledge. However, we could see the illness as a symbol of not their increasing separation and the discontent of growing up, but as an infection by the poison of suddenly becoming aware of one's difference from the community, through a type of hyperreal media imagining. The very thing that makes him loved by his first parent/creator (the Boy), his lack of independence and squishy bottom that stays wherever it is placed, is the very thing that is detested by a different community, just as swearing with adolescent peers might be an appropriate signage for acceptance but probably not with parents or teachers. This decentering of a core essence to the self accords with Judith Butler's theory of performance as a set of repertoires through which we perform gender and identity. Rabbit has actually participated through play in a real-bunny script, but in the moment of encounter, he loses his repertoire of the stage and becomes a spectator of not-velveteen-ness. The rabbits evince no awareness of his status as a toy, measuring him against their bodies and physical abilities. They do not recognize in him a model of them, at any rate. In the encounter between presumed original and simulacrum, it is no longer entirely clear which is which since each fails to recognize the other.

Therefore, *The Velveteen Rabbit* is concerned with the lack of recognition that unfolds when models simulate originals, when the referent and Real depend on each other to construct each other. Simulations and replacements (toys replacing other toys) abound in toy stories; by the end, Rabbit is a simulation of his toy self partially, but not fully, recognized by the Boy. In fact, the Velveteen Rabbit is more unique than the mass, indistinguishable groups of bunnies by virtue of his fat bunchy body and seams. The tear he sheds earlier seems to be a rupture of simulacra's pretense because, akin to the abject theorized by Julia Kristeva, it crosses boundaries between the repressed and the commodified, or the ordered body comprised of accessories and parts. The repression has to do with the nature of being unloved as a simulacrum and being damaged to the point of abuse. Yet in the final moments, he is partially recognized as a liminal figure, separate from the mass of flesh rabbits, who was once unique as a simulacrum and with whom the Boy played "original" real rabbits.

The detail that Rabbit grew "old and shabby" (Williams 12) after his encounter with the rabbits who mock him could signify the loss that accompanies detachment from nature. In fact, the more domestic affection is given to him, the more "he scarcely looked like a rabbit, . . . except to the Boy" (12), who, as we have observed, retains faith that an original exists beyond the simulacrum. Calling attention to his loss of original rabbitness, which he never had, suggests that the encounter with flesh rabbits pushes him further into a domestic relationship with the Boy and away from awareness of wild rabbits. The more you become like simulacra, the less you resemble the original.

The Boy's investment in Rabbit being a model is fascinating to ponder in the schema of virtual realities here since the Boy constructs the virtual as a model of the real, but the bunny becomes a character in it and cannot see the virtual. From a postmodern viewpoint, Rabbit is rather an avatar for the Boy, created to simulate flesh behavior through play, interacting in their virtual space through scripted performance. Teri Silvio, in her analysis of puppets, avatars, and like figures, suggests the lens of performance theory is the best approach to cultural practices of animation. Avatars are somewhere in between the real and the imaginary but "allow users to interact in social space" (Meadows 13). Losing his brown spots and whiskers, which were described as "real thread," shows how much Rabbit is being turned into the virtual, which is here the transitional reality the Boy needs. The Boy needs him to be less recognizable to flesh rabbits but linked to the real world through burrowing play. Ironically, the Velveteen Rabbit's first encounter with being (flesh) Real is in the Boy's play space, showing how much that space is ruled by the Boy, or gamer, as it were. Rabbit is merely a pawn in that space. In fact, in that space, the narrator declares him Real: "nursery magic had made him Real, and when you are Real, shabbiness doesn't matter" (Williams 12). This assertion is all the more confusing after the narrator and not just the Boy names him Real, a theory to be overturned with hyperreality later. From puppet to avatar carrying forth social interactions in hyperreality, yet returning to the Boy for recognition, Rabbit deftly challenges empirical realities and recognitions by substituting virtual communities.

Conclusion: The Avatar at Home

Rabbit's devotion during the illness reveals the narrator's respect for his agency and choice, given his lack of mobility without the Boy. Whereas Rabbit has used different voices with Skin Horse and the real rabbits, during the illness, he whispers to the Boy, and in response, the Boy gets better. When condemned to fire, he is put outside "at the end of the garden behind the fowl-house" (Williams 15), *beyond* animals kept domesticated. He despairs about the pointlessness of being Real if it ends in homelessness, abandonment, and death. However, the Fairy's declaration that he will be "real to every one" (17) involves being wild, not a pet. It is only the Fairy's commands that make the wild rabbits accept him; she tells them to be "kind" (18)—they certainly were not earlier. He does not feel the transformation, only the trauma of the earlier social shame, until instinct trumps consciousness: "before he thought what he was doing he lifted his hind toe to scratch it" (18). In other words, reality is perceived as a mechanical response to the pre-conscious flesh—the natural instinct, which is as much a matter of mechanics and design as being a toy was. Yet just as Kuznets notes the problem of living "for ever" with the flesh rabbits who are mortal (61), we note the problem of being "a Real Rabbit at last, at home with the other rabbits" (Williams 19), real as an artifact of being "at home." This is a strange word choice of at-home-ness given that he is specifically not transformed into a pet and allowed to maintain a relationship with the Boy in a domestic context.

The irony of being "at home" in the wild underscores the logic of simulation and simulacra. But the ending image is of two rabbits seeing the Boy, suggesting Rabbit has a mate and more than the joy of hind legs. The final lines, however, fuse the model with the copy, and the model infuses his presumably "flesh," original status:

> [T]he spots still showed through. And about his little soft nose and his round black eyes there was something familiar, so that the Boy thought to himself:
> "Why, he looks just like my old Bunny that was lost when I had scarlet fever!"
> But he never knew that it really was his own Bunny, come back to look at the child who had first helped him to be Real. (19)

In other words, spots show through because the original (some vague category of "real rabbits") and the model intertwine; the real bears the trace of the simulacrum, otherwise we could not understand the real at all. In the Boy's eyes, the bunny before him is a model of his original velveteen one. The word "really" in "it really was his own Bunny" smacks of irony in that "his own Bunny" now has a real status primarily because he is not owned and not a commodity, and the ending simultaneously verifies reality in the domestic relationship with the Boy and overrules it. What is missing, of course, is the pet—the possibility of being a flesh rabbit and having a relationship with the Boy.

Whereas Rabbit feels he is not a modern toy because he lacks machinery and clockwork gears, not to mention any sense of his own status as simulacrum, his story is very much a modern one: the crisis of passivity and alienation that occurs when you are at the mercy of tricks of stop motion and animation that substitute poses for the real, commodities for values, and models for originals. Within this web of simulations and prewired design issues, however, the Rabbit self-actualizes by fusing his status as virtual model with a new game, having embraced his role as avatar with the Boy. As such, his demand for recognition at the end means that he has fused the burrowing model taught in play (akin to a video game) with a hyperreal posture acquired through a new community. It may not matter if the Boy fully recognizes him in return, since the virtual space the Boy created did indeed help Rabbit first become Real. Through circulation in virtual space as a simulacrum, Rabbit achieves independence and even fetish status, for it is the very independence of simulacra that creates the confused, contingent realities that we now call hyperspace, whether or not we fully recognize and acknowledge the relationships between ourselves and the avatars we create.

Works Cited

A.I. Artificial Intelligence. Directed by Steven Spielberg, Warner Brothers, 2001.
Bakhtin, Mikhail. *The Dialogic Imagination*, edited by Michael Holquist. Translated by Michael Holquist and Caryl Emerson, U of Texas P, 1983.
Baudrillard, Jean. *Simulacra and Simulation*. Translated by Sheila Faria Glaser, U of Michigan P, 1994.
Butler, Judith. *Gender Trouble: Feminism and the Subversion of Identity*. Routledge, 2006.
Clark, Cindy. *Flights of Fancy, Leaps of Faith: Children's Myths in Contemporary America*. U of Chicago P, 1995.
Crafton, Donald. *Before Mickey: The Animated Film. 1898–1928*. MIT P, 1982.
Daniels, Steven V. "*The Velveteen Rabbit*: A Kleinian Perspective." *Children's Literature*, vol. 18, 1990, pp. 17–30.
Freud, Sigmund. "The 'Uncanny': (1919)." *Massachusetts Institute of Technology*, https://web.mit.edu/allanmc/www/freud1.pdf. Accessed 25 Feb. 2020.

Harryhausen, Ray, and Tony Dalton. *A Century of Model Animation: From Melies to Aardman.* Aurum P, 2008.

Hoffmann, E. T. A. "Automatons." *The Serapion Brethren, vol. I*, translated by Alex Ewing, George Bell and Sons, 1908. *Project Gutenberg*, https://www.gutenberg.org/files/31820/31820-h/31820-h.htm. Accessed 9 Oct. 2022.

Hoffmann, E. T. A. *Nutcracker and Mouse King. E. T. A. Hoffmann:* Nutcracker and Mouse King; *Alexandre Dumas:* The Tale of the Nutcracker, translated by Joachim Neugroschel, Penguin, 2007, pp. 1–62.

Jacobson, Kirsten. "Heidegger, Winnicott, and *The Velveteen Rabbit*: Anxiety, Toys, and the Drama of Metaphysics." *Philosophy in Children's Literature*, edited by Peter R. Costello, Lexington, 2012, pp. 1–20.

Kristeva, Julia. *The Powers of Horror: An Essay on Abjection.* Translated by Leon S. Roudiez, Columbia UP, 1982.

Kuznets, Lois Rostow. *When Toys Come Alive: Narratives of Animation, Metamorphosis, and Development.* Yale UP, 1994.

The Mascot. Directed by Wladyslaw Starewicz [Ladislas Starewicz], Gelma-Films, 1933.

Meadows, Mark Stephen. *I, Avatar: The Culture and Consequence of Having a Second Life.* New Riders, 2008.

Nelson, Victoria. *The Secret Life of Puppets.* Harvard UP, 2001.

Segel, Harold B. *Pinocchio's Progeny: Puppets, Marionettes, Automatons, and Robots in Modernist and Avant-Garde Drama.* Johns Hopkins UP, 1995.

Shershow, Scott Cutler. *Puppets and "Popular" Culture.* Cornell UP, 1995.

Silvio, Teri. "Animation: The New Performance?" *Journal of Linguistic Anthropology*, vol. 20, no. 2, 2010, pp. 422–38.

Sologub, Fyodor, and Daniel Gerould. "The Theatre of One Will." *The Drama Review*, vol. 21, no. 4, 1977, pp. 85–99.

Standage, Tom. *The Turk: The Life and Times of the Famous Eighteenth-Century Chess-Playing Machine.* Walker & Co., 2002.

Tillis, Steve. *Toward an Aesthetics of the Puppet: Puppetry as a Theatrical Act.* Praeger, 1992.

Toy Story. Directed by John Lasseter, Pixar, 1995.

von Kleist, Heinrich. "On the Marionette Theatre." 1810. Translated by Idris Parry, *SouthernCross Review*, vol. 9, Jan.–Feb. 2001, https://southerncrossreview.org/9/kleist.htm. Accessed 9 Oct. 2022.

Williams, Margery. *The Velveteen Rabbit: Or How Toys Become Real.* Heinemann, 1922. *Internet Archive*, https://archive.org/details/velveteenrabbitooobian/page/n49/mode/2up. Accessed 1 Apr. 2022.

Chapter 2

Visualizing Velveteen: Original Illustrations and Subsequent Adaptations

—Kelly Blewett and Alisa Clapp-Itnyre

> Soft and endearing as many picturebook characters may be, they exist in tougher environments than we might imagine, blank spaces of fear. It is up to us to discover their ways of meaning and form, to being-in-the world.
> —William Moebius, "Introduction to Picturebook Codes" (158)

It may be surprising to consider that when *The Velveteen Rabbit* (1922) was first published in the US, William Nicholson, the British illustrator, was more widely known than Margery Williams, the American author. Librarian and critic Anne Carroll Moore, an important early promoter of *The Velveteen Rabbit*, reported that her first question upon seeing the galley was, "Who is Margery Williams and how came William Nicholson to illustrate it?" (Moore and Miller 7). Though he rarely offered media interviews, Nicholson spoke with Moore about *The Velveteen Rabbit* at Appletree Yard, his home in England. She publicly wrote about the encounter at least twice, once in *Bookman's Magazine* (March 1923) and then again in a collection commemorating Margery Williams that was released in 1951. In that volume, Moore wrote: "Mr. Nicholson's character portrait of Queen Victoria with her little dog has been one of my treasures for years and I knew that he had painted some remarkable portraits of children. To associate his name with these fresh interpretive drawings for a children's story gave me a thrill" (Moore and Miller 8). She was so invested in the "fresh interpretive drawings" that she brought the originals back to New York and shared them publicly in the New York Children's Library's 1922 holiday display, just after the book was published. She wrote that the illustrations—seven lithographs colored in red, black, slate blue, and pale yellow—were especially important to children. When children saw the pictures, Moore wrote, they would say, "You can almost see the Velveteen Rabbit changing into a real one" (9).

At first glance, the original illustrations may seem repetitive and abstract.[1] Detailed backgrounds—e.g., the type favored by nineteenth-century artist Walter Crane—are eschewed for moody shadows and sketchy lines. The titular character is prominently placed in six of the seven lithographs as well as on the book cover and within the highly decorated initial capital of the story. Other characters— in fact all human characters, including the Boy—are absent from Nicholson's lithographs. A 1922 review in *Ladies Home Journal* refers to the pictures as "quite the most unusual illustrations of the year" (Farrar 185). Though unusual, there is undeniable power in the illustrations, which was recognized by Moore. She recommended that new parents might frame a print of the Rabbit for their nurseries (Moore, "Who" 201). Such prints are still on sale today.[2] Copies of the book with the original illustrations have been reprinted and sold in 1958, 1975, 1987, and 1991. Indeed, the book with the original illustrations has never been out of print, either in the United States or in England. Nicholson's illustrations inspired late twentieth-century children's illustrators, who often echo his approaches to the story by illustrating the same key narrative moments (such as the Rabbit in the Christmas stocking, the Boy sick in bed, and the Fairy). Clearly the original illustrations have staying power, and the reaction of the children in 1922 may help us understand why by drawing our attention to how Nicholson visualized the Rabbit's transformation.

Our analysis reveals that Nicholson's lithographs do, in fact, communicate the protagonist's transformation in vivid, visual language. For Nicholson, the central tale of *The Velveteen Rabbit* is the journey of the Rabbit himself from toy to living animal. The Boy, while important to the first part of the Rabbit's journey, is ultimately a figure from whom the Rabbit must separate to become fully real. This is not surprising given the era of Sigmund Freud, and readers' appreciation for inner depth, even of a toy protagonist.[3] Such an interpretation of the text anticipates and aligns with subsequent psychoanalytic criticism of *Velveteen* and differs significantly from the interpretations offered by late century illustrated editions of the book. As the second part of this essay explores, in the 1980s, once the copyright expired, a spate of new editions of *Velveteen* emerged in quick succession. The illustrations offered in this second wave of *Velveteen* demonstrate dramatic points of contrast with Nicholson's temperamental originals, bringing back the child as a central visual character, a vulnerable, nurturing boy-hero, psychologically rich for late century readers seeking assurances of childhood well-being. In the subsequent sections, we will first examine how these competing interpretive stances connect to larger critical discussions, and then, we will offer a closer look at both Nicholson's original seven lithographs and a handful of stand-out adaptations. Ultimately, this study brings a critical lens to *Velveteen*'s secondary aesthetic—the illustrations—first to be noticed by readers but often last to be analyzed by critics.

Critical Considerations: Rabbit vs. Boy

The ending of *The Velveteen Rabbit* is undeniably emotional. Faith McNulty, writing in *The New Yorker* in 1982, explains that, for her, the ending "evoked terrible feelings, too complicated to name" (179; see also Weales). The ending is both a reunion and a rejection between the Rabbit and the Boy, and the nature of the relationship between the two characters at this juncture is ambiguous, leading to competing critical interpretations. Psychoanalyst Steven V. Daniels uses the theories of Melanie Klein, a protégé of Freud, to argue that *The Velveteen Rabbit* is ultimately a story about the Rabbit's separation and its attendant anxieties. His desire to break away from the Boy and become a real Rabbit amounts to what Daniels calls a "betrayal of the Boy" (23). Countering Daniels, sociological critic Allan Kellehear argues that the Boy is not the antagonist but a protagonist central to the continued maturation of both characters: "Although the Rabbit was discarded by the Boy's guardians and not, it should be well noted, by the Boy himself, the love between them continues on in both their subsequent lives and memories" (46). Therefore, Kellehear continues, "the story's theme is not about the 'ambivalence of separation' but rather the robust ability of love to transcend separation, even in death" (46). Others have agreed that the second transformation is an extension of, rather than a deviation from, the first transformation (see Ehle; Guroian; Weithman), or alternatively, that the second transformation is just as much about the Boy breaking away from the Rabbit as a transitional object as it is about the Rabbit breaking away from the Boy (Jacobson). Thus, critical debates revolve both around the moments of separation and transformation as well as *whose* separation—Rabbit's or Boy's—becomes the cornerstone of the story. There's also critical disagreement about how children would interpret the illustrations. Specifically addressing Daniels's reading, Kellehear counters that children would find the love between toy and Boy to be a theme "more accessible to the emotional sensibilities of young readers" (40).

It is striking that Nicholson's original illustrations align so clearly with Daniels's psychoanalytic reading. They do so through a purposeful establishment of the tensions and the mood of the Rabbit from the opening pages of the story through the end, when he joins the world of living rabbits. The children's original reaction in the New York Public Library—"You can almost see the Velveteen Rabbit changing"—suggests that children may be more sympathetic to the psychoanalytic perspective than Kellehear imagines. Further, to the modern eye, what is most striking about this illustrated transformation is the complete omission of the

Boy, who has been argued by critics to be a parent figure to the Rabbit (Daniels 21), a stand-in for God himself (Weithman 260), or a fellow protagonist in the story (Jacobson).

In contrast, later adaptations of *The Velveteen Rabbit* more adhere to Kellehear's approach, emphasizing especially the life of the Boy himself "and the love between" Boy and Rabbit (Kellehear 46). Many illustrators include the now-older Boy within the final frame, in various poses of partial recognition of his old toy, which still bears a physical resemblance to his toy-self even though he is now real. If the Rabbit transforms, it is not complete; if the Boy ages, neither does he completely leave childhood. As per Kellehear's sociological reading, children "become socially real when they grow up to be adults and toy rabbits become real when they . . . are no longer required as playthings" (44).

A final point is consideration of the picture-book quality of the story itself. In "Suspended Animation," Nathalie op de Beeck sidelines *The Velveteen Rabbit* in her discussion of Nicholson's illustrated books, arguing that it is not a true modern picture book of balanced picture and text but rather an illustrated story in which the illustrations are subservient to the text (72n2). Later, illustrators utilize different approaches—full-page spreads, even condensing text—to correct the picture-text imbalance of the original. The visual theories of Perry Nodelman, William Moebius, and Molly Bang, as well as our own close readings of about a dozen illustrated editions of *The Velveteen Rabbit*, 1922–2013, help us "discover . . . ways of meaning and form" (Moebius 157), particularly the ways the illustrations draw out moments of fear and separation implicit in both the Rabbit's and the Boy's stories.

Nicholson and the Original Illustrations: Portraits of a Changing Rabbit

Remembered today as a landscape and still-life painter, Nicholson was a talented and prolific producer of many artistic genres. In the 1890s, he distinguished himself as a graphic designer, decorating London with bold posters made in a small print shop with his brother-in-law. Around the turn of the century, he released a popular book of woodcut portraits.[4] He began painting oil portraits, many of which were of children. By the early twenties, he was a well-regarded portraitist who had also dabbled in theater, for instance designing the sets and costumes for the first production of *Peter Pan: Or, the Boy Who Would Not Grow Up* (Schwartz 1).

The illustrations Nicholson produced for *Velveteen* were lithographs, yet similarities with his oil portraits are evident. In both portraiture and illustration, Nicholson utilizes shadow and textured surfaces to maintain a central perspective on the subject. In *Velveteen*, Nicholson offers repeated images with the Rabbit at or near the center of the frame and avoids complex, symbolic backgrounds. It is reasonable to think of his representations of the Rabbit as a kind of object portraiture, which is how some critics regard his later still-life paintings (see Reed). Yet when the illustrations are assembled side by side, a kind of visual sequence emerges—what Michael P. Grady and Emily A. Luecke call the "picture sentence" (qtd. in Nodelman 177). Subtle changes to angle and color, to line and composition and perspective, draw readers into the Rabbit's story. These changes suggest the passage of time and, as the children in the New York Public Library saw, transformation. Nicholson zeroes in on key moments of the Rabbit's journey, offering a provocative—and perhaps even counter-textual—interpretation of the story's ending.

His focus on the Rabbit begins on the first page of the story by way of a decorative letter (figure 2.1)—i.e., the initial capital—that opens the first line of the book: "There was once a velveteen rabbit, and in the beginning he was really splendid" (Williams 1922, 9). This image immediately raises a question for the reader: Who are the two rabbits? Perhaps they are the Velveteen Rabbit and a reflection of himself or perhaps the Velveteen Rabbit and one of the wild rabbits referred to later in the story. The long line of the *T* itself could be a kind of divide that the story will try to cross, which Moebius indicates exist in some illustration compositions: "between these images lies a buffer zone, an undefined 'wilderness'" (130). From the very first letter, then, the conflict of the story—as presented by the illustrations—lies primarily with the Rabbit, who is longing for another rabbit across a divide. The distance between the two rabbits is heightened by the design choices of the *T*. Rather than straight, the *T* is slanted, which can represent both motion and tension (see Bang 62). Rather than a solid line, the *T* is filled with zippered white jags, which emphasize the separation between the rabbits. As will become apparent, adjustments with shading and angles are similarly taken up in other illustrations in the book, demonstrating that these details are far from arbitrary, but instead work together to establish a central effect. As Nodelman explains, well-executed picture books "seem complete" because "the various systems of signification they evoke all seem to support and amplify the same central effect" (43). In Nicholson's *Velveteen Rabbit*, the focus is the transformation of the Rabbit, and visual patterns he establishes at the beginning and develops throughout the text draw attention to this feature of the story.

Unlike the editions of *Velveteen* that were published in the latter half of the twentieth century, Nicholson provided only seven illustrations. Each one was titled and included in a "List of Illustrations" preceding the text: no. 1 "Christmas Morning"; no. 2 "The Skin Horse Tells His Story"; no. 3 "Spring Time"; no. 4 "Summer Days"; no. 5 "Anxious Times"; no. 6 "The Fairy Flower"; and no. 7 "At Last! At Last!"

Original Illustrations and Subsequent Adaptations 43

Figure 2.1 The *T* from the opening line of *The Velveteen Rabbit*, original edition, illustrated by William Nicholson.

We could chart these illustrations along a traditional plot scheme. During the exposition, we would have image 1 ("Christmas Morning"). Image 2 would incite the rising action, as the Rabbit tries to figure out what it means to be "Real" through conversation with the Skin Horse. The incline of the action would escalate more steeply after image 4, which documents the Velveteen Rabbit's confrontation with two wild rabbits. Image 6 is the climax, as the Fairy emerges to transform the Velveteen Rabbit, and image 7 is the resolution as the Rabbit enjoys his new way of being in the world.

The narrative begins on Christmas morning. Setting a pattern that will be repeated in subsequent editions, Nicholson opens the book with an image of the Velveteen Rabbit in a Christmas stocking. The viewer's eye is drawn to the center of the picture, where the Velveteen Rabbit is featured in a portrait-like composition that will be repeated in images 3 and 5. As Bang writes, the center of the page is also the center of the reader's attention (84). The Rabbit is heavily shaded in red, with his black shadow looming against the wall. "Nicholson was really in love with shadows," art historian Sanford Schwartz writes, especially the "unpredictably shaped, self-contained, and pool-like presence that a shadow can take in a picture" (44). Shadows, visual theorists note, are often symbolic, representing unpredictability and the unknown (Bang 94; Nodelman 154). For Nicholson, they establish a melancholy, uncertain mood from the beginning of the story.

In illustration 2, "The Skin Horse Tells His Story," dramatic shadows again loom behind the characters, reflecting the text's explanation that the characters are in the closet. The toys—Rabbit, Skin Horse, books, and a clown—are shaded in red and stand out sharply against the dark backdrop. The pattern encourages readers to associate red with toys, a technique of color association often used by illustrators to encourage readers to draw connections among similar items (Bang 106). Until his transformation, when his color shifts to yellow, the Rabbit is predominantly shaded in red or ruddle (a muddier, earthier red). The staging of this illustration is also significant, as the placement of the Rabbit on the left-hand, top side of the page may indicate that he is the character with whom readers should relate. Placing the most important objects at the top left of the left-hand page is another technique used by illustrators, who understand that English readers will interpret pictures from left to right, just as their eyes track written text (Nodelman 135). Such staging is not a consistent choice across all illustrated editions (e.g., Sendak) and underscores Nicholson's focus on the Velveteen Rabbit's prominence and on developing a visual echo between these two scenes.

In the third illustration, "Spring Time," perhaps the most iconic in the book and which is also the cover image, the Rabbit's color becomes an almost mottled gray, matching the clouds in the sky. Op de Beeck refers to this color as "ochre" and notes that it evokes "the pathos and the perils of a toy becoming 'Real'" (72). Ochre, an earthy tone that can range from yellows to reds to browns, is a color choice often associated with paleolithic art, adding to its rustic, primal resonance (Leori-Gourhan 40). The ambivalent, melancholy mood Nicholson establishes through the colors and perspective should be understood as contributing to our understanding of the scene as a whole, which is a crucial hinge to the story.

Striking an almost identical pose in "Summer Days," in the fourth illustration (see figure 2.2), the Velveteen Rabbit is an ochre blur, with ears blowing off to the left and paws reaching stiffly forward. Contrastingly, the foregrounded wild rabbits are much lighter in saturation and yellow in color, with alert ears and pointed-up noses, sensing and smelling. They are in control of their bodies, while the Velveteen Rabbit is merely seeing through his stuffed eyes. The illustration thus underscores a point made by both the Williams text and literary critic Kirsten Jacobson: the Velveteen Rabbit has no control of his movements. And movement, historically, is one of the things required to be Real. Jacobson explains: "Something natural and thus real in a more primary sense, he [Aristotle] says, is something that moves itself. . . . For the velveteen rabbit, this recognition arrives when, having been made truly real by the fairy, he discovers that he can move of his own accord" (4). This journey to recognition is demonstrated in the coloration and lines of the images themselves. "Real" animals—animals who move naturally, who are not plagued with ambivalence about their place in the world—do not have long shadows, they are not colored in ochre, and they do not have what Schwartz calls "the befuddled look of being stuffed" (216), an effect achieved through tilted posture, bent ears, rigid paws, and drooping whiskers. Instead, they are caught in motion, alert and responsive, and their coloration is yellow. The Velveteen Rabbit's envy of these wild rabbits, so central to Daniels's psychoanalytic interpretation of betrayal, is vividly portrayed through the picture.

While all previous illustrations were spaced out with predictable frequency (either two or three pages apart), following "Summer Days," the text goes on for several pages without an illustration. The effect of this long omission is that the Boy's illness, vividly portrayed by some subsequent adaptations, is absent from the visuals of this book, which might encourage readers to hurry through this part of the story or to see it as less central to the main narrative. When the Rabbit appears again, it is in another centered portrait, and the elements that illuminated his earlier distress—the ochre coloring, the dark shadows, the slight listing—are more pronounced. In "Anxious Times" (illustration 5), the entire Rabbit appears to be slumped in exhaustion. The ochre coloration darkens toward black, and the image is cast in a gray shadow. The angle of the Rabbit has shifted from leaning to the right in the Christmas stocking in illustration 1 (approximately 70 degrees) to being propped-up in illustration 3 (approximately 90 degrees, though the ears are listing to the left) to leaning more pronouncedly to the left here (approximately 105 degrees). The listing of the Rabbit, subtle on first view, manifests the character's anxiety and unsteadiness.

However, a dramatic transformation is only a few pages away. Following the appearance of the fairy in illustration 6 comes the final two-page spread (figure 2.3). Like the other two-page spreads, this one features the Rabbit with other figures. This time, however, the formerly Velveteen Rabbit is not represented as smaller than the others or at a distance from them. Instead, the Rabbit is leaping in the foreground, by far the largest character in the scene, and clearly surrounded by other rabbits, two of which are racing along the ground from left to right. Echoing this motion, the Rabbit's head is twisted to the right. Unlike the ochre illustrations of the past, this Rabbit is entirely yellow. His shadow is neatly reflected below him. This illustration suggests a different interpretation of the ending than that of the text, offering what Moebius calls a "semic slippage," which happens in a picture book when "word and image seem to send conflicting, perhaps contradictory messages about the 'who' or the 'what' of the story" (143). Whereas Williams writes of the rabbits in the final scene, "One of them was brown all over, but the other had strange markings under his fur, *as though long ago he had been spotted, and the spots still showed through*" (40, emphasis added), Nicholson's final image of the Velveteen Rabbit bears no spots.

For Nicholson, then, we might say that the Rabbit's transformation is more complete than it is for Williams. In his image, the character takes center stage as a leaping figure. It is the Rabbit's passage to nature that is emphasized in form, color, and line—as well as the exclamatory picture title, "At Last! At Last!" The Boy is nowhere to be found, and neither are the old spots, and neither is the ochre, and neither are the overwhelming shadows. The "convention of recognizability" (Moebius 145), which requires characters appear visually similar across illustrations, has been abandoned. And the feeling evoked here is not one of pathos

Figure 2.2 Nicholson's illustration 4, "Summer Days."

Summer Days

Figure 2.3 Nicholson's illustration 7, "At Last! At Last!"

Original Illustrations and Subsequent Adaptations 49

At Last! At Last!

(pity, sadness), but rather triumph (joy, satisfaction). The transformation is also ongoing, rather than fully finished, as emphasized through the foregrounded Rabbit's head being twisted to the right, toward the future. As Nodelman writes, there is a long tradition of characters journeying to the right in picture books, with the future always on the next page, reflecting that English readers turn pages and read in that direction (164).

Across the seven illustrations, Nicholson uses visual conventions to emphasize the transformation of the Rabbit and to plot that transformation from an uncertain beginning to an anxious middle and finally to a triumphant ending. The ending spread, in particular, showcases Nicholson's primary interpretation that the Rabbit has fully changed, that he is no longer fixated on the Boy, and indeed no longer recognizable as the original Velveteen Rabbit. By omitting the spots that the text describes on the final page, Nicholson's moody original illustrations diverge from the text, demonstrating how illustrations may "amplify, distort, or even reverse the meanings" of the text they accompany (Nodelman 20). By offering a singular focus on the transformation of the Rabbit, Nicholson ultimately aligns with psychoanalytic criticism that treats *The Velveteen Rabbit* as predominantly a heartrending story about the anxieties attendant with separating from loved ones to fully become oneself and thus a tale that can stir the "terrible feelings" McNulty describes having when reading the book as a child. It is a powerful, Freudian reading of necessary separation appropriate for its day but clearly too disturbing by McNulty's 1980s era.

Editions from the 1980s to the Present: From a Toy Story to a Boy Story

While *The Velveteen Rabbit* enjoyed a devoted readership for the sixty years after its 1922 publication, including a reillustrated edition by Maurice Sendak in 1960, once the copyright expired in 1982, that decade saw a groundswell of new versions. Readership even expanded to toddlers when the board book publishing phenomenon struck in the 1990s. Strides in picture book publishing throughout the 1980s and 1990s, enhanced by increasing computer technologies, allowed for more intricate pictures, vivid colors, and even cutouts to attract casual buyers at chain and independent bookstores (Osnos). Here, we will consider a few selected texts, exploring them through Nodelman's concepts of "visual storytelling."[5] As he explains, "Because picture-book artists are restricted in the number of moments they can depict—usually it is fewer than fifteen, including the title page—they must choose their moments carefully" (Nodelman 183). It is upon this selection of "moments" that we focus, noting that, as op de Beeck also acknowledges, the text of this 1922 storybook is unusually long by post-1950s standards (72n2).

This requires more pictures, often larger ones, to achieve the picture-book feel, especially because illustrations for a known text are "made in response to the texts," conveying "information that causes us to reinterpret and particularize the meanings of the words" (Nodelman 217). Thus, though illustrators often outfit the Boy in knickers and a flat-cap to suggest a 1920s setting, clearly they are working under late twentieth- and early twenty-first-century ideologies to reinterpret an older story, highlighting, among other late century priorities, the centrality of home, a heightened awareness of childhood psychology, a reconsideration of gender stereotypes, and a postmodern acknowledgement of grief and trauma.

As such, most illustrators move away from Nicholson's singular focus on the Rabbit and instead focus on the interior life of the young Boy. Advancements in color printing allow for a spectrum of palettes representing photo-like resonances with real life, while late century ideals of gender equity open up that life to be focused on a Boy at once full of vibrant play and of nurturing sensitivity and vulnerability. Admittedly, all books in our study also feature a Caucasian boy clearly living a middle-class, even upper-class, life of leisure, certainly not representative of most young boys living in the 1980s nor is it even a lifestyle necessarily described by Williams, though the toys and relaxation of her story suggest the Boy does not want for much (see KaaVonia Hinton's contribution to this volume for an analysis of class and race assumptions in the original and later adaptations). In fact, almost all newer books open with an image of the Rabbit in the Christmas stocking and include illustrations of the Rabbit and Boy at play and snuggling, plus scenes of the Boy's climactic sickness in bed, all moments indirectly suggesting the family's financial security, which is also demonstrated through their employment of multiple servants. Hinton interrogates the "Whiteness" of the book incredibly well. From a childhood studies approach, which attends to power dynamics issuing from age in addition to class and race, we will consider these moments as important to developing the character of the Boy as a child with limited power. Late century illustrators are keen to embellish these moments visually so as to engage the child reader more intimately. Each illustrator imbues these scenes with unique meaning. As Nodelman reminds us, speaking of different illustrations of the same Snow White story, "it is uniqueness—in personality, in atmosphere, in attitude—that makes the pictures in picture books so enjoyable.... [T]hey achieve what Barthes called 'unity on a higher level' by making the difference between words and pictures a significant source of pleasure" (209). In other words, every picture book version of this story will bring about its own attitude and unity.

To pause momentarily at Sendak's 1960 edition, we can see a visual artist who, like Nicholson, chose (or was required to use) a limited color palette where line (hatching and cross-hatching) and shape (circles, squares) dominate. Utilizing images mainly focused on the Rabbit, Sendak reinterprets very similar moments as Nicholson: the Rabbit in a Christmas stocking, with the Skin Horse, with the real rabbits, by the sickbed, and with the Fairy. Sendak very clearly demarcates the wearing down of the Rabbit, shown through line and shape of the sagging Rabbit's figure. Sendak departs from Nicholson to introduce the Boy in two images: speaking to the Rabbit in a wheelbarrow and looking unawares at the Rabbit at the closure of the story. With his back toward us in both scenes, the Boy becomes yet another scenic encounter for the Rabbit, preventing a reader's engagement with him and creating, instead, irony—when the "pictures demand that we stand back and look . . . from a distance" (Nodelman 232). This ironic distance with the Boy is counter to the original textual engagement of the last scene: "And about his little soft nose and his round black eyes there was something so familiar, so that the Boy thought [of his old toy]" (Williams 1960, 104).

Only a few republications of the original came out in the 1960s and '70s, so that the onslaught of postcopyright 1980s editions (at least twelve that we have found) is quite noticeable. In 1983, five were even reviewed as a set in the *New York Times* by Gerald Weales, who made this interesting remark: "One can see its appeal for illustrators . . . [T]here are occasions for drawing Christmas ornaments, toys of all kinds, medicine bottles, flora and fauna; if the central events are a bit static, the backgrounds can keep busy." This suggests a very different interpretation of the visual potential: whereas Nicholson capitalized on the nature of the story to create static images focused on a single protagonist, later illustrators extend the text to create action and visually detailed environments. Further, as the 1980s saw a concentrated "focus on the family"[6] and a rededication to reading at home through Scholastic Book Clubs in schools, among other cultural pressures, the appeal of this domestic story is unsurprising. Simultaneously, the effects of feminism and attempts to break down gender norms can also be seen in the prominence of this uncharacteristically vulnerable Boy.

Notably, 1980s editions tend to more focused on the Boy, his gender qualities fluid although always depicted as White.[7] Michael Hague, illustrator of a 1983 edition, exemplifies this trend demonstrated throughout his twenty-five illustrations, five given before the story even begins. Significantly, he highlights the Boy in ten of them, including on the cover and inside-cover page. Working with a palette of pastels, Hague especially utilizes blues, yellows, and light browns to set the story in a rich, pleasing, pastoral world where the Boy plays and romps, always with the Rabbit in tow. The depiction of time—the "continuance narrative" (Joseph Schwarcz qtd. in Nodelman 166)—is shown specifically in the aging of the Boy, who appears first in a toddler's long underclothes and transitions by the end to knee-highs. Many endearing moments are depicted between this effeminized Boy, from cuddling the Rabbit in bed (Williams 1983, 6) to reading to the Rabbit in bed when sick, their noses and eyes at exactly the same height (21). Hague depicts the Fairy as a young girl of about the same age also cuddling the Rabbit in her arms in much the same nurturing posture (28–29). The Rabbit's emotional life is not diminished, but clearly the Boy's emotions are paramount, and in a two-page spread opening and ending the book, he is placed above and to the left of the Rabbit, a position often used to prioritize characters (Nodelman 134). Notably, this reverses Nicholson's staging of the Rabbit with other characters in the original edition (see illustration 2 in Williams 1922 and illustration 4, shown in figure 2.2).

Two years later, David Jorgensen illustrated the story using a more Impressionist style with blue and black and brown chalk over scratchboard, effectively showing the dreamlike world of the Boy and Rabbit (albeit a middle-class world as in the 1980s living room shown in the opening spread [Williams 1985b, 1]). This Boy demonstrates affection through hand gestures: clutching (3), hugging (12), poking the Rabbit(17); instead, the hands of the nurse and doctor create rupture in plucking the Rabbit up for the trash (27). While Hague shows a curious Boy peering around a tree at the real Rabbit (32), Jorgenson does not bring the Boy back after his illness; instead, the disembodied hands of the Fairy replace him, rescuing the Rabbit in the final scenes (34). Jorgenson furnishes very little energy to the more vulnerable Boy, instead exhibiting it in the Rabbit; for example, four still images of the Rabbit enact his slow-motion fall into the Boy's bed (11), and six stills of the real forest rabbits' dance suggest what the Rabbit will ultimately do (20). This treatment of a more passive Boy is similar to the treatment in S. D. Schindler's 1988 visual rendering where three of four images of the Boy show him asleep in bed as if to refocus the energy of the story upon the active Rabbit, who alone inhabits the final image as a live, dancing animal. The Boy is now the symbol of helplessness and vulnerability.

Michael Green, in his 1984 illustrations, brings more energy and personality to both the Boy and the Rabbit. Alternating between full-page colored acrylic paintings and sepia-etched inserts, Green imbues life into the Rabbit through facial expressions (showing open-eyed concern, peering up at the Skin Horse, and glancing up at the Boy in bed). The Boy's life is likewise connoted by visual imagery. His passivity in bed is shown in border illustrations and inserts of sepia etching and single body parts: disembodied hands reaching out of bed for the Rabbit, an upper body and pointed finger in the act of speaking to the Rabbit, and head poking out of the bedcovers with a hand on the Rabbit. In contrast, full-color spreads are used to indicate his outdoor activity as described by the text: the Boy—depicted with fair hair and skin—gives the Rabbit rides in the wheelbarrow, holds picnics on the grass for his dolls, and walks in the woods. All images of him show him in overalls or a blue sailor suit and hat (Williams 1984,16) and often in effeminate activities, as when he brings pets and toys together for a tea party on the lawn (figure 2.4).

Circles border the outdoor expanses, a design that suggests containment and safety in Nodelman's way of reading (127). Only in the last images—of the Rabbit

Figure 2.4 Illustration by Michael Green (1984). From *The Velveteen Rabbit* by Margery Williams, copyright © 1997. Reprinted by permission of Running Press Kids, an imprint of Hachette Book Group, Inc.

running free and of the Boy playing alone—are squares used, now to show the enlarged world into which the Rabbit will move and in which an older Boy now plays. In their last encounter, the illustration shows the Boy and Rabbit staring at each other in bewilderment and, as shown in the Boy's face, even disgust; in fact, the Boy's toy sword lies dangerously close to the Rabbit. Clearly effeminate

Original Illustrations and Subsequent Adaptations   55

Figure 2.5 Illustration by Katherine Wilson (1987). Reprinted by permission of Katherine Wilson.

tea parties with stuffed animals have been replaced by more "gender-appropriate" sword fighting where wild animals may themselves now be in danger.

A final edition of the 1980s deserves attention not only because it is illustrated by the only female of this group of illustrators but also because of its approach: Katherine Wilson's 1987 rendering of childhood and its world of toys. Through rich, watercolor, primary-colored paintings, Wilson completes the space of the room with details of toys and windows, gives the Rabbit a charmingly adorable face and a series of emotions told through its expressions, and makes the Boy nearly androgynous with longer hair and a cherubic appearance. Clearly a toddler in this story, the Boy reaches up to grasp the Rabbit with chubby hands and snuggles in bed with him. The Rabbit is anthropomorphized even more than in other renditions, with eyes closed in sleep and sitting up in bed with an open book and teacup at his bedside. The Rabbit thus aligns more strongly with the Boy and vice versa in this edition, even in the penultimate image when they discover each other in the woods. Though the Boy now has an older, clipped haircut and the Rabbit is clearly alive, Wilson still indicates their closeness by placing them only inches away from each other, the Boy's arms wrapped around a tree emblematic of the love he once gave to the Rabbit. In fact, in her attempt to render the entire picture book pleasing and with childhood comforts, Wilson depicts Nana as a kindlier mother figure (or possibly even his mother) comforting the Boy and tucking him into bed with his doll (figure 2.5), a pleasing reinterpretation, even contradiction, of Nana's lines "Here . . . take your old Bunny! He'll do to sleep with you!"

The publishing initiative to put books into more children's hands, and thus expand the purchasing audience of children's books, led 1990s publishers to the genre of the board book for republication of earlier classics. The text of *The Velveteen Rabbit* was substantially abridged to privilege the size and number of images, although this did not always produce superior illustrations. Thrift editions, like those produced for Random House (Williams 1993) and Dover (Williams 1997), show simplistic illustrations with often unproportioned bodies and "cutesy" Rabbits. Other times, the result was a shortened text with better-quality images from earlier publications: both Dragonfly and Candy Cane Press rereleased their illustrated editions by Jorgensen and Wilson as board books (Williams 1989; Williams 2013, respectively).

The 2000s continued the ideologies begun in the 1980s of refocusing on the Boy's child life and growth, if still a White, middle-class Boy, along with the transformation of the Rabbit. Now, though, with advanced publication technologies allowing for inexpensive art reproduction and with eye-catching illustrations often being the selling point, picture books interpret the story with full spreads and in full color. This is true of Pat Thompson's 2006 beautiful illustrations in gouache and watercolor to "humanize" the Rabbit "birthed" in a flame-red stocking (Williams 2006, 2). We also see a pensive Boy, legs tucked, sitting on the lawn (9, 21) and the Fairy now as a little girl, as if in dress-up (18), all reproduced in full-page spreads to balance the length of text. Charles Santore created full-color, representational/realistic paintings for Applesauce's 2012 hardcover edition and 2014 board-book edition, which use most of his illustrations and truncate the text. Santore's illustrations display many moments of the Boy's inner life, albeit a White and leisured one: lovingly holding the Rabbit to his chest, his eyes closed in reverence (Williams 2012, 14) or sitting listlessly on a porch chair during his convalescence (17). The former image is, in fact, featured on the book's cover to highlight a boy's tender feelings for a contemporary audience seeking confirmation of such gender-role reversals. The latter acknowledges the trauma of illness for the Boy now unable to play.

Finally, a 2016 adaptation of *The Velveteen Rabbit*, illustrated by Sarah Massini, uses a cartoon style to depict what might be the most true-to-life portrayal of childhood. Through long shots cut across rooms and even into the yard, Massini resurrects the parents and home life of this 1920s young boy that is omitted from the text ("it is striking that the story makes no explicit reference to parents," writes Daniels [18–19]). For instance, in a two-page spread with the hint of a Christmas tree in the left-front corner, Massini uses a hall light as a stage light upon the forgotten Rabbit on the floor, then uses a diagonal light-and-shadow line to point us to the true action of the Christmas scene: the Boy greeting his

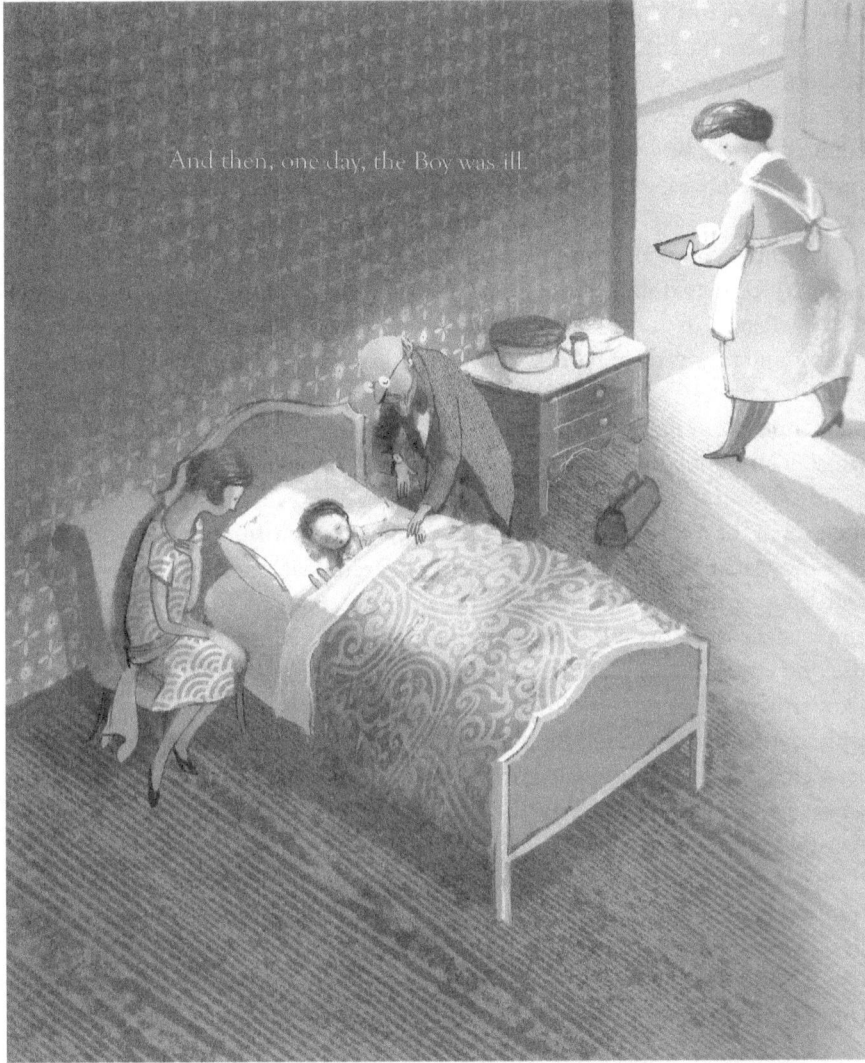

Figure 2.6 Illustration by Sarah Massini (2016). Copyright © Sarah Massini 2016. Reproduced with permission of the publishers, Candlewick Press, Somerville, MA, and Nosy Crow Ltd.

"Aunts and Uncles" who bring "all the new presents" that lead him to forget the Rabbit—one of the few illustrators to register that neglect. This Rabbit is the most anthropomorphized of all versions through his wearing of a red jacket throughout the story. Further, the Boy's activities are amplified in Massini's version: we witness him through a window playing in the snow as Nana picks up his toys, hiding under the bed covers with Rabbit, throwing the Rabbit through the air, prancing about the playroom while Nana is tied up in a paper chain, and building a log fort in the yard—examples of what Moebius terms "plate tectonics" (143), illustrations that extend beyond the original text that made no mention of these activities. Full views thus draw the readers into the Boy's world, albeit a 1920s privileged one, with nannies and gardeners bustling around a three-story country manor. But Massini invites empathy for the sick Boy even more so than earlier close-up depictions: in Massini's rendering, the viewer looks down on the sickroom (figure 2.6) where we see Nana, the doctor, the medicine bag, and, most significantly, a mother, never mentioned in the text but surely involved (Williams 2016, 33). Only two slips of ears remind us that the Rabbit snuggles down under the covers next to the ashen-faced Boy. It is a powerful image rarely shown of the anxiety and near grief of parents at a dear child's sickbed, what perhaps Nicholson could not bear to register in the 1920s following the horrors of the Spanish flu pandemic (1918–1920, which killed a disproportionate number of children) but which a 2016 illustrator feels empathy now to acknowledge.

The Boy and Rabbit are so indelibly aligned in Massini's illustrations that their separation is more significant. The Rabbit's transformation to a real animal is made visually by the Rabbit shedding his red coat, entering the lush forest, and reappearing as a real rabbit. In the final two-page spread, Massini likewise emphasizes the Boy's vital understanding of this event. First, she places him peeking around a tree on the far-left page, which is often the place of significance (Nodelman 136) and then shows understanding on his face as he sees his Rabbit with another rabbit-friend among the forest ferns. Though they must go their separate ways, their friendship is immortalized in the last illustration of the book: an image in a picture frame of the Boy hugging his Rabbit to remind us of the two-fold heroes of this story.[8]

In conclusion, if the original illustrations prioritize the Rabbit and his individual transformation, more recent illustrators bring the Boy back into the transformative process, reminding readers that love for a toy, even and especially from a boy, might be an integral part of childhood. Ultimately, this visual connection with boyhood—and a more gender-fluid one at that—no doubt injected new life into a well-worn story, reviving *The Velveteen Rabbit*'s relevancy for a new century of readers. By including the Boy and tracing his development alongside the Rabbit's, the later editions promote different textual identification for child readers and subtly reframe the central message of the story from one of individual transformation and self-actualization to one about the inner life of a boy, both boyishly exuberant and uncharacteristically sensitive. If he transforms at all, into an older, potentially "tougher" young male, many late century illustrators elide that moment. Their common emphasis aligns with Kellehear, who wrote that "both children and their toys live on as memories and dreams, the past a living social presence and influence on the present" (45). Since the story's inception, the flexible language of illustration has allowed *The Velveteen Rabbit* to speak to myriad generations of children and thus allowed the Rabbit itself to be reborn over and over again.

Notes

1. For a good representation of the original illustrations in full, which are also those used in this analysis, see Williams 1922. Note that the coloration varies across editions.

2. As of the time of this writing, they could be purchased on the Etsy marketplace from the sellers bmarinacci, ShopDvorak, and MySolluna (websites available in the works cited list), who emphasize that the "Classic Vintage Art Poster" is appropriate for "Birth, Christening, Nursery Gift," or "Nursery Décor."

3. Freud's publications began as early as 1891, with his famous *The Interpretation of Dreams* published in 1899 and with nine more books to follow in the next decades, including his *Introductory Lectures on Psycho-Analysis* (1915–1917). By the 1920s, he was publishing *Beyond the Pleasure Principle* (1920) and *Group Psychology and the Analysis of the Ego* (1921). We are working under the cultural-studies assumption that his basic theories would have infiltrated the consciousness of citizens and artists alike, including that of Nicholson.

4. Nicholson's book of woodcut portraits was titled *London Types* (1898). Among the subjects he memorialized was, as Anne Carroll Moore recollects, the Queen of England. For more information on the title, see Schwartz.

5. Additional, contemporary picture books not analyzed in this study include those illustrated by Graham Percy (Octopus Books, 1987); Allen Atkinson (Alfred A. Knopf, 1992); Sherry Neidigh (Dalmatian, 1999); and Justin Todd (Puffin Books, 2015).

6. James Dobson's conservative Christian organization, Focus on the Family, was established in 1977 and gained prominence in the 1980s. Its focus on the family included advocating prayer in schools and conventional male-female marriage, but also included aspects of an ultra-right-wing agenda not tied to the family.

7. See KaaVonia Hinton, "Whiteness and the Selective Tradition in *The Velveteen Rabbit*" in this volume for much more about this issue.

8. We wish to thank Mr. Matt Dilworth, coordinator of reference and media services at the IU East Library, who went out of his way to procure and even purchase editions of *The Velveteen Rabbit* picture books for our essay when all the lending libraries had closed down during the spring 2020 COVID lockdown.

Works Cited

Bang, Molly. *Picture This: Perception & Composition*. Little, Brown and Company, 1995.
bmarinacci. "Velveteen Rabbit Cover Wall Decor, Digital Print, Nursery Decor, Dictionary Page Art, Wall Art, Sheet Music Print 2354." *Etsy*, https://www.etsy.com/listing/493995684/velveteen-Rabbit-cover-wall-decor?gpla=1&gao=1&. Accessed 10 Dec. 2021.
Daniels, Steven V. "*The Velveteen Rabbit*: A Kleinian Perspective." *Children's Literature*, vol. 18, 1990, pp. 17–30.
Ehle, Maryanne. "*The Velveteen Rabbit, The Little Prince*, and Friends: Posacculturation through Literature." Annual Meeting of the Professional Clinic Association of Teacher Educators, 13–19 Feb. 1982, Phoenix, AZ. Conference Presentation.

Farrar, John. "New Books for the Children's Christmas." *Ladies Home Journal*, Dec. 1922, p. 185.
Guroian, Vigen. "Love and Immortality in *The Velveteen Rabbit* and *The Little Mermaid*." *Tending the Heart of Virtue: How Classic Stories Awaken a Child's Moral Imagination*, edited by Tom Burns, Oxford UP, 1998, pp. 62–70.
Jacobson, Kirsten. "Heidegger, Winnicott, and *The Velveteen Rabbit*." *Philosophy in Children's Literature*, edited by Peter R. Costello, Lexington Books, 2011, pp. 19–34.
Kellehear, Allan. "Death and Renewal in *The Velveteen Rabbit*: A Sociological Reading." *Journal of Near Death Studies*, vol. 12, no. 1, 1993, pp. 35–51.
Leori-Gourhan, André. *The Art of Prehistoric Man in Western Europe*. Thames & Hudson, 1968.
McNulty, Faith. "Children's Books for Christmas." *New Yorker*, 6 Dec. 1992, pp. 176–82.
Moebius, William. "Introduction to Picturebook Codes." *Word & Image: A Journal of Visual Inquiry*, vol. 2, no. 2, 1986, pp. 144–58.
Moore, Annie Carroll. "Who Is Writing Books for Children?" *The Bookman*, Oct. 1922, p. 201.
Moore, Anne Carroll, and Bertha E. Mahoney Miller, editors. *Writing and Criticism: A Book for Margery Bianco*. Horn Book, 1951.
MySolluna. "The Velveteen Rabbit Print, INSTANT DOWNLOAD, Birth, Christening, Nursery Gift, Nursery Decor, Velveteen Rabbit Classic Vintage Art Poster." *Etsy*, https://www.etsy.com/listing/855416401/the-Velveteen-Rabbit-print-instant?ga_order=most_relevant&ga_search_type=all&ga_view_type=gallery&ga_search_query=velveteen+Rabbit+wall+art&ref=sr_gallery-1-23&organic_search_click=1&pro=1. Accessed 12 Oct. 2022.
Nodelman, Perry. *Words about Pictures: The Narrative Art of Children's Picture Books*. U of Georgia P, 1988.
op de Beeck, Nathalie. "Suspended Animation: Picture Book Storytelling, Twentieth Century Childhood, and William Nicholson's *Clever Bill*." *The Lion and the Unicorn*, vol. 30, no. 1, 2006, pp. 54–75.
Osnos, Peter. "How Book Publishing Has Changed Since 1984." *The Atlantic*, 12 Apr. 2011, https://www.theatlantic.com/entertainment/archive/2011/04/how-book-publishing-has-changed-since-1984/237184/. Accessed 12 Oct. 2022.
Reed, Patricia. "Some Aspects of William Nicholson's Portraiture." *The Art of William Nicholson*, by Colin Campbell et al., Royal Academy of the Arts, 2004, 35–42.
Schwartz, Sanford. *William Nicholson*. Yale UP, 2004.
ShopDvorak. "The Velveteen Rabbit by Margery Williams 1980s Childrens Picture Book in Color." *Etsy*, https://www.etsy.com/listing/775305223/the-velveteen-Rabbit-by-margery-williams?ga_order=most_relevant&ga_search_type=all&ga_view_type=gallery&ga_search_query=velveteen+Rabbit&ref=sr_gallery-1-16&organic_search_click=1&cns=1. Accessed 10 July 2022.
Weales, Gerald. "Children's Books." *New York Times*, 3 Apr. 1983, section 7, p. 13, https://www.nytimes.com/1983/04/03/books/children-s-books-069929.html. Accessed 1 June 2020.
Weithman, Paul. "God's Velveteen Rabbit." *Journal of Religious Ethics*, vol. 37, no. 2, 2009, pp. 243–60.

Editions of Margery Williams's *The Velveteen Rabbit*

Williams, Margery. 1922. *The Velveteen Rabbit: Or How Toys Become Real*. Illustrated by William Nicholson, Doubleday. A Celebration of Women Writers. *University of Pennsylvania Digital Library*, https://digital.library.upenn.edu/women/williams/rabbit/rabbit.html. Accessed 31 Oct. 2022.

Williams, Margery. 1958. *The Velveteen Rabbit: Or How Toys Become Real*. Illustrated by William Nicholson, Doubleday, 1991.
Williams, Margery. 1960. *The Velveteen Rabbit*. Illustrated by Maurice Sendak, *Best in Children's Books*, Doubleday, pp. 85–105.
Williams, Margery. 1975. *The Velveteen Rabbit*. Illustrated by William Nicholson, Avon, 1987.
Williams, Margery. 1983. *The Velveteen Rabbit: Or How Toys Become Real*. Illustrated by Michael Hague, Fitzhenry and Whiteside.
Williams, Margery. 1984. *The Velveteen Rabbit: Or How Toys Become Real*. Illustrated by Michael Green, Running Press.
Williams, Margery. 1985a. *Velveteen Rabbit*. Illustrated by David Jorgensen, board book ed., Random House, 1989.
Williams, Margery. 1985b. *The Velveteen Rabbit: Or How Toys Become Real*. Illustrated by David Jorgensen, Alfred A. Knopf.
Williams, Margery. 1987. *The Velveteen Rabbit: Or How Toys Become Real*. Illustrated by Katherine Wilson, Ideals Publishing.
Williams, Margery. 1988. *The Velveteen Rabbit: Or How Toys Become Real*. Adapted by David Eastman, illustrated by S. D. Schindler, Troll.
Williams, Margery. 1993. *The Velveteen Rabbit*. Adapted by Kimberly Kass, illustrated by Nancy Carpenter, board book ed., Random House.
Williams, Margery. 1997. *The Velveteen Rabbit*. Adapted and illustrated by Marty Noble, sturdy book ed., Dover.
Williams, Margery. 1998. *The Velveteen Rabbit: Or, How Toys Become Real*. 1984. Illustrated by Michael Green, condensed ed., Running Press.
Williams, Margery. 2006. *The Velveteen Rabbit: Or How Toys Become Real*. Illustrated by Pat Thompson, Dalmatian Press.
Williams, Margery. 2012. *The Velveteen Rabbit*. Illustrated by Charles Santore, board book ed., Applesauce Press.
Williams, Margery. 2016. *The Velveteen Rabbit: Or How Toys Become Real*. Illustrated by Sarah Massini, Nosy Crow.

Chapter 3

Plush, Plastic, and Plato: Purpose and Being in *The Velveteen Rabbit* and *Toy Story*

—Melanie Hurley

Toy narratives, as well as narratives featuring sentient objects more generally, have a tendency to turn philosophical, whether explicitly or implicitly. As its discarded windup mice struggle to survive and to become "self-winding," Russell Hoban's *The Mouse and His Child* (1967) ponders both what it means to be alive and the power of the self. Pixar's short CGI (computer-generated imagery) film *Knick Knack* (1989) is a disconcerting comedy because of its focus on a decorative snowman who is unable to escape his glass snow globe: it laughs at his entrapment and his consequent inability to connect with the other souvenirs on the shelf.[1] Similarly, another of Pixar's CGI shorts, namely *Tin Toy* (1988), turns fears of chaos, intimacy, and abandonment into fun. Tinny, the eponymous toy, initially fears the baby, Billy, who appears to be a harmful individual. Tinny runs away and hides but then decides that he does actually want to play with Billy. Unfortunately, the baby now ignores him in favor of an empty shopping bag. Toy narratives, although seemingly simple, portray existential angst and offer deep reflections on the nature of human life and emotion.

Two toy narratives that use strikingly similar motifs to arrive at profound yet vastly different philosophical conclusions are Margery Williams's *The Velveteen Rabbit* (1922) and Pixar's *Toy Story* franchise. Despite the seventy-three years spanning the publication of Williams's book and the release of the first *Toy Story* film (1995), they both feature sentient toys questioning who and what they are; an intense bond between a child and a toy (or toys); the toy(s) becoming trash; and the toy's (or toys') seemingly imminent but finally avoided annihilation. The presence of these motifs is not limited to these toy narratives; for example, the toy mice in the aforementioned *The Mouse and His Child* break and become trash early in the narrative and question their own nature, and A. A. Milne's *Winnie-the-Pooh* (1926) and *The House at Pooh Corner* (1928) feature an intense bond between Christopher Robin and his toys. One could justifiably study the presence of these motifs across a range of toy narratives and examine what philosophies they develop in each one, but Williams's classic book and Pixar's flagship franchise mirror each other so closely that they are worthy of special consideration with regards to their philosophical positions.

The Velveteen Rabbit employs a model of reality markedly similar to that which Plato offers in his *Republic*, albeit with hints of his *Phaedo* and *Symposium*, an idealist philosophical system that today reads as idealistic. In Williams's book, a toy rabbit is a copy of a flesh-and-blood rabbit (17–21), just as for Plato art is a deficient copy of the material world and all phenomena are deficient copies of the eternal Ideas (or Forms) (*Republic* 595a–599c).[2] For example, Plato's fictionalized Socrates reasons that the beds that artists paint are copies of the beds that carpenters make and the beds that carpenters make are copies of the Idea "bed," which the gods make (596e–597d). As the Idea "bed" is the most Real of all the beds and the artist's painted bed is twice removed from the Idea, the artist's bed contains little reality.[3] Similarly, the Rabbit learns he is a deficient copy of a flesh-and-blood rabbit when he meets wild rabbits with hind legs and a scent that he lacks (Williams 19–20). In order to be truly Real, the Rabbit must become a flesh-and-blood rabbit, a transformation achieved through the love of a child, the Boy (29, 33), and an event that reflects the importance of love in the philosopher's journey to knowledge (Plato, *Symposium* 210a–212a). However, *The Velveteen Rabbit*'s ontology renders it myopic, for the Rabbit's escape from the bonfire makes the text blind to the reality that our objects, even our beloved toys, become waste.

Toy Story eschews such a metaphysical system in favor of existentialist philosophy, echoing but not replicating Albert Camus's arguments in "The Myth of Sisyphus" (1942). These films do not include magical transformations and they unflinchingly present the realities of a toy's "life." The anthropomorphized toys' existence is a continuous battle against obsolescence and destruction, just as Camus argues that human life is endless struggle. For example, a boy named Sid attempts to blow up Buzz Lightyear with a rocket (*Toy Story*) and Sheriff Woody worries that his owner, Andy, will throw him away after his arm rips (*Toy Story 2* [1999]). In *Toy Story 3* (2010), the corrupt teddy, Lotso, even voices what *The Velveteen Rabbit* omits, for he declares that toys are "trash," objects "made to be thrown away." Unlike Camus's philosophy, though, the films include love, loyalty, and hope and show that these things are a part of what makes life meaningful. When one reads the *Toy Story* films in conjunction with *WALL-E* (2008), a Pixar film about a trash-compacting robot who becomes sentient through its routines, one finds that Pixar's films argue that struggles like those of the toys and the robot, WALL-E, are necessary if we are to maintain life on Earth and not find ourselves overwhelmed and devastated by the same plastics that form our possessions and become our waste materials.[4] Ironically, Pixar uses trash to illustrate the threat that trash poses to both our personal survival and the survival of our planet as a whole, sending a powerful message about the necessity of action against overproduction and unnecessary waste.

When compared to *The Velveteen Rabbit*, the *Toy Story* films as well as the Pixar canon more generally show a profound shift in their understanding of not just toys, but of reality and life. All these texts show that one can be happy despite and even because of struggles, and they all have a sophisticated underlying philosophy, but the Pixar films leave idealism, in both senses of the word, behind and take the toy narrative in its necessary direction for the 1990s, 2000s, and beyond.

The Velveteen Rabbit's Plush Platonism

Through its "magic metamorphic" story—that is, a story in which a toy transforms into a flesh-and-blood creature (Kuznets 59–62)—about the eponymous Rabbit, *The Velveteen Rabbit* presents a tale that has deep affinities with Plato's idealism. The Rabbit's journey closely parallels *Republic*'s cave allegory, with both the cave's prisoner and the Rabbit gaining more knowledge of the Real as the stories progress. While this parallel makes for an impressive philosophical tale, its conclusion is not entirely satisfying, either narratively or philosophically. Death haunts but never explicitly enters *The Velveteen Rabbit*, giving the story a happy but unrealistic ending. In keeping its focus always on the great good of "becoming Real" (Williams 6) and understanding this state, the book presents a consistent ontology but not one that includes the realities of death, obsolescence, or destructive trash.[5]

Critics have not always been kind to *The Velveteen Rabbit*, although it is for a stronger reason than simply because they read it as a saccharine story; rather, it is because they see it as a failed fable of childhood psychological development, an interpretation to which an ontological reading provides a more positive alternative by providing insight into the book's philosophical value. Steven V. Daniels reads the story through Melanie Klein's psychoanalytic writings on child development. He argues that the Rabbit, whom he sees as representative of the developing child, fails to gain full independence from the Boy, representative of the parent, and so falls into a depressive anxiety for which the final transformation is not an adequate cure (Daniels 24–26). Daniels takes the book's central question to be the one that the Rabbit asks as he awaits his end: "Of what use is it to be loved and lose one's beauty and become Real if it all ended like this?" (Williams qtd. on 26), a question that he reads as an expression of "the Rabbit's feelings of abandonment in the face of annihilation by persecutory agents" and as indicative of the depressive position (25). Lois Rostow Kuznets agrees with the first part of Daniels's assessment, suggesting that the narrative likely does not adequately work through and resolve the Rabbit's anxiety because the book's "young reader whose anxiety level may be elevated through identification with both the faithless Boy and the abandoned Rabbit" needs "a quick, happy, unexamined ending" (62). She then suggests: "the powerful attraction of this toy narrative may actually lie in its apparent weaknesses. Readers of all ages have been known to adore resolutions that are 'bad for them' or only 'wishful thinking' in psychological terms" (62). If one reads the book psychoanalytically, Daniels's conclusions and Kuznets's suggestions do make a great deal of sense. However, one does not need to read *The Velveteen Rabbit* psychoanalytically; indeed, the book's subtitle, *How Toys Become Real*, invites an ontological reading. Analyzing the book through Plato's philosophy decentralizes the question on which Daniels focuses and shifts the story's perceived major concerns from childhood psychological development to an interrogation of the nature of reality. Reading *The Velveteen Rabbit* through Plato thus makes it more than just a children's book filled with "wishful thinking."

The Velveteen Rabbit conveys the same basic message as *Republic*'s cave allegory for it endows the Rabbit with a similar state of ignorance as the cave's prisoners, showing that one's philosophical journey begins with limited knowledge of the Real. In *Republic*, in order to contemplate the effects of education, Socrates asks his interlocutors to imagine a scenario in which humans are chained in a deep cave, always fixed in the same position and staring at the cave wall. There is a fire burning far above and behind the prisoners, and between the fire and their backs, there is a low wall, behind which people pass with objects that cast shadows on the wall before the prisoners. The prisoners have never been outside, so they believe that "the truth is nothing other than the shadows" (Plato, *Republic* 515c). Similarly, when Williams's book begins, the Rabbit thinks that he is a true rabbit for he has never seen a flesh-and-blood rabbit. He cannot "claim to be a model of anything" for he thinks that all rabbits are "stuffed with sawdust like himself" (Williams 3–4). The more solid, more Real sources of shadows and velveteen rabbits remain unknown to these characters, and their understanding of the world is consequently severely limited.

The Velveteen Rabbit diverges from the cave allegory after establishing the Rabbit's initial state of ignorance in that it follows a character who is becoming Real rather than one who is learning about the nature of reality; still, the Rabbit learns about the Real through his becoming, and he even begins the process with a questioning exercise that resembles the conversation between Socrates and his interlocutors. After describing the cave, Socrates asks Glaucon to consider what would happen if one of the prisoners suddenly gained freedom from his bonds. Socrates suggests (and Glaucon readily agrees) that when the released prisoner looks into the light of the fire for the first time, his eyes will hurt and his initial experience with sunlight will produce even greater pain; consequently, when first out in the light, he will be unable to see anything clearly. Later, as his eyes adjust to the light, he will be able to see and distinguish between the things of the world, and eventually he will be able to look upon the sun, and he will understand it as the source of all things (Plato, *Republic* 515c–516c). The prisoner's story is, of course, an allegory for the philosopher's journey from ignorance to wisdom, from the illusory, changing world to the eternal, intelligible world of Ideas, with the sun representing the Good, the source of all (517b–518b, 519c, 532a–b). The Rabbit and the Skin Horse conversing in the nursery are similar but not identical to Socrates and his friends. The temptation is to equate the Rabbit with Socrates in this scenario for, like Socrates, the Rabbit asks questions about the nature of reality to advance the philosophical discussion. However, the Rabbit is unlike Socrates because he does not yet have any firm opinions of his own and is dependent on the Skin Horse for information. The Skin Horse is actually more like Socrates for he has wisdom, while the Rabbit is truly more like the interlocutors for he is ignorant. Curious, the Rabbit bluntly asks the Skin Horse, "What is REAL? . . . Does it mean having things that buzz inside you and a stick-out handle?" to which the Skin Horse replies, "Real isn't how you are made. . . . It's a thing that happens to you." The Rabbit continues, "Does it happen all at once, like being wound up . . . or bit by bit?" The Skin Horse responds, "It doesn't happen all at once. . . . You become. It takes a long time," and sometimes, he admits, the becoming is painful (Williams 6). Both learning about the Real and becoming Real are journeys that require patience and endurance and that are sometimes uncomfortable. These points are true for the Rabbit, the prisoner, and the interlocutors. Furthermore, these journeys are linked since the cave prisoner, living among the shadows in ignorance, seems hardly more alive than the stuffed Rabbit and so also, in a sense, becomes more Real as he learns about the Real. Finally, all these journeys are tantalizing despite their painfulness because they promise greater knowledge and a superior state of being.

Later in the narrative, *The Velveteen Rabbit* appears to offer a new definition of the Real, one that is dependent on magical metamorphosis and that Kuznets believes raises critical eyebrows because it seemingly undermines the earlier conversation between the Rabbit and the Skin Horse. However, this "second" definition has, in fact, been present since almost the beginning of the story and has created a problem in need of resolution. Kuznets argues, "Some of the trouble [for the critics] seems to arise from its [the book's] change in midstream from the notion of a toy becoming animated through child love—but remaining a toy—to that of one undergoing magical metamorphosis into a flesh-and-blood animal" (60). In her opinion, the Fairy's statement that only beloved toys undergo magical metamorphosis clears up the inconsistency (Kuznets 61). On the contrary, though, it is actually the toy's animation through a child's love that is the story's second definition of the Real. The reader presumably knows that there are flesh-and-blood rabbits, and, in case not, the book itself mentions them *before* the Rabbit's conversation with the Skin Horse. Early in the text, the narrator says, "he [the Rabbit] didn't know that real rabbits existed" (Williams 3–4). It is therefore after the pivotal conversation with the Skin Horse that one must first wonder, "Can there really be *two* versions of Realness?"—a question that the Rabbit himself must eventually consider. When the Rabbit meets the wild rabbits and learns that he is a model of a flesh-and-blood animal, he also discovers that even though the Boy loves him dearly, he is an imperfect rabbit: he lacks hind legs, cannot jump of his own accord, and does not have the scent of a flesh-and-blood rabbit (19–20).[6] He becomes distressed when one of the rabbits declares that he is "not real," insisting that he knows he is: "The Boy said so!" (20). The wild rabbits reject his notion of Realness, running away and leaving him sorely disappointed (20–21). The Rabbit must now question whether the Skin Horse's definition of the Real, and therefore also his own Realness, is lacking. The narrative now has to resolve this crisis and reconcile the Skin Horse's statements and the Rabbit's resultant beliefs with this other definition of the Real, one that has been haunting the narrative and has now, finally, become explicit.

The Rabbit's continued questioning of the world and the narrative's upholding of the flesh-and-blood definition of the Real correspond to Plato's arguments in *Republic* for it is only in these ways that both the philosopher and the Rabbit can grow in understanding and get closer to the truth. According to Plato, continuous interrogation of the world is necessary for growing in knowledge. As discussed above, the cave prisoner learns by stages, a process that is elucidated by passages in book VI of *Republic*, the book before the one containing the cave allegory. Toward the end of book VI, Socrates argues that the things of the world are divided between the realm of the visible and that of the intelligible. The visible is further divided into images (e.g., art, shadows, and reflections) and the sources of those images (e.g., animals, plants, and manufactured things), and the intelligible is further divided into mathematical principles and Ideas. Socrates says that a particular type of mental activity corresponds to each of the divisions: imagination (images), belief (sources), thought (mathematics), and understanding (Ideas). Socrates asks Glaucon to imagine these divisions as a line divided into two unequal sections and then to imagine each of these sections divided in the same ratio as the line. These divisions correspond to the degree to which the mental activity leads one to truth; thus, understanding occupies the largest portion of the line and imagination the smallest (Plato, *Republic* 509d–511e). If one reads the cave allegory in conjunction with the line, one finds that the prisoner moves from imagination (represented by the shadows) to belief (the objects that cast the shadows), then to thought (the things of the world outside the cave), and finally to understanding (the sun). Things further up the line, which correspond to the things that the prisoner sees outside the cave, are more Real and much closer to the truth than the things lower on the line, which correspond to the things inside the cave. Since images are far removed from understanding, within this system, art does not contribute much to the discovery of truth. In *The Velveteen Rabbit*, the Skin Horse does not recognize that an image can never be as Real as a flesh-and-blood creature, so unlike Socrates, he falls for the trickery of art and the imagination (Plato, *Republic* 598c, 602c–d). The Rabbit, by contrast, overcomes this deception by continuing to learn through his encounters with the wild rabbits and the Fairy and then through becoming a flesh-and-blood rabbit. He moves closer to the truth in body and mind, completing the philosophical journey to the Real and to understanding. The perceived change in the book's direction is therefore not a change at all but rather a necessary part of the Rabbit's growing understanding of Realness and of the book's development of its version of philosophical idealism.[7]

This development continues through the book's argument that love is a necessary part of the journey to Realness, an argument that combines elements of Plato's *Symposium* with the basics of the *Republic* and shows their consistency with one another. The Rabbit would not have been able to complete his journey without love, a situation that echoes Diotima's statements to Socrates in *Symposium*. Diotima argues that love is a state between the ugly and the beautiful, a state in which one desires what is beautiful and good because one is *not yet* in possession of it (one does not desire that which one already possesses). The philosopher is thus a lover in pursuit of the wisdom he wants to acquire (Plato, *Symposium* 200a 200e, 202b, 204b). According to Diotima, one moves from loving beautiful bodies to beautiful souls and then to contemplating the Idea "beauty" (210a–211b). Although *The Velveteen Rabbit* does not map onto *Symposium* nearly as well as it does onto *Republic*, the Rabbit is like the philosopher in that he desires the Real, that which he does not yet possess; he pursues it wholeheartedly; and he completes his journey because the power of love allows the Fairy to make him Real (Williams 29). The difference between the Rabbit and Diotima's philosopher is that the latter needs only to love to reach the beautiful and good, while the Rabbit must be both lover and beloved to reach his destination. Nonetheless, *The Velveteen Rabbit* eloquently, if unintentionally, shows that *Symposium*'s statements about love complement *Republic*'s cave allegory and form a consistent philosophical system. Thus, Williams's book is both an endearing children's story and a refined philosophical narrative.

While *The Velveteen Rabbit* presents a complex ontology, its philosophy of toys is not a happy one as toys remain images only, replaceable and barely Real items that will ultimately find themselves in the trash. When the Fairy saves the Rabbit from his seemingly imminent end in the coming bonfire, she actually saves him from death altogether. She tells the wild rabbits that she has brought them a "new playmate" who will live with them "for ever and ever!" (Williams 29). Kuznets critiques this immortality on the grounds that it is "a violation of the mythic metamorphic tradition" (61); that is, in stories from pagan tales to Carlo Collodi's *The Adventures of Pinocchio* (1883), metamorphosis does not allow the changed individual to live forever. This immortality is, however, consistent with Plato's philosophy, especially as laid out in *Phaedo* (65c–66e) since one can only truly contemplate Ideas when one is free of a mortal body. The Rabbit must become eternal if he is to be fully Real and able to fully understand this condition. Nevertheless, it is here that philosophical idealism causes Williams's narrative to turn idealistic. The Fairy's transformation of the Rabbit into an immortal wild rabbit allows the narrative to gloss over the death and destruction that trouble the text. Mechanical toys arrive in the nursery "to boast and swagger, and by-and-by break their mainsprings and pass away" (Williams 4); the Boy contracts scarlet fever, a deadly illness (23); and, although the Rabbit escapes the planned conflagration, presumably the old picture books still burn. The book may wish to deny it, but a toy's end is in the trash and a human's end is death. What is more, toys, unlike humans, are replaceable objects. The Rabbit takes the place of a china dog in the Boy's bed as a consequence of both the Boy being unable to find the dog and Nana being unwilling to look for it (9), and when the doctor declares the Rabbit "a mass of scarlet fever germs" (23), the Boy gets a new bunny to sleep with him, "a splendid bunny, all white plush with real glass eyes" (24). Toys break, become outdated, or even become dangerous because of contact with germs. Once they have fulfilled their purpose, which may be as a beloved comfort object and playmate, or, ostensibly like many of the Boy's toys, may be limited to only a few play sessions, they become garbage. No amount of love and ontological interrogation can change the fact that toys create waste. Dan Fleming observes that, as of the time of his writing, most toy lines had only a two- to three-year lifespan (116), becoming junk when a new trend started. When a child's desires and interests change, the toys become either dust collectors or trash. While the toys-to-waste transition may not have been particularly troubling in 1922, it is disconcerting today because of the higher availability of toys and the quick turnover in trends, which together create a larger numbers of waste objects.

It is not surprising that a book that corresponds so closely to Plato's philosophy does not show much concern for the general fate of toys, given the low status that Plato assigns to images. As *The Velveteen Rabbit* is a *toy* narrative though and as we live in a world concerned with the waste produced by the planned obsolescence of consumer objects, this glossing over of the doom of most toys is unsatisfactory. Pixar's *Toy Story* franchise takes a much darker approach to the toy narrative, abandoning idealism in favor of anxiety-ridden existentialism, and in this way, it meets questions of obsolescence head-on. Thus, the *Toy Story* films update the toy narrative, particularly *The Velveteen Rabbit*'s pattern of that narrative, to address our present-day concerns.

Toy Story's Existential Angst

The gods sentenced the mythic King Sisyphus to an eternity of hopeless, useless labor. He is forever rolling a huge rock to the top of a mountain only to watch it roll back down to the bottom. The toys in the *Toy Story* films are like Sisyphus for their struggles, too, are futile. No matter how many times they escape their demise, the threats of obsolescence and obliteration return.[8] In the *Toy Story* films, plastic will only ever be plastic. Likewise, in Camus's philosophy, there is no afterlife: for him, the only certainty is that we will die (57). This section begins from Ellen Scott's assertion that, despite their G ratings, the *Toy Story* films do not dispatch the forces of doom, but rather leave death and decay to "spread throughout their largely peakless narrative structures" (151). It builds on this idea by analyzing the films through and against Camus's philosophy, thus revealing the extent of their existential angst. It argues that, as Camus says of Sisyphus, the toys are ultimately happy despite their struggles and their pain. Yet, the films do not correspond precisely to "The Myth of Sisyphus," instead developing their own existential position that includes hope, loyalty, and purpose. Finally, by reading across Pixar's canon with specific reference to *WALL-E*, this section shows the relevance of the films' existential position to a world facing climate crisis and ecological disaster. We fear destruction, particularly by the plastics that *Toy Story*'s CGI mimics, and so, like the toys and *WALL-E*'s eponymous robot, we must continue to struggle against the forces that threaten us if we are to have a future.

In every one of the four *Toy Story* films, Andy's toys, especially Sheriff Woody, the cowboy doll, struggle to prevent their own obsolescence and complete ruin, but with each film, they come closer to death, with the fourth film even symbolically killing Woody. Despite their physical durability, the toys cannot win against these inexorable forces, making their lives a series of ultimately futile struggles. In *Toy Story 2*, as Woody tries to escape from Al's apartment to return to Andy and avoid becoming an item in a museum display,[9] Stinky Pete, an unopened prospector doll, asks him: "How long will it last, Woody? Do you really think Andy is going to take you to college or on his honeymoon?" Stinky Pete then observes, "Andy's growing up, and there's nothing you can do about it." Scott argues that "against this booming statement, Woody's attempts to rationalize his own obsolescence do and will ring hollow" (158). The next film, in fact, begins with Andy preparing to go to college, seemingly to leave his remaining toys with the options of storage in the attic, which would mean a boring life as dust-collecting junk; life at Sunnyside daycare, a place that exposes them to destructive toddlers; or going to the dump. At the end of the film, Andy pursues a fourth option, transferring the toys' ownership to a little girl named Bonnie, thereby prolonging their usefulness for a little while longer. However, by the beginning of *Toy Story 4* (2019), Bonnie has lost interest in Woody, and there is no way for him to regain her love. In the end, Woody surrenders his voice box to the broken doll Gabby Gabby, allowing her to finally function properly and find a child of her own, and he joins his love interest Bo Peep as a "lost toy," a childless toy who wanders the earth. The G rating prevents the film from annihilating Woody altogether, but there is a strong sense in which the loss of his voice box and his resultant inability to return fully to playtime constitutes his death. Unlike the Rabbit, who gets to live carefree forever, Woody remains an object made of plastic, cloth, and stuffing that will eventually fall apart. The extension of playtime is just that, an extension: it will end, and the toys will still be left with unappealing options followed by their final ruin.

Woody's body may not be eternal, but his loyalty is enduring, and it is this quality that both burdens him and endows him with nobility, aligning him with Camus's Sisyphus, who likewise rises above his burden and is happy in spite of it. Camus says that Sisyphus always returns to his rock at the bottom of the mountain and takes up his burden once again without becoming depressed by that burden. He argues that Sisyphus "teaches the higher fidelity that negates the gods and raises rocks.... The struggle itself toward the heights is enough to fill a man's [sic] heart. One must imagine Sisyphus happy" (Camus 123). Woody, like Sisyphus, continually picks up his burden: his faithfulness to his child owners provides him with purpose yet wounds him emotionally because the children grow up and leave him behind. In *Toy Story 2*, when Woody passes up the opportunity to become an object of adoration for generations of children passing through the Konishi Toy Museum, it is a sacrifice made in the name of being true to his role as Andy's toy. In *Toy Story 4*, even though Bonnie now leaves him in the closet, Woody is compelled to help her the first time she goes to school, sneaking into her backpack and stealthily providing the shy little girl with the materials from which she makes Forky, a toy whose foundation is a discarded spork. Woody then spends his time preventing Forky, who does not understand what it means to be a toy, from flinging himself back into the trash and educating him on the purpose of toys. Despite his own demoted status in her life, Woody cannot stand to see Bonnie suffer the loss of her new favorite toy. After the toys' struggle in the dump in *Toy Story 3*, it is humorously ironic that Forky wants to return to the trash rather than be Bonnie's toy. At the same time, it highlights the fact that all toys, no matter what their construction, are ultimately trash and that Woody is once again becoming an unwanted item. Woody's labor is as futile as that of Sisyphus for he will never overcome his gradual loss of esteem in the eyes of the children who own him. Still, he perseveres in the task of making children happy, thereby rising above his own problems. That is not to say that Woody never becomes caught up in his own troubles: in *Toy Story 2*, in a nightmare sequence, he worries about Andy throwing him away, and in *Toy Story 4*, Bo Peep recognizes that Woody is protecting Forky so that he can feel important. Nonetheless, Woody always grows as a character, always picking up his burden once again until the end of the last film.

While Woody is the most poignantly Sisyphean of Andy's toys, the toys' collective struggles speak to the absurdity of life and to Camus's argument that revolt is the only coherent philosophical position in the face of this absurdity. Camus argues that the absurd arises from the clash between the human heart's "wild longing for clarity" (21) and the unreasonable outside world that cannot meet this demand. He says that awareness of the absurd begins with the question, "Why?" (13)—Why am I here? Why am I doing what I am doing? From there, the absurd can become a "harrowing" passion (22). Still, he believes that suicide is not the rational response to this situation. An individual who commits suicide settles the absurd for himself, herself, or themself and succumbs to the reality of the death that awaits us all. Camus argues that it is, instead, revolt that is the rational response because an individual who revolts, in contrast to a suicidal one, "challenges the world anew every second," aware of, yet rejecting, death (54). It is therefore revolt against the absurd, the choice to live in spite of it, that gives life its value and its majesty. The anthropomorphic toys possess reason and emotions, making them capable of recognizing the absurd. In the first film, the "Strange Things" sequence gestures to the peculiarity of being a toy. This sequence shows a montage of moments in which Buzz supersedes Woody in every possible way and Woody's aghast reactions to these moments. Woody's reactions highlight the difficulties of a sentient being with no control over his destiny and who suffers because of the whims of an uncaring, unreasonable world.[10] Woody rebels against this situation when he tries to trap Buzz behind a desk so that Andy will choose him for the trip to Pizza Planet. Woody's pain here is only the tip of the proverbial iceberg as existential pain and struggle become pervasive in *Toy Story 3*. In this third installment, Andy is preparing to leave for college, setting the stage for the toys' literal fight for their lives. They must battle from start to finish to maintain relevance to someone and to escape annihilation, whether by Sunnyside Daycare's toddlers or by the dump's incinerator. The *Toy Story* films dramatize both the pain of living with the absurd and the revolt against it, aestheticizing them perhaps even more than Sisyphus's myth through their detailed CGI animation, excellent voice acting, and intensely emotional plots, thus making the strange majesty of such a life abundantly clear.

Despite the many resonances between Camus's "The Myth of Sisyphus" and the *Toy Story* films, the films do not as closely parallel Camus's philosophy as *The Velveteen Rabbit* does Plato's for the films entertain hope and maintain a clear purpose for the toys' lives, whereas Camus does not make room for either hope or purpose. Camus argues that it is possible to live "without appeal," that is, *without* a known purpose and *without* even the possibility of finding one because revolt is a sufficient reason for life (53, 55, 119). By contrast, the *Toy Story* films keep hope and purpose alive. As in *The Velveteen Rabbit*, in the *Toy Story* films, toys are objects for children's play and comfort, but unlike Williams's book, the films celebrate toys for what they are in and of themselves. In the first film, Buzz believes that he is truly a space ranger rather than a toy, but the film does not validate this belief or the desire to be other than a toy. Buzz becomes depressed after learning from a television advertisement that he is a mass-produced object and then even more depressed after discovering that he cannot actually fly. Woody then explains to Buzz that it is awesome to be such a "cool toy" and consequently to have the love of a child, a lesson that Buzz eventually accepts. Time and again, the films return to the idea that a toy's role as a play object is immensely valuable and gives a toy purpose. For example, Buzz protests Woody's decision to go to the museum (*Toy Story 2*), and Mrs. Potato Head objects to Woody's choice to accompany Andy to college instead of staying with them in the daycare (*Toy Story 3*) because museums and colleges are not places for play. Even though a toy's role comes to an end when a child grows up or simply loses interest or when the toy breaks, a toy nevertheless has a clear, enjoyable role. Furthermore, there is always hope for starting over. Wheezy, the broken penguin toy, receives a new squeaker and rejoins the rest of Andy's toys at the end of *Toy Story 2*. Jessie starts over twice after her original owner, Emily: first, with Andy (*Toy Story 2*) and then with Bonnie (*Toy Story 3*). The toys do not live completely without appeal as they love it when children play with them and live for these moments. Instead of being an animated replica of Camus's philosophy, the *Toy Story* films develop their own philosophical position, one in which purpose exists but is constantly threatened by obsolescence and in which hope, love, loyalty, and struggle all endow life with meaning and majesty.

Toy Story's existential position is particularly relevant to a world threatened by overconsumption and the resultant waste materials for, in conjunction with Pixar's *WALL-E*, it shows that we must struggle against hostile forces if we are to survive and have meaningful lives. *Toy Story 3*'s extended dump sequence, in which the toys almost meet their end in an incinerator, is a microcosm for the trash-clogged, uninhabitable world we see at the beginning of *WALL-E*. The dump sequence is a slice of time that gestures toward the detrimental nature of trash, providing a glimpse of the coming trash apocalypse against which we must fight if we do not want our planet to be as lifeless as *WALL-E*'s Earth. As noted in the introduction, toys becoming trash is a consistent motif in toy and other related narratives, usually signaling the end of a toy's purpose as a plaything—its symbolic death—as it does in *The Velveteen Rabbit*, Hans Christian Andersen's "The Sweethearts (The Top and the Ball)" (1843), *The Mouse and His Child*, and, in Scott's opinion, *Toy Story 3* (160–61). However, some related narratives use a different kind of trash motif: namely, trash as signifier of large-scale or post-apocalyptic destruction. For example, in Giovanna Riccio's "North Pacific Garbage Gyre," the final poem in *Plastic's Republic* (2019), the trash-clogged ocean is a dying place, and in *WALL-E*, the whole Earth is an uninhabitable dump.[11] In *Toy Story 3*, the trash and the dump's mechanisms for dealing with it, the conveyor belt and the incinerator, overwhelm the toys, just as in these other works trash overwhelms the ocean and the Earth. The trash consists mostly of metal and plastic objects, such as food cans, labels, golf clubs, and pots, making it a similar mix as that which the tin mice encounter in *The Mouse and His Child* (Hoban 15–22) and which fills the ocean in Riccio's poem (113–15, lines 4–6, 21–23, 26–27). Discarded manmade objects are the source of damage or signal doom in several narratives, and they will engulf us and devastate us, as has happened in *WALL-E*, if we do not struggle as the toys do.

WALL-E shows that if we do not struggle, if we do not love our world and have hope for the future as the toys love their lives with children and maintain hope for their futures and as WALL-E loves exploring the world around him, we will, in a sense, commit suicide. In *WALL-E*, humans live on "starliners," spaceship versions of cruise ships. Onboard the Axiom Starliner, the flagship of Buy n Large's (BnL's) fleet, morbidly obese humans are at the mercy of the corporation that owns the fleet, the same corporation that, as the opening shots establish, came to dominate the world and whose junk seems largely responsible for destroying it. The humans spend their days looking at the screens that BnL provides for their entertainment, slurping the shakes that BnL gives them for food, and responding uncritically to BnL advertising. They have ceased to struggle or truly care about anything. They may breathe, but they seem less alive than the curious WALL-E, who investigates the trash that he is meant to compact, collects the pieces that he finds interesting, enjoys the cockroach Hal's companionship, and falls in love with EVE, a robot who comes to earth to investigate potential plant life. It is WALL-E's presence on the Axiom that disrupts the humans' routines, bringing them to greater awareness, and causing them to struggle against BnL and the robots ruling the ship. The film shows that the less we struggle against corporations and consumerism and the more plastic and other refuse we put in the dump, the less we live and the less chance we have of living in the future. Existential crisis proves necessary to the fight against ecological and climate crisis: it is only by revolting against the world that we can maintain an inhabitable world.

Conclusion: Toying with Philosophy and the Future

Through their depictions of questioning, anxious, sentient toys, the love between toys and children, the toy characters' conversion into trash, and their subsequent brushes with death, *The Velveteen Rabbit* and the *Toy Story* films develop strikingly different philosophies. *The Velveteen Rabbit* presents a philosophy that is markedly similar to Plato's, but its similarity to an ancient thought system causes it to look backward rather than forward, and it is thus often unsatisfying to contemporary audiences. The *Toy Story* films, however, take the concerns of *The Velveteen Rabbit*—Realness and the nature of toys—and respond to them through developing their own existential philosophy. The toys struggle against the world and therefore live meaningfully. However, toys become trash, one of the hostile forces against which we must fight if our lives and our world are to continue. We, like the toys in *Toy Story 3* and the eponymous character in *WALL-E*, must not allow the trash to overwhelm or stop us. The *Toy Story* films and other entries in Pixar's canon, such as *WALL-E* and the short films I mentioned in the introduction, are therefore the inheritors of *The Velveteen Rabbit*, the necessary versions of the toy narrative for inspiring revolt against the forces that threaten our doom.

Notes

1. Although children sometimes like to play with snow globes, *Knick Knack*'s snowman is not technically a toy, but rather a souvenir from Nome, Alaska. However, like the toys in toy narratives, the snowman is a sentient material object, and both his struggle against forces larger than himself and his desire for connection with others is similar to the *Toy Story* toys' fight against destructive forces and their longing for a child's love.

2. I am indebted to Giovanna Riccio's *Plastic's Republic* (2019) for this theoretical lens as well as for the title of this chapter. Although I am not dealing with Riccio's poems about Barbie here, they have been a major inspiration for my interpretation of toy narratives.

I would also like to thank everyone who read this chapter and gave me feedback, and my first philosophy professor, Seamus O'Neill, who introduced me to both the discipline and Plato's works.

3. I use the spelling "Real" throughout this essay rather than "real" to be consistent with the capitalization in *The Velveteen Rabbit*. The only exceptions are quotations that use the latter letter case. Since I give a Platonic reading of Williams's text and argue that the "Real" of Williams's text is essentially synonymous with Plato's "Ideas," I see no reason not to apply this capitalization to a discussion of Plato's philosophy.

4. In the final chapter of *When Toys Come Alive* (1994), Lois Rostow Kuznets analyzes stories about toy-like automata, looking at these stories as an extension of toy narratives because they share the common concern of objects gaining sentience, which in turn raises questions of what it means to be alive and to be human. Consequently, I believe that my brief discussion of *WALL-E* at the end of this chapter is justified.

5. I am not actually directly quoting the text here but rather paraphrasing the conversation between the Skin Horse and the Rabbit (Williams 6). However, both words are key to this conversation and the text as a whole.

6. The Rabbit should have actually known of the existence of flesh-and-blood rabbits before this point because, in his play, the Boy makes tunnels for the Rabbit in the bedclothes that he likens to the burrows of "real rabbits" (Williams 10). Despite this reference, when the Rabbit

first sees the wild rabbits, he thinks they are some kind of amazing toy with well-hidden seams and clockwork (17). Here, the book's philosophy turns rather Humean, for without the impression of a wild rabbit (that is, without personally seeing a wild rabbit), the Rabbit is unable to recognize one or understand its reality. This sudden switch in philosophical schools would be worth exploring and critiquing, but such an exercise is beyond the scope of this chapter.

7. Since the book adopts the Rabbit's perspective, the reader theoretically grows in knowledge of the Real along with the Rabbit. Even if the reader does not accept the Skin Horse's position, or the book's overall position for that matter, he, she, or they must at least contemplate these divergent understandings of the Real. As the book presents a philosophical position without being a work of philosophy (that is, it does not explicitly make a philosophical argument or declare itself to be a philosophical text), it is likely to be less effective in arguing its case than Plato's *Republic*, which openly uses allegory to make an argument about the nature of reality and thereby guides the reader, along with the in-text interlocutors, through Socrates's logic. A study based in reader-response theory would help to explore how the reader interprets and reacts to *The Velveteen Rabbit*'s ontological meditation.

8. Brushes with death and obsolescence include Jessie's fear in *Toy Story 2* of being put back into storage and therefore forgotten in the dark and Andy's remaining toys finding themselves in a trash incinerator in *Toy Story 3*.

9. Early in the film, Woody rides Andy's dog, Buster, into a yard sale to rescue Wheezy, a broken penguin toy. Al, a toy dealer, finds Woody on a table, and when Andy's mom refuses to sell him because he is an old family toy, Al steals him. Al needs him to complete his Woody's Roundup collection (a collection of toys based on a fictional television series from the 1950s) and sell it to the Konishi Toy Museum.

10. One can read the children in the *Toy Story* films as representatives of Camus's unreasonable world for they are not particularly well-developed characters and most of their behavior goes unexplained. While they have some discernible characteristics (Andy is happy and playful, Sid is destructive, and Bonnie is timid but deeply imaginative), they do not express the same depth of character or range of emotions as the toys, and the toys are subject to and victims of their ever-changing fancies.

11. These different uses of the trash motif are worthy of further consideration, but I do not have the space to enter into such a consideration here.

Works Cited

Andersen, Hans Christian. "The Sweethearts (The Top and the Ball)." *Andersen's Fairy Tales*. Translated by Pat Shaw Iversen, Signet Classics, 2013, pp. 132–35.
Camus, Albert. "The Myth of Sisyphus." 1942. *The Myth of Sisyphus and Other Essays*. Translated by Justin O'Brien, Alfred A. Knopf, 1969, pp. 1–138.
Daniels, Steven V. "*The Velveteen Rabbit*: A Kleinian Perspective." *Children's Literature*, vol. 18, 1990, pp. 17–30. *Project MUSE*, https://muse.jhu.edu.qe2a-proxy.mun.ca/article/246200. Accessed 6 Oct. 2022.
Fleming, Dan. *Powerplay: Toys as Popular Culture*. Manchester UP, 1996.
Hoban, Russell. *The Mouse and His Child*. Illustrated by Lillian Hoban, Harper & Row, 1967.
Knick Knack. Directed by John Lasseter, performance by Mel Blanc, Pixar Animation Studios, 1989.
Kuznets, Lois Rostow. *When Toys Come Alive: Narratives of Animation, Metamorphosis, and Development*. Yale UP, 1994.

Milne, A. A. *The House at Pooh Corner*. 1928. Dutton, 2018.
Milne, A. A. *Winnie-the-Pooh*. 1926. Dutton, 2017.
Plato. *Phaedo*. Translated by Benjamin Jowett, ARC Manor, 2008.
Plato. *Republic*. Translated by G. M. A. Grube, revised by C. D. C. Reeve, Hackett, 1992.
Plato. *Symposium*. Edited by M. C. Howatson and Frisbee C. C. Sheffield, translated by M. C. Howatson, Cambridge UP, 2008.
Riccio, Giovanna. *Plastic's Republic*. Guernica, 2019.
Scott, Ellen. "Agony and Avoidance: Pixar, Deniability, and the Adult Spectator." *Journal of Popular Film and Television*, vol. 43, no. 3, 2014, pp. 150–62. *Taylor & Francis*, https://doi.org/10.1080/01956051.2014.881773.
Tin Toy. Directed by John Lasseter, performances by Andrés Couturier, Mel Blanc, and Sárközi Olivér, Pixar Animation Studios, 1988.
Toy Story. Directed by John Lasseter, performances by Tom Hanks and Tim Allen, Walt Disney Pictures and Pixar Animation Studios, 1995.
Toy Story 2. Directed by John Lasseter, performances by Tom Hanks, Tim Allen, Joan Cusack, and Kelsey Grammar, Walt Disney Pictures and Pixar Animation Studios, 1999.
Toy Story 3. Directed by Lee Unkrich, performances by Tom Hanks, Tim Allen, Joan Cusack, Don Rickles, Wallace Shawn, and John Ratzenberger, Walt Disney Pictures and Pixar Animation Studios, 2010.
Toy Story 4. Directed by Josh Cooley, performances by Tom Hanks, Tim Allen, Annie Potts, and Christina Hendricks, Walt Disney Pictures and Pixar Animation Studios, 2019.
WALL-E. Directed by Andrew Stanton, performances by Ben Burtt, Elissa Knight, Jeff Garlin, and Sigourney Weaver, Walt Disney Pictures and Pixar Animation Studios, 2008.
Williams, Margery. *The Velveteen Rabbit: Or How Toys Become Real*. 1922. Illustrated by Michael Green, Running, 1984.

Chapter 4

Personhood and Love: Interrogating "Realness" in *The Velveteen Rabbit*

—Claudia Mills

The philosophical concept of "personhood" was put forward by Immanuel Kant in his 1785 *Groundwork for the Metaphysics of Morals*. There he writes that all rational beings have the special status of being *persons*: "rational beings are called persons, inasmuch as their nature already marks them out as ends in themselves, i.e., as something that is not to be used merely as a means" (36). By "ends in themselves" Kant means beings that have their value *in themselves*, rather than merely possessing instrumental value for achieving the purposes of others. The contrast here is between persons and things: "In the kingdom of ends [Kant's idealized vision of moral community] everything has either a price or a dignity. Whatever has a price can be replaced by something else as its equivalent; on the other hand, whatever is above all price, and therefore admits of no equivalent, has a dignity" (40). *Things*, then, have a *price*—either a market price or what Kant calls an "affective price," a value measured in terms of someone's desire for it. *Persons* alone have a *dignity*.

Margery Williams's 1922 classic *The Velveteen Rabbit* can be read as a story about a toy rabbit's yearning for the moral status of "personhood." In seeking to become "Real," the Rabbit seeks the moral standing of a being who has value in *itself*—value for its *own* sake. To achieve this moral status is, in the sense most fundamental to Williams's narrative, what it is to become Real.[1]

Reality as Personhood

The Velveteen Rabbit presents a heartbreaking example of toys treated only as disposable and replaceable things. "For at least two days," the Velveteen Rabbit is loved by the Boy and then completely forgotten until the Boy's impatient Nana can't find "the china dog that always slept with him" (Williams 1). Casting about for any available alternative, she seizes upon the Rabbit: "take your old Bunny! He'll do to sleep with you!" (9). One toy animal will "do" as well as another to serve the instrumental purpose at hand; to echo Kant's language, one toy can be "replaced by something else as its equivalent" (40). After the Boy's long illness comes the devastating announcement that "all the books and toys that the Boy had played with in bed must be burnt" (Williams 22), including the Boy's now-cherished Rabbit: "Burn it at once. What? Nonsense! Get him a new one" (24). And so, once again, one *thing* is replaced with another *thing*; the shabby Velveteen Rabbit is replaced with a "a splendid bunny, all white plush with real glass eyes" (25).[2] There is no more poignant expression of what it is to be a mere thing, lacking the dignity of personhood, than when the discarded Velveteen Rabbit is "put into a sack with . . . a lot of rubbish" (24). Then halfway through the story comes a night when the Boy absolutely cannot go to sleep without the Velveteen Rabbit, and this time Nana has no choice but to go out hunting for him in the darkness. When Nana grumbles, "You must have your old Bunny! . . . Fancy all that fuss for a toy!" (12), it is at this moment that the Boy declares that the Velveteen Rabbit "isn't a toy. He's REAL!" (13). That is to say, the Velveteen Rabbit is not a replaceable thing with only instrumental value, but rather a nonreplaceable *person* who matters for his own sake.

Note that personhood is not the same thing as being a member of the species *Homo sapiens*. In introducing the concept of personhood, Kant took pains to write that it is not only "man" but "in general every rational being" that possesses this moral status (35). For Kant, rationality, not humanity, is the essential criterion for personhood. (Kant himself did not even consider recognizing sufficient rational capacity in nonhuman animals to include them in the category of persons and so did not accord them independent moral status in their own right.) Over the past half century, more recent philosophers have followed Kant in distinguishing personhood (often called "full moral standing" or "full moral status") from mere species membership. While there is widespread agreement that all adult human beings with normal levels of cognitive functioning count as persons, questions arise about whether some human beings, such as fetuses, infants, or those lacking a measurable IQ or suffering from advanced dementia, may *not* qualify to be persons. Questions also arise regarding whether certain nonhuman animals (perhaps even most nonhuman animals) should be judged as meeting the relevant standard for personhood, depending on what it is deemed to be. Indeed, the contemporary concept of personhood was developed and refined in part precisely to assess the degree to which nonhuman animals might (or might not) merit inclusion as members of the moral community.[3] So, in becoming "real" as he does at the end of the story, this time in the sense of becoming an actual, living rabbit, the Velveteen Rabbit is actually transformed into a creature that has a controversial moral status and is often treated entirely as a mere thing; consider the widespread use of animals for meat production and laboratory experimentation.

What, then, are the criteria that mark out some entity as a "person"? For Kant, as we have seen, the key is rationality; within the larger framework of Kantian ethics, rationality is exalted for its role in enabling autonomous action, where moral agents act autonomously if they obey the moral law that they have legislated for themselves. Presumably not even dolphins or primates have the capacity to function at this highly sophisticated level. More recent writers have nominated as sufficient criteria for personhood sophisticated cognitive capacities, such as the capacity to will (e.g., Quinn), to experience self-awareness (e.g., McMahan), and to care for others (e.g., Jaworska). Debate then ensues over what level of these abilities is required for personhood and whether animals can meet the necessary standard for crossing the threshold. One of the best-known advocates for animal rights, Tom Regan, argues that the crucial feature for granting the kind of full moral status associated with personhood is the capacity to be "the experiencing subject of a life" (24). This in turn requires the ability "to want and prefer things, believe and feel things, recall and expect things" and above all to have these things in some sense *matter* to you. Regan argues that animals are clearly "experiencing subjects of a life" and thus have an "inherent value of their own" (24). Here, of course, the fictional Velveteen Rabbit already meets all the criteria for being an experiencing subject of a life as much as any living rabbit ever could, indeed vastly more so. Presumably, no actual living rabbit is capable of engaging in extended conversations and meditations about what it is to be Real!

A different group of philosophers, also seeking to defend moral standing for nonhuman animals, have proposed the more minimal standard of mere sentience: the mere ability to feel pleasure and pain.[4] Jeremy Bentham, the founder of utilitarianism and one of Kant's contemporaries, famously wrote that the relevant question to ask for drawing the "insuperable line" between beings that have independent moral status versus "the class of *things*" is "not, Can they *reason*? nor, Can they *talk*? but, Can they *suffer*?" (283n1, emphasis original). When the Velveteen Rabbit asks the Skin Horse, "Does [being Real] hurt?" the Skin Horse replies, "Sometimes" (Williams 5), but if we understand "being Real" to correspond with "having moral status in one's own right," the ability to be hurt, to feel pain, to feel anything, is not a possible *consequence* of being Real, but rather the *precondition* for it. For utilitarians, like Peter Singer, the capacity to feel is the capacity to have "interests"—to care about what happens to you: "The capacity for suffering and enjoyment is *a prerequisite for having interests*" (8). A rabbit can have interests; a stone cannot. The rabbit minds if you kick it; the stone does not. The interests of all affected by a potential action, Singer argues, need to be weighed and balanced in determining what it is right or wrong to do.

Now, as a fictional character in the world created by Williams, the Velveteen Rabbit (unlike toys in the real world) already possesses all the qualities offered above for moral status: he can reason, reflect, and feel deeply. Within the framework of the story, what the Rabbit chiefly lacks is the power of locomotion, of moving himself according to his own will and being able "to hop on [his] hind legs" (Williams 17). The ability to "run and play" (29) is what he gains in becoming a real rabbit in the story's conclusion, to go "springing about the turf on [his hind legs], jumping sideways and whirling round as the others did" (32). But nowhere in the philosophical literature on personhood has the capacity for self-generated locomotion been proposed as the definitive marker for full moral standing; it would be ludicrous to mount a serious argument for the view that, in losing her legs, a human amputee loses her full membership in the moral community. However, the experiences of many who live with physical limitations on mobility bear witness to the extent to which *recognition* of one's humanity can be diminished through perceived disability (as discussed in the chapter by Scott T. Pollard and Kara K. Keeling in this volume), so the Rabbit's yearning for full mobility as enhancement of his personhood sadly engages with the reality of widespread social reactions toward physical impairment. The story's ending also seems to suggest that by becoming a living rabbit, the Velveteen Rabbit will acquire some kind of immortality: the Fairy tells the other rabbits, "[H]e is going to live with you for ever and ever" (Williams 29). Of course, the precise opposite is true. To be a live rabbit is to be mortal, not only capable of feeling pain but capable of dying—indeed, guaranteed to die. An entity that is alive is an entity that will someday not be alive.

Of the capacities that have been advanced as criteria for personhood, I want to focus on those necessary for *caring* about something or somebody—caring about what happens to oneself and also what happens to others. Agnieszka Jaworska argues that "the emotional capacity to care is a sufficient condition of an individual's FMS [full moral standing] as a person" (460). She includes as typical components of caring such things as "joy and satisfaction when the object of one's care is doing well and advancing and ... fear when the object is in jeopardy and relief when it escapes untouched" (483). At the close of her discussion, Jaworska provides empirical evidence that great apes, such as the legendary gorilla Koko,[5] are "capable of the cognitively sophisticated kind of caring" necessary for full moral status (495). *Caring* is close enough to *love* that, following Jaworska, we could say that the crucial capacity for personhood is the capacity to love.

The Velveteen Rabbit, however, inverts this claim. Williams's authority on Realness, the well-worn Skin Horse, explains to the Rabbit (and to the child reader) that the key to becoming Real is not loving, but being loved: "Real isn't how you are made.... It's a thing that happens to you. When a child loves you for a long, long time, not just to play with, but REALLY loves you, then you become Real"

(Williams 5). The Boy makes the Rabbit Real by loving him. But following my trail through the philosophical literature on personhood, if Realness is identified with personhood, and personhood is conditional upon the ability to love, it would be the Boy, as the active loving agent, who shows the Realness of his personhood here. Persons are not those who are loved; they are those who do the loving. To connect this back to the Rabbit's original conversation with the Skin Horse, it is for this reason that being Real sometimes hurts. It is not being loved that exposes us to hurt; it is loving that does this. It is having a loving heart of one's own that can be broken. Viewed through the lens of the literature on personhood, the Skin Horse's pontifications about Realness get things precisely backward.[6]

Love and Value

The Skin Horse's account of Realness fares considerably better if we turn from the philosophical literature on personhood to the philosophical literature on love. In Aristotle's discussion of *philia* (a form of love) in the *Nicomachean Ethics*, he defines "love" (often translated as "friendship") as wishing good to another for the other's own sake (121). This definition has been taken up by recent writers. Aaron Smuts, for example, argues that "what is common to all different kinds of love is a concern for the beloved for her own sake" ("Part II" 518).

This analysis of love resonates with the analysis of personhood, for on this account only persons can be objects of love. Persons are beings who have interests, beings who are capable of caring about what happens to them and about what happens to others. If love is wishing good to another for the other's own sake, the other has to be the kind of object capable of having a distinct and independent good. Despite how we fling the term about in ordinary language, strictly speaking we can love only persons, not things. We may say that we love fried chicken or a beautiful sunset or a Beethoven piano sonata, but as Smuts is defining love, we cannot really mean this. We can intensely *like* these things, we can have deep and powerful emotions regarding them, but "we can only love what we perceive to have a good" (Smuts, "Part I" 509). Smuts points out that we cannot wish good to fried chicken for the fried chicken's own sake simply because there is nothing that is good *for* a piece of fried chicken for its *own* sake. We may say, for example, that it is bad for fried chicken to be overcooked, but this is not bad for the fried chicken; it is bad for those who will now be disappointed when they go to eat it. A dead chicken (whether fried or fricasseed) has no wants or desires, feels nothing, cares about nothing, so there is nothing that can matter to it for its own sake. On Smut's definition of love, however, it is not only human beings to whom we can wish good for their own sake; we can wish good to a live, feeling, experiencing chicken for the chicken's own sake (ditto for live, feeling, experiencing rabbits) because there are things that matter to live chickens and rabbits. So just as only persons are capable of loving, only persons are capable of being loved.

The Fairy states that the Boy loves the Rabbit: "You were Real to the Boy ... because he loved you" (Williams 29). It is not completely clear, however, that the Boy wishes good to the Rabbit for the Rabbit's own sake. When the Rabbit goes missing on the fateful night on which his Realness is declared, Nana must go searching for him "because the Boy couldn't go to sleep unless he was there" (12). This could be read that the Boy values the Rabbit only for the Boy's own sake, for the Rabbit's usefulness as a reliable remedy against insomnia. We can also lie sleepless, however, out of worry for another's well-being and out of sheer longing for the other's cherished presence. When the Rabbit is carted off with the other germ-infested toys to be burned, admittedly the Boy makes no protest. But his lack of any expression of concern for the Rabbit's imminent demise suggests that he now no longer loves the Rabbit, that he has outgrown that love.

Does the Rabbit love the Boy? The text at one point explicitly says that he does. Immediately after the Boy confers Realness upon the Rabbit, "That night [the Rabbit] was almost too happy to sleep, and so much love stirred in his little sawdust heart that it almost burst" (13). When the Boy becomes ill, the Rabbit hides beneath the bedcovers, "afraid that if they found him someone might take him away, and he knew that the Boy needed him" (21). Admittedly, the Rabbit seems more concerned about the Boy's recovery in anticipation of the "delightful things" the two of them will be able to do together than out of consideration for the Boy's own well-being (21); one could say the same thing about the Boy's love for the Rabbit. But I have argued elsewhere that "[in] personal relationships we do and should desire to be valued at least in some sense instrumentally" (Mills 4); it is not only permissible, but desirable that there be some selfish as well as selfless motivation for love. I love you in part for the joy you bring to my life; I would hope that you love me in part for the joy I bring to yours; we can both love each other for the joy we share together.

To love something is to see that thing as valuable: love can be understood "to be a distinctive mode of valuing a person" (Helm). This provokes a much-debated question: Do I love someone because of the ways in which she is valuable (i.e., because of her intrinsic attractive features that I have now come to recognize)? Or is someone valuable because I love her (i.e., does my love itself confer value upon her?) Which came first, the value or the love? It is not only philosophers who puzzle over this chicken-and-egg question about love; it is relevant in other classics of children's literature and culture as well as *The Velveteen Rabbit*. In Oscar Hammerstein and Richard Rodgers's *Cinderella*, for example, the Prince and Cinderella engage in a musical dialogue on this very subject, asking each other, "Do I love you because you're beautiful? Or are you beautiful because I love you? ... Do I want you because you're wonderful? Or are you wonderful because

I want you?" In a way that connects with our discussion here, they frame these as questions about whether the other can *really* be as beautiful or wonderful as they seem or whether their seeming perfection is merely imaginary, part of a "lover's dream." But another possibility is that love actually invests the other with beauty and wonder that have their own reality.

The view that we love another in recognition of that person's already existing merits is initially appealing. As Harry Frankfurt writes: "Love is often understood as being, most basically, a response to the perceived worth of the beloved.... We begin loving the things that we love because we are struck by their value, and we continue to love them for the sake of their value. If we did not find the beloved valuable, we would not love it" (38). Most of us can provide a catalog of attractive features that make our beloveds worthy of our love: intelligence, beauty, a sense of humor, moral integrity, being a good listener, etc. On further consideration, however, this view can leave us uneasy. If we love someone because of how they rank on some scale of attractiveness, there seems no reason not to transfer our love to someone who ranks even higher on that scale: someone who is more intelligent or more beautiful, funnier, with even more irreproachable integrity or more empathetic listening skills. But "the objects of our love are irreplaceable" (Smuts, "Part II" 520). When we love someone, we love that *person*, not that person's particular constellation of virtues. Nor is the genuine lover willing to "trade up" upon locating someone with a greater degree of these same traits and characteristics (Smuts, "Part II" 520).

Returning to the Rabbit and the Boy, the Boy's love for the Rabbit—shown in his declaration that the Rabbit is "REAL"—is part and parcel of his refusal to accept any substitutes for him, threadbare though he is. Earlier in the story, the Boy accepted the Rabbit as a substitute for the china dog, sharing Nana's judgment that any toy "will do." Later the Boy will accept the new "splendid bunny, all white plush with real glass eyes" (Williams 25). But that he can allow this substitution implies that he loves the bunny no longer. Following Smuts, to truly love someone is to be indifferent to any proffered alternatives, however plush their fur or glassy their eyes. During the course of their loving relationship, the Boy loves and wants the Rabbit not because the Rabbit is beautiful or wonderful; he loves the *Rabbit* regardless of whether a more beautiful or wonderful stuffed toy is available.

These kinds of considerations lead Frankfurt to argue for the alternative answer to the chicken-and-egg question about the relationship of love to value. He writes: "The truly essential relationship between love and the value of the beloved goes in the opposite direction. It is not necessarily as a *result* of recognizing their value and of being captivated by it that we love things. Rather what we love necessarily *acquires* value for us *because* we love it" (Frankfurt 38–39). He gives as his central example the love of parents for their children. In many cases, parents (both biological and adoptive) love their children even before they are born, with no "relevant information about their particular characteristics or their particular merits and virtues" (39); whatever relationships they envision developing with these children are based on no specific fact whatsoever about them, as no such facts yet exist. Nor would such information, even if available, be the grounds for parental love. Frankfurt writes, "It is quite clear to me that I do not love [my children] more than other children because I believe they are better" (39). Nor is parental love unique in this regard. As Irving Singer writes of love more generally, "love . . . confers importance no matter what the object is worth" (273).

Nonetheless, value conferred in this way seems to remain value only in the eyes of the lover; it is not objective value that the rest of us have any reason to recognize. If Cinderella becomes beautiful to the Prince because of his love for her, this does not necessarily make her beautiful to her stepsisters. Thus, love confers value only in a limited, lover-specific sense. The Fairy acknowledges this when she says, toward the end of the book, that the Bunny was "Real to the Boy . . . because he loved you. Now you shall be Real to every one [sic]" (Williams 29). Being Real to the one who loves you does not make you "really" Real (truly valuable) to anyone else.[7] In order for this final step in the journey toward Realness to be accomplished, the nursery magic Fairy needs to summon her powers to bring about the Rabbit's final transformation into a living, breathing, moving rabbit. At this point in the story the original sense of Realness put forward by the Skin Horse is being replaced by a quite different—and far less interesting and thought-provoking—understanding of the term. Now "real" means something like "natural," where the opposite is "artificial" or "human-made." Being real in this new sense has nothing to do with being a person who is an end in himself or a source of value or an object of value or an object of love.

Let me set this aside. Williams was not intending to produce a philosophical treatise but a story for children, animated by a message about love and personhood that she was clearly invested in sharing: the message is, as we have seen, that we become persons and that we acquire value by being loved. Let us now, in closing, examine that message more closely.

Ethical Implications

If we move from thinking about the metaphysics of Williams's account of becoming Real to its ethical dimensions, how should we respond to the message about self-worth that this story has imparted to young readers for the past century? To recapitulate: I have argued that in seeking to become Real, the Velveteen Rabbit seeks to become a person with what Kant would call a *dignity*, a source of value in his own right, rather than a thing of only instrumental value to others that can be used as a mere means and then discarded. We have considered two ways in which someone might attain that goal. The first (drawn from philosophical writings on personhood) is by being the kind of creature capable of loving. The second (drawn from philosophical reflections on love) is by being a creature who has in fact been loved. Williams, via the Skin Horse, explicitly endorses the second of these alternatives. Realness "is a thing that happens to you" (5). However, her text gives us materials for endorsing the first alternative, as the Rabbit's love for the Boy can be read as a sign of his already present personhood.

In my view, there is something deeply unsatisfying about the Skin Horse's answer, that we become Real, someone who *matters*, by being loved. This is the same answer given in Dean Martin's hit song, "You're Nobody 'til Somebody Loves You," which continues after this line with "You're nobody 'til somebody cares," a song that made me deeply discouraged when I spent most of my high school years without a boyfriend. Even though the song concludes with the instruction, "So find yourself somebody to love," I knew at sixteen that even if I found somebody to love, there was no guarantee that somebody would love me back. Loving is simply not the same thing as being loved.

It seems to me problematic to encourage young readers to think that they grow in "Realness" as a form of self-worth only by being lucky enough to be loved. (It has always seemed to me equally problematic when the wizard tells the Tin Man, at the end of the MGM film *The Wizard of Oz* (1939), "A heart is not judged by how much you love; but by how much you are loved by others.") As the great Stoic philosopher Epictetus reminds us in the opening sentence of his *Handbook*, "Some things are up to us and others are not" (287), where the first category contains only "whatever is our own action," and the second category contains everything else on this Earth, including (most relevant for our purposes) other people's thoughts, feelings, and actions. Epictetus proceeds to offer this advice: "[I]f you desire any of the things that are not up to us, you must necessarily be unfortunate" (288). Following Epictetus, we can say that, rather than hoping someone will come along some day and love us, our lives will go better if we ourselves undertake the undeniable risk of loving someone else fiercely and fully. Reflecting on the question, not of what makes some entity count as a person at all, but what makes each of us into the *specific* persons we are, I define myself more by what and whom I have loved than by whether I was lucky enough to have someone else's love "happen to me." In any case, it seems preferable to recommend to young readers activity rather than passivity in pursuing those things that are most important for a life well lived.

Iris Murdoch offers this apt observation of the relationship between love and Realness: "Love is the extremely difficult realization that something other than oneself is real" (51). Love consists in seeing the other as a person and in honoring and celebrating their personhood. Perhaps it is via this realization that one becomes "Real" oneself as well—more fully a person in one's own right. This chapter has focused on understanding the "Reality" of the Rabbit, but the Boy himself also engages in a journey toward becoming "Real" in the course of Williams's story. The Boy shows his love for his well-worn toy when he comes to see the Velveteen Rabbit as Real; note that the Boy's *realizing* that the Rabbit is Real means that the Rabbit was *already* Real. In coming to this realization, in recognizing the Rabbit's Reality, the Boy also becomes more Real himself. He finds his own voice in challenging Nana's dismissal of his "old Bunny"; he exercises his own agency not in passively being loved by others but in actively loving them. As a person acknowledging the Reality of another person, the Boy himself has become more capable of love and growth, more capable of pain and loss, and more fully, and *really*, alive. This focus on the power of loving, rather than the Skin Horse's much-quoted reflection on the hope of being loved, is the more valuable message at the heart of this book beloved by children and their parents for the past century.

Notes

1. Throughout this chapter, I capitalize "Real" when I am using the term in the sense discussed by the Skin Horse in Williams's text or trying to explore the term, as used in that sense, as a philosophical concept. I lowercase "real" when used in the more ordinary sense of "real" as opposed to "artificial," as in the Rabbit's transformation from toy rabbit to living rabbit at the end of the story, or in a more ordinary sense more generally.

2. It is worth noting that its white color seems to count as one of the features that make this new bunny a "splendid" upgrade from the merely "spotted brown and white" fur of the now shabby Velveteen Rabbit. The "realness" of the glass eyes invokes a different sense of realness from the one previously advanced in the text; here the "real glass eyes" seem to contrast with eyes made of some imitative alternative. This is the sense of realness akin to the one that comes into play with the Rabbit's transformation into a real (nonimitation) rabbit at the end of the story.

3. A helpful overview of philosophical argumentation on how to determine the moral status of animals is provided in Lori Gruen's entry on "The Moral Status of Animals" in the *Stanford Encyclopedia of Philosophy*. An equally helpful overview of philosophical argumentation on how to determine moral status more generally appears in Agnieszka Jaworska and Julie Tannenbaum's entry on "The Grounds of Moral Standing," also in the *Stanford Encyclopedia of Philosophy*.

4. These philosophers, most famously Peter Singer, tend not to use the language of "personhood" in mounting this defense, but they share the goal of trying to ground the moral significance of animals as beings valuable in their own right.

5. Jaworska references not only Koko's ability to converse extensively with her caregiver in sign language but also Koko's tender play with her companion kitten and expressions of grief even months after the kitten's death.

6. The claim that we become Real—that we count as persons with full moral standing— by being loved does have some support in the philosophical literature on personhood. For

example, Eva Feder Kittay, writing about her relationship with her profoundly disabled daughter, Sesha, rejects the view that any "intrinsic psychological capacities . . . are the principal qualification for membership in a moral community of individuals deserving equal respect and dignity" (100). For Kittay, social relations play a crucial role "in the constitution of identity" (110). Even an anencephalic infant, born without the brain components to enable consciousness, "is someone's child"; "It is morally (and emotionally) appropriate to care for one's child for the child's own sake" (111). That said, Kittay goes on to characterize her own daughter as having the "capacity to embrace those who show her love and care," and whose "infectious love of life enriches the lives of others" (123); "Sesha is capable of great joy and great love" (129). So, the capacity for love remains relevant, even if full moral standing may be granted in a very few highly exceptional cases to a being only because this being is "someone's child."

7. This dispute in the philosophical literature about whether love appraises value or confers value remains unresolved, as most disputes on most topics have been throughout the history of philosophy. For two especially nuanced accounts that give credit to both sides of the argument, see Setiya and Jollimore.

Works Cited

Aristotle. *Nicomachean Ethics*. Translated by Terence Irwin, 2nd ed., Hackett, 1999.

Bentham, Jeremy. *Introduction to the Principles of Morals and Legislation*. Edited by J. H. Burns and H. L. A. Hart, Metheuen, 1982.

Cinderella. Directed by Charles S. Dubin, song performed by Lesley Ann Warren and Stuart Damon, CBS, 1965.

Epictetus. *The Handbook of Epictetus*. *The Discourses of Epictetus*, edited by Christopher Gill. Everyman, 1995, pp. 287–306.

Frankfurt, Harry. *The Reasons of Love*. Princeton UP, 2004.

Gruen, Lori. "The Moral Status of Animals." *The Stanford Encyclopedia of Philosophy*, edited by Edward N. Zalta, fall 2017, https://plato.stanford.edu/archives/fall2017/entries/moral-animal/. Accessed 8 Oct. 2022.

Hammerstein, Oscar, and Richard Rodgers. "Do I Love You Because You're Beautiful?" *Cinderella*. Directed by Charles S. Dubin, song performed by Lesley Ann Warren and Stuart Damon, CBS, 1965.

Helm, Bennett. "Love." *The Stanford Encyclopedia of Philosophy*, edited by Edward N. Zalta, fall 2017, https://plato.stanford.edu/archives/fall2017/entries/love/. Accessed 8 Oct. 2022.

Jaworska, Agnieszka. "Caring and Full Moral Standing." *Ethics*, vol. 117, no. 3, Apr. 2007, pp. 460–97.

Jaworska, Agnieszka, and Julie Tannenbaum. "The Grounds of Moral Status." *The Stanford Encyclopedia of Philosophy*, edited by Edward N. Zalta, spring 2018, https://plato.stanford.edu/archives/spr2018/entries/grounds-moral-status/. Accessed 8 Oct. 2022.

Jollimore, Troy. *Love's Vision*. Princeton UP, 2011.

Kant, Immanuel. *Grounding for the Metaphysics of Morals*. Translated by James W. Elllington, 3rd ed., Hackett, 1993.

Kittay, Eva Feder. "At the Margins of Moral Personhood." *Ethics*, vol. 116, no. 1, Oct. 2005, pp. 100–131.

Martin, Dean. "You're Nobody 'til Somebody Loves You." *This Time I'm Swingin'!* Capitol Records, 1960.

McMahan, Jeffrey. *The Ethics of Killing: Problems at the Margins of Life*. Oxford UP, 2005.

Mills, Claudia. "Are There Morally Problematic Reasons for Having Children?" *Philosophy & Public Policy Quarterly*, vol. 25, no. 4, fall 2005, pp. 2–9.
Murdoch, Iris. "The Sublime and the Good." *Chicago Review*, vol. 13, no 3, autumn 1959, pp. 42–55.
Quinn, Warren. "Abortion: Identity and Loss." *Philosophy & Public Affairs*, vol. 13, no. 1, winter 1984, pp. 24–54.
Regan, Tom. "The Case for Animal Rights." *In Defence of Animals*, edited by Peter Singer, Basil Blackwell, 1985, pp. 13–26.
Setiya, Kieran. "Love and the Value of a Life." *The Philosophical Review*, vol. 123, no. 3, July 2014, pp. 251–80.
Singer, Irving. "From *The Nature of Love*." *The Philosophy of (Erotic) Love*, edited by Robert C. Solomon and Kathleen Higgins, Kansas UP, 1991, pp. 259–78.
Singer, Peter. *Animal Liberation*. Avon, 1975.
Smuts, Aaron. "Normative Reasons for Love, Part I." *Philosophy Compass* vol. 9, no. 8, 2014, pp. 507–18.
Smuts, Aaron. "Normative Reasons for Love, Part II." *Philosophy Compass* vol. 9, no. 8, 2014, pp. 518–26.
Williams, Margery. *The Velveteen Rabbit: Or How Toys Become Real*. Doubleday, 1922.
The Wizard of Oz. Directed by Victor Fleming, performances by Judy Garland, Frank Morgan, Ray Bolger, Bert Lahr, and Jack Haley, Metro-Goldwyn-Mayer, 1939.

Chapter 5

Becoming Real through Matter That Matters: An Onto-Epistemological Analysis of *The Velveteen Rabbit*

—Adrianna Zabrzewska

As a soft toy filled with sawdust and coated with brown, spotted fur, the Rabbit of *The Velveteen Rabbit* (1922) understands himself and other toys living in the nursery through notions of texture, material, surface, stuffing, and winding mechanisms. The ways in which these toys are made, how they look, and how they can be used in a child's play give rise to a unique social hierarchy. This hierarchy is based on the toys' ability to move and their connection to real-world referents. The claim to realness is placed on a scale of likeness to a living animal or a full-sized vehicle. The Velveteen Rabbit eventually achieves the highest possible form of realness and becomes a living, breathing animal once the story takes on a more religious, didactic turn. But before the Velveteen Rabbit becomes a rabbit in its proper sense, the book is driven by a different kind of Realness—the privilege and the expense of becoming "Real" in the eyes of those who love us (Williams 17). Per the book's logic, "Realness" and "Real," when capitalized, refer to the process of becoming a unique, unrepeatable, and meaningful being for another unique being. Whereas "small *r*" realness denotes the condition of being similar or even identical to another entity or group of entities, "big *R*" Realness signifies the dynamic, embodied process of gradually becoming something that is unlike anything and anyone else.

Acknowledging the "return to the body" (Nikolajeva 132) in children's literature scholarship (Harde and Kokkola) and its intersections with feminist new materialism (Trites), this essay aims to explore the problem of embodiment and realness in Margery Williams's classic book. Using selected notions from

Karen Barad's new materialist philosophy, I provide an analysis of the Velveteen Rabbit's changing relationship with his own body, the bodies of others, and the material world as such. The chapter is intended to serve as a map for an onto-ethico-epistemological reading of one of Anglo-American literature's most famous rabbits. As I will argue, the book illustrates both the principles of Barad's philosophy and the order that this philosophy seeks to subvert. Up until the Boy's illness and the Rabbit's death sentence, the book shows us that to exist as a distinct, authentic, and meaningful self—and to be loved as that self by someone else—is an active, gradual, and potentially hurtful process of becoming that invites reciprocity, interdependence, and vulnerability. It is a material-discursive process that has its roots in the experience of being a body in all its imperfections and finitude. The second part of the book, however, contradicts this message. Instead of acknowledging love as a material practice between two embodied beings, the story eventually embraces a logic of transcendence in which something that is a mere representation of something else becomes that which it represented. With the appearance of the Fairy, the Rabbit leaves the limited existence of a toy and embraces the elevated ideal of a real animal—but that renders his relationship with the Boy meaningless. The story's ending completely obliterates the everyday embodied existence of both protagonists, the love that stems from their mundane encounters, and love's power to make the Rabbit Real in the eyes of the Boy. Once the story reveals itself as a Christian fable about redemption and eternal life, love—and materiality as such—have no more place in it.

The Velveteen Rabbit: An Onto-Epistemological Reading of What It Means to Become Real

In a nursery full of modern mechanical toys, the Velveteen Rabbit initially feels inferior to other toys. Even though he is a brand-new plaything with fluffy fur and artfully crafted details, he quickly gets forgotten by the Boy, and that does not make it any easier for him to develop self-esteem. Mechanical toys, model replicas of vehicles, and wooden animal figurines with movable joints all claim their right to superiority based not only on the fact that they are frequently used but also on their ability to move and/or their connection to a real-world referent. This connection usually entails physical resemblance, but it can also pertain to a toy's knowledge of the world outside of the nursery—or confabulated knowledge, as in the case of "Timothy, the jointed wooden lion, who . . . pretended he was connected with Government" (Williams 16–17). What makes the Velveteen Rabbit an outcast within the society of toys are thus two things. First, as a plush toy, the Rabbit is incapable of moving on his own, and hence, he does not *do* anything in the ordinary sense of the word; and second, since the Rabbit is not aware of the existence of real-life rabbits, he is convinced he has no real-life referent and cannot be classified as a "model" of any animal.

I argue that the hierarchy of the nursery is driven by a belief in both representationalism and active agency conventionally understood. According to the feminist philosopher and theoretical physicist Karen Barad, representationalism is a philosophical, scientific, and cultural order found in both social constructivist and realist beliefs. This order not only assumes a privileged position of language in the processes of knowledge and power production, but also draws clear-cut boundaries between entities and *relata*, the observer and the observed, the name and the named. As Barad notices, representationalism gives rise to a "triadic structure of words, knowers, and things" in which each of the categories is perceived as a separate entity ("Posthumanist Performativity" 131). Only the knower can be an active agent in relation to inherently passive matter, broadly understood as the natural world, human-crafted artifacts, nonsentient living beings, and nonhuman animals. By ascribing value to resemblance and sameness, representationalism constructs an arbitrary, hierarchical relationship between self and other, in which the self stands for positively valorized sameness, while otherness stands for difference and inferiority—and this philosophical paradigm entails grave and tangible social consequences whenever otherness is stigmatized.[1] As an alternative to representationalism, Barad proposes a theory of performativity that shows that matter (i.e., everything that exists in a physical sense) not only *is* but rather constantly *becomes* as it acquires different meanings though different cultural, social, linguistic, and scientific practices and, at the same time, actively influences these practices through its own materiality. As a toy that interacts with a child's world of play and imagination, Williams's Rabbit is also always actively becoming, constantly morphing into yet another version of himself, obtaining and then losing the Realness that, according to the mythos of the nursery, is a special kind of magic that happens through a child's love. In the words of the Skin Horse, the Velveteen Rabbit's personal guide to "big *R*" Realness: "It doesn't happen all at once. . . . You become" (Williams 17).

In their philosophical project, Barad is looking for "a relational ontology that rejects the metaphysics of relata, of 'words' and 'things'" ("Posthumanist Performativity" 130). Barad's objective is to shift "the focus from questions of correspondence between descriptions and reality (e.g., do they mirror nature or culture?) to matters of practices/doings/actions" (121–22). My objective for this reading of *The Velveteen Rabbit* is not to focus on how to infuse an inanimate object with animate essence, but rather—following Baradian logic—how to discuss the protagonist as a dynamic and relational phenomenon that is always already doing something, because it is involved in constant processes of becoming.

As a fictional character, the Rabbit is written as a sentient, speaking being whose status of a toy does not change the fact that he lives within an intricate net of relations that connect him to everything else that exists. His ontological status (what he is) demonstrates the blurring of clear-cut dichotomies—animate and inanimate, active and passive, object and subject, matter and language, while his epistemological status (what he knows) shows how the entirety of his knowledge draws on the experience of being a physical body in a world of other physical bodies. Instead of being just a "thing," the Velveteen Rabbit can be perceived as a phenomenon (Barad's basic ontological category) that reaches determinacy and meaning through intra-action with other phenomena. While interaction "presumes the prior existence of independent entities/relata" (Barad, "Posthumanist Performativity" 133), intra-action points to the fact that phenomena are complex ebbs and flows in which matter (all that is) and discourse (all that can be said and thought) are mutually entangled. Since *The Velveteen Rabbit*'s narrative remains silent about any previous experiences of the main protagonist, we can assume that the Rabbit "awakens" into consciousness only when he arrives at the Boy's nursery. The intra-action between self and other, individual and environment, being and knowing occurs within a limited setting. The Rabbit needs to make sense out of that setting by means that are accessible to him, and one of those means—the most accessible and immediate one, one that conditions the very possibility of understanding—is his own body. The relation between being and knowing—which, to use a Baradian term, can be described as "knowing in being" (Barad, "Posthumanist Performativity" 147)—becomes apparent when the Velveteen Rabbit imagines all rabbits to have bodies just like his. "The Rabbit could not claim to be a model of anything, for he didn't know that real rabbits existed; he thought they were all stuffed with sawdust like himself, and he understood that sawdust was quite out-of-date and should never be mentioned in modern circles" (Williams 15).

The Rabbit knows his own boundaries and the boundaries of other material objects, but those boundaries are constantly renegotiated whenever the protagonist discovers something new about the world around him, and he learns something new about himself as well. The Rabbit's perception of his internal and external reality begins to change when the Skin Horse introduces him to a different kind of realness. For the Skin Horse, an old rocking horse who used to belong to the Boy's uncle, Realness is not defined by similarity to a nontoy equivalent, but rather by the meaning that a child assigns to their favorite toy. From a toy's perspective, this process comes with a price. Since this kind of meaning can arise only from a long-lasting experience of regular and intensive play, it severely impacts a toy's longevity by wearing it out. Looking at the Skin Horse's balding coat and loose seams, the Velveteen Rabbit seems to experience both yearning and anxiety: "He longed to become Real, to know what it felt like; and yet the idea of growing shabby and losing his eyes and whiskers was rather sad" (Williams 20). The thought that Realness happens at the expense of becoming deformed, off-colored, and shabby-looking makes him uncomfortable because he imagines it to be a hurtful process. Faced with something he has not yet lived through, the Rabbit tries to appropriate it to familiar experiences by asking the Skin Horse tentative questions: "Does it hurt?" and "Does it happen all at once, like being wound up, . . . or bit by bit?" (17). This way, the Rabbit learns that becoming Real has nothing to do with being wound up, since it is not an easy, mechanical act that brings immediate results. Rather, it is a long, potentially painful process of becoming that takes a lot of patience and a lot of resilience on part of the toy. "That's why it doesn't happen often to people who break easily, or have sharp edges, or who have to be carefully kept," explains the Skin Horse (17).

The physical, external boundaries and properties that define a toy's material condition become entangled in the above passage with phenomena that we would traditionally connote with internal, psychological ones. What occurs is the blurring of the lines between inside and outside, body and mind, but also self and other since these phenomena implicitly point to the quality of a relationship, or even the likeliness of forming a relationship, between individual and society. Toys whose bodies break easily evoke emotional fragility that prevents one from opening oneself to others in an act of vulnerability and trust. Toys that have sharp edges remind us of callousness, harshness, and cynicism. Toys who need to be carefully kept indicate extreme dependency and a constant, excessive need to be sheltered from harm. In a set of metaphors that extend beyond the world of toys and beyond this particular book, we can observe how the ontological condition of being a material body in a world of other material bodies influences the ways in which we think and talk about phenomena that also include nonmaterial components. What arises from those onto-epistemological entanglements are material-discursive practices, i.e., apparatuses, through which we conceptualize and differentiate between our experiences of the world (see Barad, "Posthumanist Performativity" 138). When I interpret the passage from *The Velveteen Rabbit*, I build an apparatus that delineates the meaning of that passage. This apparatus arises from everything I am and everything I know. It combines different types of knowledge collected across the years on both empirical and theoretical levels, experienced on a first-hand or second-hand basis, mediated through literature, perceived through the senses, and deepened during encounters with people, animals, and things. To attain this knowledge, I (just like any human being) had to experience different types of physical and emotional hurt, to learn about the physical properties of different material objects—their weight, elasticity, temperature, solidity, and finally, to observe, explore, and acknowledge the psychological needs and emotional reactions of humans and other sentient creatures. Even though they are just figments of Williams's imagination, the Velveteen Rabbit and the Skin Horse are depicted as onto-epistemological beings who function along the very same lines as people do, albeit building their knowledge upon their embodied experiences as toys.

Not long after the conversation with the Skin Horse, the Velveteen Rabbit finds himself thrown into the Boy's bed by his caretaker, Nana. This fateful night constitutes the beginning of what will soon turn out to be the Rabbit's journey to Realness. As in a romantic relationship, the Velveteen Rabbit first needs to get used to lying beside somebody else at night. "At first he found it rather uncomfortable, for the Boy hugged him very tight, and sometimes he rolled over on him, and sometimes he pushed him so far under the pillow that the Rabbit could scarcely breathe" (Williams 21). The Rabbit needs to compromise some of his own physical comfort in order to experience the complex satisfaction that stems from physical and emotional proximity as established through the warmth of touch, whisper, breath, and intimate play.

The relationship between the Velveteen Rabbit and the Boy deserves a detailed discussion, but before that, let me introduce one more term from Barad. We already know that according to Barad the basic ontological category is called a phenomenon. Phenomena are characterized by "inherent ontological indeterminacy" (Barad, "Posthumanist Performativity" 133); a given object does not mean anything specific until it is exposed to the processes of observation that delineate its boundaries and define its properties. At this point, the phenomenon reaches determinacy. What conditions the possibility of determinacy is an act of the agential cut that locally differentiates a given phenomenon in the process of observation. For example, if a toy rabbit catches my eye in a store, I might take notice of its shape, size, and color. In an act of agential cut, the toy that attracted my gaze becomes differentiated from other phenomena around me. If I look at the same toy rabbit again, but this time with the intention of gifting it to a child, I will take more time to study its texture, weight, and quality, to see how it feels against the skin, to check how soft and fluffy it is, all that while trying to imagine how a child would relate to the stimuli that I am experiencing. These two instances of observation will be different, even though technically nothing changed in the object of observation. The physical and chemical properties of the toy rabbit have remained the same, but it is not exactly the same toy rabbit—at least not to me.

To recapitulate, whenever matter, discourse, and apparatus come together, we, as thinking human bodies, find ourselves in the realm of the agential cut, i.e., in a moment in which our temporal and spatial situatedness in a given context allows us to experience a moment of meaning in an otherwise changing topology of phenomena in their inherent ontological indeterminacy. Finding oneself in a moment of the agential cut, a person can observe a given phenomenon; they can make it intelligible or even measure it. The latter seems especially important since, without the possibility to measure a phenomenon in an objective way, Barad's theory could be attacked for advocating an extreme kind of relativism where anything can be defined in any way at any time or where nothing can be ever defined in any way at any time. With the knowledge of a natural scientist, Barad asserts: "The notion of agential separability is of fundamental importance, for in the absence of a classical ontological condition of exteriority between observer and observed, it provides the condition for the possibility of objectivity" ("Posthumanist Performativity" 133). This approach is useful when thinking about human bodies because it acknowledges both their physical limitations and potentialities *and* a whole nexus of meanings that can be attached to those bodies. In other words, the fact that human bodies have different properties that come across as objective (e.g., that they can be male, female, or intersex, black, white, or brown bodies) can be theorized in a way that does not give rise to essentialism, but rather acknowledges the problematic complexity of meanings attributed to those particular features of bodies. But what would it mean for the Velveteen Rabbit?

As a sentient toy, the Rabbit finds himself within the agential cut pretty much all the time—he is constantly experiencing and making sense out of the world around him in a never-ending sequence of agential cuts that occur from moment to moment, but only some of these moments are singled out in the process of self-reflection. The Velveteen Rabbit is aware of some of the changes he undergoes while pursuing his relationship with the Boy. He grows fond of having the Boy around and experiences a sense of joy he has not yet known. Other changes, however, pass unnoticed: "And so time went on, and the little Rabbit was very happy—so happy that he never noticed how his beautiful velveteen fur was getting shabbier and shabbier, and his tail becoming unsewn, and all the pink rubbed off his nose where the Boy had kissed him" (Williams 22). The process of wearing out in the course of play happens without the Rabbit purposively reflecting upon it. Given the anthropocentric frame of reference for this story, the toy's experience is analogous to how human beings keep losing track of aging processes that occur in their bodies. Even though those processes are *lived* and, in a sense, felt all the time, they are *noticed* only occasionally whenever a person finds themselves containing that ongoing process in reflecting upon a specific, tacit physical manifestation of that process. A strand of gray hair or a new line on the face do not usually appear overnight, just like a bald patch on one's favorite velveteen toy does not appear overnight, but when we take notice of them, they nevertheless strike us as sudden and somewhat surprising. What the Velveteen Rabbit once feared does not worry him at this stage because he is too busy exploring his relationship with the Boy. All possible existential fears blend into the background as the Rabbit gets to love and be loved. This mutual relationship is sanctioned when the Boy declares the Velveteen Rabbit Real, that is, when the Boy differentiates this toy from all other playthings by assigning exceptional meaning to it.

The definition of Realness introduced by the Skin Horse thus pertains to a mutual, relational process of becoming meaningful in the eyes of the loved one by intra-actively experiencing each other's physical presence. But the Velveteen

Rabbit discovers yet another meaning of realness when the Boy takes him to the woods. As the toy rabbit sits in the grass, two mysterious, mesmerizing creatures approach him. He finally recognizes them as real-life rabbits, but before that realization occurs, the Velveteen Rabbit initially reads the rabbits as if they were toys: "They were rabbits like himself, but quite furry and brand-new. They must have been very well made, for their seams didn't show at all, and they changed shape in a queer way when they moved; one minute they were long and thin and the next minute fat and bunchy, instead of always staying the same like he did" (Williams 25, 28). Since this is the first time that the Velveteen Rabbit sees this kind of organic, muscle-driven movement of real-life animals, he has a hard time making sense out of it. The image of how the hopping rabbits change from "long and thin" to "fat and bunchy" is especially interesting for a Baradian reading since this difference can be used as an illustration of the wave-particle duality paradox. What is understood by that paradox is that, under certain conditions, particles can behave like waves, and conversely, light (a wave) can occasionally display particle behavior (Barad, *Meeting the Universe* 83).

These findings in quantum physics help us to think of matter in more dynamic, subtler terms. After all, if matter can occasionally display characteristics of waves, this means it is technically not a stable, immobile "thing" because waves are not things but rather oscillations or disturbances that have the capacity to overlap, bend, and spread, consequently producing what is known as diffraction patterns. Darker and lighter concentric ripples forming on the surface of water when a pebble is thrown into a pond or white and black lines that superimpose around the edges of a razorblade's shadow are all diffraction patterns.[2] In Barad's book *Meeting the Universe Halfway: Quantum Physics and the Entanglement of Matter and Meaning* (2007), diffraction and the wave-duality paradox become figures of thought that help us to think about the material world not in terms of black-and-white entities with clear-cut boundaries, but rather in terms of gradients and spectrums of mutually entangled phenomena. Drawing on Donna Haraway's discussion in *Modest_Witness@Second_Millennium: FemaleMan©_Meets_OncoMouse^{TM}* (1997), Barad adopts diffraction as a model alternative to reflexivity and all that it entails, that is, reflection, mimesis, reproduction, and representationalism. Haraway's "suspicion is that reflexivity, like reflection, only displaces the same elsewhere, setting up the worries about copy and original and the search for the authentic and really real" (16). Echoing Haraway, Barad adds: "diffractive methodology is a critical practice for making a difference in the world. It is a commitment to understanding which differences matter, how they matter, and for whom. It is a critical practice of engagement, not a distance-learning practice of reflecting from afar" (*Meeting the Universe* 90).

When the Velveteen Rabbit sees real-life rabbits for the very first time, he is faced with a difference that he seeks to understand. The rabbits puzzle him because they exhibit two different and inherently contradictory characteristics. In one moment, as they sit on their hind legs, they look like points in space (particles), but in another moment, as they stretch out and make a leap, they become lines (waves). What the Velveteen Rabbit does not know, however, is that he should not be ashamed of his status as an inanimate object because a diffractive reading turns him into an active, dynamic, and differential becoming of matter that matters. The Velveteen Rabbit matters in a two-fold sense. First, he matters in a Baradian way, as matter involved in intra-active "practices of mattering through which intelligibility and materiality are constituted" ("Posthumanist Performativity" 138)—he matters because he is matter ("physical substance"), which comes to matter ("to have significance"). Second, the Velveteen Rabbit starts to matter like no other material object once the Boy grows to love and cherish him—he matters because he is significant to that one person. While the Rabbit shares mattering in the first sense with the totality of physical substance, the second sense is reserved only for him and his unique existence as the Boy's favorite toy.

Unfortunately for the Velveteen Rabbit, real-life rabbits make fun of him due to his otherness. He does not have any hind legs to hop on; he does not look like a real rabbit; he does not smell like one. Ostracized by his real-life equivalents on the basis of his material condition and the meaning they attach to it, the Velveteen Rabbit experiences a traumatic moment when all that he thought to be true crumbles into pieces with one cruel judgment of the rabbits: "You are not real." Despite the Velveteen Rabbit's pleas and his faith in love that made him feel Real to the Boy—"Come back and play with me!" called the little Rabbit, "Oh, do come back! I *know* I am Real!" (Williams 30)—the rabbits denounce the protagonist's Realness and, it would seem, so does the whole narrative.

In the parts of the book that follow, we are once again forced to play the reductive game of what is "really real" but this time without any potential for subversion. The Velveteen Rabbit gets to spend a couple more weeks with his beloved Boy before disaster strikes. After the Boy comes down with scarlet fever, his doctor orders that all toys and picture books be burned to prevent the spreading of germs. As Steven V. Daniels observes in his Kleinian interpretation of the book, "the prospect of annihilation by burning has its own precedent in the Boy's fever" (26). It is also foreshadowed by the Velveteen Rabbit's sensation of unpleasant warmth that he feels when still lying in the Boy's arms: "His face grew very flushed, and he talked in his sleep, and his little body was so hot that it burned the Rabbit when he held him close" (Williams 32). After the doctor's command, the Velveteen Rabbit gets shoved into a bag and carried outside—and the Boy forgets him easily since he has been promised a trip to the seaside for his recovery. Faced with a death sentence, the Rabbit spends a restless night in a sack behind the fowl house, waiting for the morning to come and the gardener to set up the bonfire. His entire life flashes before him, filling him with a sense of grief and making him shed a tear over his own fate. According to Gerald Weales in his 1983 essay for the *New York Times*, it is rather disappointing that "the final transformation is brought about not by love but by self-pity" (13). The fragment in which the Velveteen Rabbit sorrowfully reflects on his life exemplifies this self-pity especially well: "Of what use was it to be loved and lose one's beauty and become Real if it all ended like this?" (Williams 37).

As much as I share Weales's disappointment with that final transformation, I find it surprising that he does not take the opportunity to notice that the Rabbit's sorrow is not an ideologically transparent self-pity. Like Christ crying "Eloi, Eloi, lema sabachthani?" (My God, my God, why have you forsaken me?) when he awaits his death on the cross (*The Holy Bible*, Mark 15:34, Matt. 27:46), the Velveteen Rabbit goes through a dark moment of self-pity that heralds his ascension into a different, better realm. It is thus not enough to say that the Rabbit "cries a real tear that sprouts into a flower and disgorges a Fairy who saves him from the auto-da-fé and turns him into a genuine rabbit" (Weales 13) because this is not exactly the existence of a genuine rabbit that the protagonist is being given. The Fairy grants the Velveteen Rabbit the form of a rabbit but one living for the rest of eternity somewhere on the fringes between reality and the hereafter. "I take care of all the playthings that the children have loved. When they are old and worn out and the children don't need them any more, then I come and take them away with me and turn them into Real," says the Fairy as she appears in front of the Velveteen Rabbit like an interventionist God ready to lead her beloved son into the afterlife (Williams 38). "I've brought you a new playfellow," says the Fairy as she introduces the Rabbit—once velveteen, now lifelike—to all the other rabbits who dance in a beautiful, moonlit forest where "the fronds of the bracken shone like frosted silver" (40). "You must be very kind to him and teach him all he needs to know in Rabbit-land, for he is going to live with you for ever and ever!" she adds, leading the protagonist into what is most likely a heaven for rabbits (40). The meaning of realness thus shifts once again as transcendence supersedes the realness of a living, breathing, and mortal animal. As Platonic and Christian traditions inform us, transcendence can be reached only after departing a flawed, limited, sinful, and utterly uninteresting mortal body for an external reality of perfect and eternal ideals. The story obscures that transcendental logic by suggesting that the Rabbit lives on in a reality perceivable by the Boy, but in light of the reading I have proposed here, it might be a hallucinatory presence of the supernatural kind, reminiscent of spirits, ghosts, and souls.

The story's overall conclusion that the love of a god is the most superior and perfect one of all is a conviction that stands at the core of most religions, including Catholicism, the religion to which Margery Williams converted. I am not arguing with that conviction. What makes *The Velveteen Rabbit* problematic is the implication that material love is completely insignificant in the larger scheme of things. The very possibility of an embodied mind being able to libidinally invest itself in people, animals, plants, things, physical and intellectual activities; its ability to desire and to be desired; the infinite ways in which it can grow emotionally, mentally, and physically attached to human and nonhuman beings; all its infinite outlets and demonstrations of care—all this is nullified by *The Velveteen Rabbit*'s ending.

Conclusions

Barad's theories prove fruitful when it comes to analyzing Williams's story. The Velveteen Rabbit's understanding of himself arises in a perpetually moving, morphing knot of meaning and matter, in both its human and nonhuman forms. The protagonist's embodied condition, his situational embeddedness in the physical world of toys, boys, nurseries, and forests, and the discursive apparatus applied by the narrator of the story to focalize the hero's self-perception all dictate the Rabbit's local determinacy through which he defines himself in a given moment, and he does so always in an intra-active relation to the world in which he exists and which he repeatedly gets to know over and over again. By exploring the protagonist in his materiality, we get to observe how his onto-epistemological status changes in the first part of the book in three crucial steps: first, he is a charming gift, next a discarded toy, and then a beloved friend. As I tried to demonstrate, the last two stages of the Rabbit's development that occur in the remaining part of the book go against the grain of the logic of materiality. Once the toy rabbit is thrown away—even despite being Real in the eyes of the Boy—the book evokes a spiritual paradigm in which the Velveteen Rabbit is first coded as a redeemed/resurrected animal and then as an eternal soul. The problem with *The Velveteen Rabbit*'s ending is not so much that it leaves "no hint that there is any way to meet the tragedy of lost love and betrayal other than letting the heart break," as Faith McNulty argues (180). Rather, its fault lies in using the logic of transcendence to renounce the validity of love as a material-discursive practice between two embodied, finite beings who exist in a given here and now and who form a meaningful, even if flawed and temporal, relationship.

But even for those of us for whom the ending of the book might be somewhat disappointing, *The Velveteen Rabbit* can still be reclaimed for the purposes of new materialist philosophy if we acknowledge the story's ambiguous nature. The ambiguity stems from the fact that the story demonstrates both the principles of new materialist philosophy and the conceptual order that this philosophy seeks to battle. Williams's book can become a powerful teaching tool that explains complex philosophical concepts using easy and accessible examples. Moreover, from within a new materialist reading, it becomes clear that the strength of

The Velveteen Rabbit as a narrative lies not in the fact that it is a story about the triumph of love over loss based, as Allan Kellehear argues, on the "message that love is a social relationship where material conditions are not necessarily determining factors" (46). Quite the contrary, the book can be used to show that love is a constitutively material practice, but that does not make it any less social or relational precisely because a material practice is always already a discursive practice. Love can be experienced only in materiality—and not in transcendence.

Notes

1. To explain how the logic of representationalism permeates social life, it might be useful to turn to another new materialist feminist thinker, Rosi Braidotti. In her book *The Posthuman* (2013), while examining the relation between sameness and difference in Western philosophical visions of personhood, Braidotti writes: "Subjectivity is equated with consciousness, universal rationality, and self-regulating ethical behaviour, whereas Otherness is defined as its negative and specular counterpart. In so far as difference spells inferiority, it acquires both essentialist and lethal connotations for people who get branded as 'others.' These are the sexualized, racialized, and naturalized others, who are reduced to the less than human status of disposable bodies" (15). The dichotomy between the privileged self and the marginalized other is something more than a mere conceptual distinction. It translates directly into lived experiences of oppression, discrimination, exploitation, and violence. Gender inequality, ableism, racism, anti-Semitism, Islamophobia, homophobia, transphobia, violence against animals, or destruction of the natural environment all stem from and build on that divide.

2. For photographs of diffraction patterns, see Barad, *Meeting the Universe* 76–77.

Works Cited

Barad, Karen. *Meeting the Universe Halfway: Quantum Physics and the Entanglement of Matter and Meaning*. Duke UP, 2007.

Barad, Karen. "Posthumanist Performativity: Toward an Understanding of How Matter Comes to Matter." *Material Feminisms*, edited by Stacy Alaimo and Susan Hekman, Indiana UP, 2008, pp. 120–54.

Braidotti, Rosi. *The Posthuman*. Polity Press, 2013.

Daniels, Steven V. "*The Velveteen Rabbit*: A Kleinian Perspective." *Children's Literature*, vol. 18, 1990, pp. 17–30.

Haraway, Donna. *Modest_Witness@Second_Millennium: FemaleMan©_ Meets_OncoMouse™. Feminism and Technoscience*. Routledge, 1997.

Harde, Roxanne, and Lydia Kokkola. *The Embodied Child: Readings in Children's Literature and Culture*. Routledge, 2018.

The Holy Bible. English Standard Version. Crossway, 2016.

Kellehear, Allan. "Death and Renewal in *The Velveteen Rabbit*: A Sociological Reading." *Journal of Near-Death Studies*, vol. 12, no. 1, 1993, pp. 35–51.

McNulty, Faith. "Children's Books for Christmas." *New Yorker*, 6 Dec. 1982, pp. 176–82.

Nikolajeva, Maria. "Recent Trends in Children's Literature Research: Return to the Body." *International Research in Children's Literature*, vol. 9, no. 2, 2016, pp. 132–45.

Trites, Roberta Seelinger. *Twenty-First-Century Feminisms in Children's and Adolescent Literature*. UP of Mississippi, 2018.

Weales, Gerald. "Children's Books." *New York Times Book Review*, 3 Apr. 1983, p. 13.

Williams, Margery. *The Velveteen Rabbit: Or How Toys Become Real*. 1922. Illustrated by William Nicholson. Doubleday, 1958.

Chapter 6

"Real" Stuffed Animals: Rabbit Tales in the Anthropocene

—Jiwon Rim

Against common sense and intuition, Margery Williams's *The Velveteen Rabbit* (1922) makes the predicament of the stuffed toy rabbit feel real. How can the stuffed animal be as real as flesh-and-blood rabbits in the wild? Taking seriously *The Velveteen Rabbit*'s claim that its story of the toy rabbit is an account of the real animal, this chapter proposes to read *The Velveteen Rabbit* as a valid record of the historical reality of commodified animals of the twentieth century. I begin by placing both wild rabbits and toy rabbits in the history of the technological domination and violent molding of animal bodies. The stuffed toy rabbit is not a fake animal that has nothing to do with the real animal, but rather it is one of the animal products of the all-encompassing system of animal commodification, as is the image of the authentic wild animal. Victorian taxidermist Walter Potter's stuffed rabbits point to the common origin of the denaturalized bodies of toy animals and the image of the authentic wild animal—in being taxidermic displays of once-living, historically real animals that do not look realistic but resemble the rabbits of Beatrix Potter. B. Potter's picture book *The Tale of Peter Rabbit* (1902) also testifies to the uncomfortable historical origin of now-familiar toy rabbits, given that Peter looks disturbingly like he is modeled from real, captured rabbits. B. Potter's verisimilar sketches of cornered, chased rabbits hint that Peter Rabbit is the product of the same violent process of molding of living animal bodies as that which was used to make images of the authentic animal in museums and textbooks at the turn of the twentieth century. After establishing this history, I proceed to contextualize *The Velveteen Rabbit* and its claim to reality. *The Velveteen Rabbit* is an animal tale of the Anthropocene in which all animals are made in the system of industrial capitalism, and "natural" animals can hardly be said to exist.

In bringing to life the plight of the thingified animal caught up in the system, *The Velveteen Rabbit* forces its readers to come face-to-face with the ethical problem of manufactured and commodified animals that cannot be returned to nature.

Walter Potter and the Denaturalization of the Animal Body

W. Potter's taxidermic diorama "The Rabbits' Village School" (1888) displays rabbits that look distinctively like B. Potter's rabbits and their toy descendants, the only difference being that W. Potter's rabbits are literally made of once-living, historically real rabbits.[1] The diorama piece was displayed as part of Mr. Potter's Museum of Curiosities in Sussex, England—a museum full of taxidermic animals dressed and posed in unnaturalistic costumes—until the museum closed in the 1970s. Taxidermy is a legitimate profession that takes skins of dead animals, stuffs them, and stitches them up seamlessly to create the visual illusion of aliveness. What sets Potter's diorama apart from more orthodox taxidermic mounts is that it dresses its stuffed rabbits up and poses them like Victorian people, staging them in a miniature Victorian schoolroom.

Potter's stuffed rabbit diorama is a snapshot of the messy historical process of making animals into things under emerging industrial capitalism, a rare work that makes apparent the violence on living animals involved in the process of producing animal-things. Conor Creaney writes that there is an indelible "taint of cruelty, even brutality" in Potter's taxidermic dioramas (7) and that this has to do with a sense that "the tableau is taking unwarranted liberties" with animal bodies, tampering "with the bodily sovereignty of these creatures for merely comic purposes" (8). It is too obvious that these rabbit bodies have been captured and forced into unnatural positions for no other purpose than human entertainment. At the same time, Potter's rabbits point to the disturbing common origin of the denaturalized bodies of toy animals and the image of the authentic natural animal, tracing both products back to the late nineteenth-century practice of violent fiddling with—and molding of—animal bodies. The techniques that have been used to construct the still-current vision of the natural animal have also been used to make something entirely different: unnaturalistic animals that are to populate the twentieth-century world as toys, accessories, and images, such as characters in picture books.

On the one hand, Potter's work denaturalizes the naturalistic taxidermy and the image of the natural animal constructed through it, exposing the vision of the natural animal to be as much a product of destruction and reconstruction of animal bodies as killed and stuffed rabbits in Victorian clothing and posture are. The taxidermic displays in natural history museums have been essential in producing the ahistorical vision of the authentic natural animal,[2] the authentic animal that is in "the Edenic state before or outside human presence" (Desmond 33). The authentic animal is considered "restored" in naturalistic taxidermy when all marks and traces of human engagement with—that is, human violence on—the animal body are eliminated (Desmond 33). The illusion of the untouched and untouchable authentic animal is further perpetuated in museums, where naturalistic taxidermic displays are kept under the stipulation that they may be viewed but never touched.

Potter's taxidermic diorama breaks the illusion of the untouched authentic animal in suggesting that the naturalistic image of the animal is a product of the violent molding of animal bodies as much as its "unnatural" taxidermic rabbits are. Potter's rabbits tell us that stuffed animals in museums, which form the basis of our vision of the natural animal, have also been captured and forced into positions not their own—for the purpose of human consumption. Michelle Henning reads Potter's taxidermic rabbits as testifying to "the fragile coexistence of English wildlife and human life" in the historical moment of ongoing industrialization and attendant "decimation of British wildlife" (671). The overabundance of rabbits in Potter's diorama also exposes the status of taxidermic animals as mere animal-things that may be subjected to whatever use people may see fit.

On the other hand, W. Potter's work gives backstory to B. Potter's rabbits and their toy descendants, placing popular denaturalized stuffed rabbits in the tradition of cruel play with living animal bodies that also produced these disturbing stuffed rabbits. The denaturalized animals are considered ahistorical and also somehow innocent of the violent history of technological domination and commodification of animals. W. Potter's rabbits' disturbing similarity to—and contemporaneity with—B. Potter's rabbits makes us see the nocuous historical origin of the supposedly harmless animal products usually associated with children. W. Potter's rabbits provide a link that connects supposedly innocent play with stuffed toy animals to the broader historical context of ethically questionable play with flesh-and-blood animals that humans collectively practice. As such, W. Potter's work opens a way to read *The Tale of Peter Rabbit* as another record of the messy historical process of molding of animal bodies into commodifiable forms at the turn of the twentieth century in England.

Beatrix Potter and Commodification of the Animal Body

B. Potter's rabbits' resemblance to W. Potter's unnatural rabbits is more than skin deep. B. Potter also makes use of naturalistic toy-animal-production techniques to manufacture unnaturalistic animal-things.[3] In the end, what enables the production of both the unnatural and the natural animals in her rabbit tales are the technological domination and appropriation of rabbit bodies. It has been noted how Potter's sketches of animals, despite the common characterization of her animals as anthropomorphic animals that have nothing to do with real animals, often turn out to be masterful works of reproduction of the naturalistic animal.[4] Peter Hollindale points out that Potter's drawings meet the standard of "exact behavioral realism" in their depiction of rabbit bodies (163). Judy Taylor describes Potter's works as "carefully observed drawings of the life around her" (34). Testifying to "the care taken over them" to make "the animals . . . accurately drawn" (Whalley 47), Potter's animal drawings look like careful reproductions of animals in their natural state.[5]

The Tale of Peter Rabbit shows how the violent appropriation of animal bodies informs the process of production of both denaturalized animal commodities (best represented in stuffed toy animals for children) and the image of the natural animal (once represented in stuffed museum displays of "real" animals). Throughout the picture book, Peter transforms back and forth between looking like a naturalistic rabbit and looking like one of the commercialized animal toys for children. Lisa Rowe Fraustino points out that "human-animal ambivalence" is the defining characteristic of Potter's drawing style (152). I read this ambivalence as a shift in the mode of rendering of the rabbit that points to the common historical origin of two very different species of animals: the natural animal and the denaturalized animal.

Peter enters Mr. McGregor's garden fully clothed, walking on hind legs. When he runs away from Mr. McGregor on two feet with outstretched arms, wearing his iconic jacket (B. Potter 27), he is a precursor of twentieth-century animal cartoons for children. But he loses his jacket in the process of the chase and gets visually captured in the naturalistic pose of a rabbit on the run (35). When Peter, unclothed, stands on the flower bed, the sketch looks as if it succeeded in capturing the moment of unmediated encounter with a wild rabbit (43). The next page again goes back to depicting the rabbit body in an unnatural posture; Peter is crying, leaning on the door, and stifling his mouth with a paw (44). Playful switches in the mode of rendering of the rabbit body testify to the illustrator's sheer power over rabbit bodies—the power to mold and bend animal bodies into shapes both natural and unnatural. The human illustrator is in possession of skills as well as freedom to make use of animal bodies as she thinks fit in the same way the taxidermist of "The Rabbits' Village School" had animal bodies as materials at his disposal.

The Tale of Peter Rabbit is thus a testimony to how both natural animals and unnatural animals are made out of captured and appropriated animal bodies. The hunt and chase of the rabbit provides occasion for both naturalistic studies of the biological rabbit and denaturalized sketches of the character Peter Rabbit.

The surface narrative of the picture book is about Peter's successful escape from Mr. McGregor's rake; Peter somehow escapes being "put in a pie" in the manner of his father (10). But the picture book itself is the product of the sadder history in which rabbits have been successfully captured and reproduced as commodities. The picture book is the record of Mr. McGregor's failed chase of Peter at the same time as being the record of a more successful chase that parallels the farmer's: that of the maker of the picture book.

Though Mr. McGregor keeps losing Peter, the illustrator's eyes do not lose him for a second, following him to every nook and corner of the garden. The illustrator's eyes follow the rabbit's frightened run in Mr. McGregor's garden with amused attention that borders on cruelty, as the rabbit body "ran into a gooseberry net" (30), "wriggled out" of a sieve (34), threw itself into a can (36), "jumped out of a window" (41), and ended up standing dumbfounded in the corner of the garden (43). The chase produces sketches of rabbits, some in the lines of naturalistic study and some in the lines of a denaturalizing caricature of the rabbit that we love and consume to this date. The close observation and skillful reproduction of the animal are predicated on the violation of the animal body, as the object in question is a cornered, lost rabbit that is "out of breath and trembling with fright" (42–43).

The concluding pages of *The Tale of Peter Rabbit* show Peter returned to his home in the wood and reunited with his family. But does this mean that he has returned to nature safe from human hands? Or does the existence of this scene show that he has been captured and preserved as a rabbit-thing for our entertainment? The evidence points to the latter. Even if the rabbit had returned to the wood, it is likely that he will soon have been incorporated into the human economy either as vermin or as property, whether it be by Mr. McGregor or not, given our knowledge of the fate of the British rural wildlife caught up in the process of industrialization. Rose Lovell-Smith points out that the "book's subtext" is an "underlying awareness that rabbits . . . commonly die violently, the prey of men or other animals" and that "the market value of rabbits" shapes the rabbits' relationship with men in B. Potter's works (22). Besides, in the last pages of the picture book, Peter's family looks suspiciously like rabbits out of W. Potter's diorama, as they stand surrounding the miniature bowl, holding spoons and dressed in aprons (58). And we know how *The Tale of Peter Rabbit* caused its rabbits to be incorporated in the endless cycle of commercial reproduction of rabbits in stuffed and other forms. B. Potter ambiguously remarks on how there has been produced "an appalling quantity of Peter" regardless of the model's death (qtd. in Taylor 40). Twenty years later comes *The Velveteen Rabbit*, in which the animal body is truly a commodity—and just that, free to be used and disposed of at the human consumer's whim.

The Velveteen Rabbit and the Plight of the Thingified Animal

Even though all other toys in the nursery, the doctor, and the Rabbit himself do not consider the Velveteen Rabbit real, Williams's narrative consistently asserts that what it records is the unembellished truth. The representation of rabbits by W. Potter and B. Potter helps place this real story of a human-made rabbit in the history of "thingification" of animal bodies. The stuffed toy rabbit is the descendant of the rabbits that got caught up in the process of technological domination and the making of animal bodies; and its story is that of the thingified animal incorporated in the now-fully-fledged system of industrial capitalism. If the two Potters' works show the natural animal and the unnatural animal together in construction via the technique of animal stuffing and caricature, *The Velveteen Rabbit* takes us to the world in which animals are things at human disposal. There is no authentic natural animal, or untouched nature, that remains outside of the system of commodification; and the image of the authentic animal, it is suggested, is but one of the products of the system that produces and circulates thingified animals. *The Velveteen Rabbit* makes the predicament of its stuffed toy rabbit feel strangely real, while making the wild rabbits—and the wild Rabbit-land—feel like phantoms more than anything. In thus bringing to life the plight of the thingified animal caught up in the all-encompassing system of animal production and use, *The Velveteen Rabbit* forces its readers to come face-to-face with the problem of manufactured and commodified animals in the Anthropocene.

The story introduces the protagonist: "There was once a velveteen rabbit" (Williams 1). This rabbit lives in the "once" of a specific age, that is, in the time of twentieth-century consumer culture. Going on to describe the toy rabbit in terms of what it is made of and how it is appealing as a consumer good, *The Velveteen Rabbit* shows that the animal body is a manufactured and commodified thing in this age. The description shows the Velveteen Rabbit is a thing assembled according to human need. Readers are told that he is stuffed "fat and bunchy," his coat color is "spotted brown and white," his ears are "lined with pink sateen," and this is how "a rabbit should be" in the system of animal commodification when a rabbit is made, not born (1). The commonsense understanding of the animal's realness in terms of naturalness is subtly challenged, given that "real thread whiskers" help to make the Velveteen Rabbit "really splendid" (1).

In the process of following the quest of the Velveteen Rabbit to achieve the elusive "Real" state of being, the story shows what kind of reality this animal-thing finds himself in. From the onset of the narrative, the Velveteen Rabbit is a consumer good among an abundance of other consumer goods, as he sits in the stocking as a Christmas present with "nuts and oranges and a toy engine, and chocolate almonds and a clockwork mouse" (1). As a mere consumable, the Rabbit's body is essentially expendable and replaceable, the same way that mass-produced and circulated animal bodies of our age are, such as meat animals and lab animals. He is loved and consumed "for at least two hours" and then gets forgotten among "a great rustling of tissue paper and unwrapping of parcels, and in the excitement of looking at all the new presents" (3)—that is, the swirl of consumerist pleasure. What brings change to the Velveteen Rabbit's fate as a forgotten thing is again the interchangeability of thingified animal bodies. The Velveteen Rabbit gets picked up as a random replacement of the Boy's normal bedtime companion, a now-missing china dog, another expendable thing that the nanny decides not to look for as it is not worth "too much trouble" (9). And the Velveteen Rabbit remains an expendable thing despite how much the Boy gets to "love" him, as we will see in the Rabbit's final turn of fate.

The Velveteen Rabbit's reality is present from the start; it is just that this reality is unpalatable and, in fact, unacceptable to the animal. In the world of the nursery, the only world the Velveteen Rabbit knows, all animals are unquestionably commodities and toys at that. But the concepts of animal-authenticity and the commodity value of the animal body are inextricably tied together. In a nursery room full of "toyified" and commodified animal bodies, the body of the Velveteen Rabbit is considered less valuable, and "being only made of velveteen, some of the more expensive toys quite snubbed him" (Williams 3). He is made of "out-of-date" technologies (4) and less expensive materials and thus supposedly less authentic. We hear that "the mechanical toys were very superior, and looked down upon everyone else; they were full of modern ideas, and pretended they were real" (3). The irony is that, unbeknownst to the toys, the authentic natural animal is the ultimate animal product. Also, the stuffed toy animal is not a product of a more premodern or "out-of-date" technology than the model boat or the jointed wooden lion. It is in fact a new thing that belongs to the new mode of technological processing of animal bodies[6]—and a thing even newer than naturalistic taxidermic displays in being part of the system of mass production and consumption of "insignificant and commonplace" animal bodies (Williams 4). The erroneous periodization of the different animal products pervading the nursery room conceals the shared "modern"—and artificial—origin of denaturalized animals and the natural animal. Showing that the most well-made stuffed animal functionally replicates the real, natural animal, *The Velveteen Rabbit* helps deconstruct the idea of the authentic animal down to its material and historical foundations. The Velveteen Rabbit comes to encounter the "authentic" wild rabbits, but the words used to describe the encounter imply that the authentic animal might be no more than another animal-thing constructed through human technological meddling with animal bodies. The Velveteen Rabbit observes: "They were rabbits like himself, but quite furry and brand new. They must have been very well made because their seams didn't show at all, and they changed shape in a queer way when they moved . . . instead of staying the same like he did" (17–18). The authentic rabbits look "brand new" and "well made" and almost like naturalistic taxidermic dummies staged in natural history museums—with seamless skins, illusion of movement, and ultimate untouchability.

The wild rabbit bodies also remain out of real reach, just as the taxidermic display of "a living, about-to-charge bear" would in a natural history museum (Desmond 33). The naturalistic look imbues the animal with the indisputable authority of realness. The wild rabbits taunt the Velveteen Rabbit: "He isn't a rabbit at all! He isn't real!" And the rabbit desperately argues for his realness, while thinking to himself that "he would give anything in the world to be able to jump about like these rabbits did" (Williams 20). The scene is loaded with hints that the authentic animal is an unattainable vision in its essence and not just for the Velveteen Rabbit. The wild rabbits hover tantalizingly around him without ever being touchable. In one moment, a wild rabbit comes "so close . . . that his long whiskers brushed the Velveteen Rabbit's ear," but the wild rabbit quickly jumps backwards without touching him (20). The wild rabbits appear out of nowhere, only to vanish like dreams at the first sign of human approach, leaving behind "a funny new tickly feeling," an inexplicable and unslakable longing for nature/naturalness (20). *The Velveteen Rabbit*, as much as it deconstructs the vision of the real, natural animal, is a record of the visceral violence of the real system of use and circulation of animal bodies that the Velveteen Rabbit is subject to. The narrative takes note of how this system makes use of the commodified animal body and how it affects the animal: "He [the Boy] loved him [the Velveteen Rabbit] so hard that he loved all his whiskers off, and the pink lining to his ears tuned grey, and his brown spots faded. He even began to lose his shape, and he scarcely looked like a rabbit any more, except to the Boy" (22). Though the Velveteen Rabbit attempts to understand his use in the Boy's hands through the romantic language of love, the Boy's love, in the end, is a form of consumption. The Boy's love of the Velveteen Rabbit takes place within the established practice of molding animal bodies into various unnaturalistic (and naturalistic) shapes: the Boy is playing with the product of two Potters, himself violently molding the animal body for his own pleasure. The technological domination and the commercial thingification of the animal body inform every aspect of the Velveteen Rabbit's relationship with the child, making it impossible to distinguish authentic love for the animal from mere use of the animal in the system.

The emergency situation of scarlet fever brings into the fore the true social status of bodies: the Velveteen Rabbit cannot but come to a realization that he is, and has always been, an expendable and easily replaceable thing. The Velveteen Rabbit gets disposed of and replaced by "a new bunny to sleep with" (26) after being used up as an object of comfort during the Boy's illness. The narrative follows the Rabbit to where he "lay among the old picture books in the corner behind the fowl-house," "very lonely," the night before he is to be incinerated

(27). This is the kind of sight that is usually kept out of our view behind walls of facilities for animal processing—in meat industries, pet farms, and sanctioned and unsanctioned laboratories. Readers are brought uncomfortably close to the real violence of the system of use of animal bodies in the form of "a real tear" that trickles down the "little shabby velvet nose" of the threadbare and shapeless toy that "scarcely looked like a rabbit anymore" (28). The Velveteen Rabbit's question—asked with "a great sadness" (27)—"Of what use was it to be loved and lose one's beauty and become Real if it all ended like this?" (28) is a question that touches on the ethics of using animals and a question that we do not have an answer to.

The narrative answers the plea of the commodified animal and rescues the Velveteen Rabbit (and readers) out of this ethical and narrative dead end by magically transforming the Velveteen Rabbit into a natural rabbit and freeing him to the wood. But the sadness lingers because *The Velveteen Rabbit*'s happy ending points to its own impossibility. Not only is magical intervention required to renaturalize the commodified animal in *The Velveteen Rabbit*, but also the Fairy who administers the magic looks artificial in the original illustrations by William Nicholson. She appears out of a flower that looks strangely fabricated with "the colour of emeralds" and "a blossom like a golden cup" (28). The Fairy in effect declares herself to be a contrivance and a deus ex machina when she explains her role: "I take care of all the playthings that the children have loved. When they are old and worn out and the children don't need them any more, then I come and take them away with me" (30). She is there to free human readers from all the moral baggage of used-up and no-longer-needed animal bodies.

The romantic depiction of Rabbitland also flags the nature that animals can return to as what environmental critic William Cronon might consider to be a harmful fiction: "the false hope of an escape from responsibility, the illusion that we can somehow wipe clean the slate of our past" (16). The Fairy frees the Rabbit to Rabbitland where he will be able to "for ever and ever" "run and play" (Williams 31) and where he will be "at home with other rabbits" (35). However, has there ever been a Rabbit-land? Rabbits have been enmeshed in a long history of violent making of animals into things. The wood for rabbits has not been a place safe from human hands, as the fate of rabbits in "The Rabbits' Village School" and *The Tale of Peter Rabbit* make glaringly clear.

With these implanted wake-up calls, *The Velveteen Rabbit* returns its readers from the dream of unviolated and ever-present nature to the moment of truth, the night before the burning of the animal and its morally loaded query. What should we do with these human-made and real bodies of animals that we have made into things at our disposal?

Notes

1. Unless otherwise specified, "Potter," in this section, hereafter refers to W. Potter.
2. Susan Leigh Star argues that "the realism instantiated in taxidermy" served as "a necessary base" for the new science of biology at the turn of the twentieth century (281) and that "the otherworldly transcendental dioramas" of natural history museums continue to inform our "sanitized vision of nature" (258). Jane Desmond shows how taxidermic mounts were supposed "to present a scientific 'truth'" of the animal to the public with "the authority of the [natural history] museum, [and] its scientific staff" at the turn of the twentieth century (31).
3. Unless otherwise noted, "Potter," in this section, refers to B. Potter.
4. It is intentional that this paper refrains from the term "anthropomorphic" in describing the animals of the two Potters and the stuffed animal toys. What defines the stuffed toy animal (and its forebearers) is not its resemblance to the figure of humans but the fact that it is made to meet human needs. The visual anthropomorphism is but one of the features that makes the stuffed toy animal more palatable and appealing as a product. Also, the term "anthropomorphic" connotates that the animal in question is somehow a false or inaccurate *representation* of the model animal. My objective in this paper is to consider different stuffed animals not as more or less accurate representations of the animal, but rather as different-looking animal products made by and for humans.
5. The care and observation that went into the reproduction of the rabbit figures is more apparent when you compare Potter's sketches of Peter, for example, with her sketches of Mr. McGregor in *The Tale of Peter Rabbit*. Peter is always in proportion and drawn to the tip of his toes, while Mr. McGregor has glove-like hands and a mere hint of facial features, on top of being out of proportion in the two scenes in which we see his body.
6. Stuffed toy animals, just as the animals of factory farms, belong to the industrialized system of animal production. The toy-making industry has been a "sector of the highly concentrated industrial economy" since the turn of the twentieth century (Kline 150) and is designed to make toys "available in large numbers" in a "mass market" (Cross 17). Stuffed toy animal production employed "a conveyer-belt system" since Steiff Inc.'s introduction of it in 1921 (Maniera 91), and production has developed into even more intensified forms after "the emergence of multinational toy companies" in the 1960s (138).

Works Cited

Creaney, Conor. "Paralytic Animation: The Anthropomorphic Taxidermy of Walter Potter." *Victorian Studies*, vol. 53, no. 1, 2010, pp. 7–35.

Cronon, William. "The Trouble with Wilderness: Or, Getting Back to the Wrong Nature." *Environmental History*, vol. 1, no. 1, 1996, pp. 7–28.

Cross, Gary. *Kids' Stuff: Toys and the Changing World of American Childhood*. Harvard UP, 1999.

Desmond, Jane C. *Displaying Death and Animating Life: Human-Animal Relations in Art, Science, and Everyday Life*. U of Chicago P, 2016.

Fraustino, Lisa Rowe. "The Rights and Wrongs of Anthropomorphism in Picture Books." *Ethics and Children's Literature*, edited by Claudia Mills. Routledge, 2014, pp. 145–62.

Henning, Michelle. "Anthropomorphic Taxidermy and the Death of Nature: The Curious Art of Hermann Ploucquet, Walter Potter, and Charles Waterton." *Victorian Literature and Culture*, vol. 35, no. 2, 2007, pp. 663–78.

Hollindale, Peter. "Humans Are So Rabbit." *Beatrix Potter's* Peter Rabbit: *A Children's Classic at 100*, edited by Margaret Mackey, Scarecrow Press, 2002, pp. 161–72. Children's Literature Association Centennial Studies.

Kline, Stephen. *Out of the Garden: Toys, TV, and Children's Culture in the Age of Marketing.* Verso, 1993.

Lovell-Smith, Rose. "Peter, Potter, Rabbits, Robbers." *Papers*, vol. 19, no. 1, 2009, pp. 17–29.

Maniera, Leyla. *Christie's Century Teddy Bears*. Pavilion, 2001.

Potter, Beatrix. *The Tale of Peter Rabbit*. 1902. Frederick Warne, 1987.

Potter, Walter. "The Rabbits' Village School." 1888. *A Case of Curiosities*, http://www.acaseofcuriosities.com/pages/01_2_00potter.html. Accessed 21 Oct. 2022.

Star, Susan Leigh. "Craft vs. Commodity, Mess vs. Transcendence: How the Right Tool Became the Wrong One in the Case of Taxidermy and Natural History." *The Right Tools for the Job: At Work in Twentieth-Century Life Sciences*, edited by Adela E. Clarke and Joan H. Fujimura, Princeton UP, 2014, pp. 257–86.

Taylor, Judy. "The Story of *The Tale of Peter Rabbit*." *Beatrix Potter's* Peter Rabbit: *A Children's Classic at 100*, edited by Margaret Mackey, Scarecrow Press, 2002, pp. 33–42. Children's Literature Association Centennial Studies.

Whalley, Joyce Irene. "Beatrix Potter's Art." *Beatrix Potter's* Peter Rabbit: *A Children's Classic at 100*, edited by Margaret Mackey, Scarecrow Press, 2002, pp. 43–51. Children's Literature Association Centennial Studies.

Williams, Margery. *The Velveteen Rabbit: Or How Toys Become Real*. 1922. Illustrated by William Nicholson, Dover Publications, 2011.

Chapter 7

Illustrations and the Eco-Reality of *The Velveteen Rabbit*

—Wenduo Zhang

In the fall of 2019, I asked a friend traveling to Tokyo to bring me a copy of the 2007 Japanese adaptation of *The Velveteen Rabbit* (1922), a thirty-two-page picture book abridged and illustrated by Komako Sakai. After searching every shelf of the children's section in vain, my friend asked a bookstore employee for help, only to find the exact book in the hands of the clerk, who was arranging a special display platform for the book. Nothing can speak better for a book's popularity than having a table of its own a decade after its initial publication. In Japan, Sakai is known as a writer and illustrator for adults as well as for children (Gussan). Although the book is recommended for ages six to seven in Japan, a web poll indicates that most readers in Japan encounter this book as an adult (*EhonNavi*).[1] The bellyband on my copy (a 2019 ninetieth reprint edition) displays praises from readers between eighteen and sixty-five, with only one commenting on reading with children as a mother. "It is a story that makes you want to read it over and over again as an adult," says Miyuki, a blogger, mother, and promoter of children's picture books in Japan. The book won first place in two Japanese picture book awards, "The 30 Best Picture Books in 2007" in *MOE*, a monthly magazine on picture books published worldwide, and "I Like This Picture Book! 2008 Edition," a selection made by 106 Japanese picture-book lovers out of thirteen hundred picture books published in Japan in 2007 (*Bronze Publishing Inc.*).[2]

Sakai's edition was such a huge success that, in 2012, the Japanese book based on Margery Williams's English tale was translated back into English by Yuki Kaneko and published in the United States by Enchanted Lion, a New York based independent children's publisher, on the tenth anniversary of their founding. This English edition quickly became a Bank Street College of Education Best Children's

Book of 2013. As in Japan, this book received a warm welcome from adult readers in the US but for a different reason. While the Japanese audience is attracted by Sakai's fame as a versatile artist, American adults approach the book from a more nostalgic and comparative perspective, as most of them already know the original tale from childhood.

Despite its popularity among readers and award committees, Sakai's edition has not received much critical attention in English-speaking countries. Reviewers praise the pictures as "richly textured" (*Publishers Weekly*) and "a force of nature" (Danielson), yet no close reading has been done to explore the relation between the visual aspects of nature as presented by the drawings, the concept of nature as told in the words, and the existence of nature outside of the book. Pictures speak for themselves, and they also inspire the reader to think beyond the text. This chapter explicates and offers an eco-critical reading of Sakai's *The Velveteen Rabbit*.

The focus of eco-critical reading in this chapter is twofold: on the structural level, the notion of an ecosystem as dynamic and flexible inspires the reader of picture books to explore meanings that shift and come in layers of text and illustration; on the thematic level, the story itself invites the reader to reflect on the intertwinement of human and nonhuman others, raising the reader's awareness that nonhuman animals have interests of their own.

David Lewis suggests that a picture book "acts as a kind of miniature ecosystem" (48):

> First, it encourages us to see how the words and pictures in picturebooks act upon each other reciprocally, each one becoming the environment within which the other lives and thrives. Second, the notion of ecosystem as a dynamic structure helps us to understand how the word-picture relationship might shift and change, page by page and moment by moment. Third, the recognition that ecosystems can be complex as well as flexible helps us to appreciate the heterogeneity that we can sometimes find within the picturebook. (54)

Lewis uses "ecosystem" as an analogy to show the interaction between words and pictures in picture books. For Lewis, the notion of ecosystem expands the reader's view of picture books as words and pictures form a dynamic system reminiscent of nature. The content of the picture book does not need to be about the environment for it to be considered a "miniature ecosystem" (48).

For a text to be "environmentally oriented," Lawrence Buell gives four "ingredients":

1. The nonhuman environment is present not merely as a framing device but as a presence that begins to suggest that human history is implicated in natural history.

2. The human interest is not understood to be the only legitimate interest.
3. Human accountability to the environment is part of the text's ethical orientation.
4. Some sense of the environment as a process rather than a constant or a given is at least implicit in the text. (7–8)

Buell does not include picture books in his sampler texts, but the "sense of the environment as a process rather than a constant or a given" is in line with Lewis's dynamic ecosystem (8). What marks a text as "environmentally oriented" is the weight of nonhuman content and a constant reevaluation of the human part in it. Although Sakai may not intend *The Velveteen Rabbit* to be an "eco-themed" picture book, the lavish depictions of animals, human-animal interactions, and both built and natural environments invite eco-critical interpretations.

In the following reading of Sakai's *The Velveteen Rabbit*, I will first look at the ways pictures support and subvert the words as well as how both pictures and words convey different meanings of the tale when considered together. Then I will examine the environmental message that this book may imply, including the influence of consumption culture on the environment and an alternative way of treating toys, which I propose as the book's ethical message on human and nature relations. Because Sakai is retelling a text already familiar to readers of this chapter, I will focus primarily on the visual narrative, namely Sakai's use of color and light, relative sizes, and distance and frames in her paintings.

Characterization through Color and Light

In *How Picturebooks Work* (2013), Maria Nikolajeva and Carole Scott conclude that "the picturebooks that employ counterpoint are especially stimulating because they elicit many possible interpretations and involve the reader's imagination" (24). Counterpoints can be found within words or pictures alone, but because picture books require both words and pictures, counterpoint between them is a distinguishing feature of the form. Nikolajeva and Scott's approach of analyzing counterpoints to reveal what they call the "word-picture dynamic" (8) correlates with Lewis's "miniature ecosystem" (48) consisting of words and pictures. On the surface, what contributes to the word-picture dynamic are observable counterpoints; yet in essence, the dynamic is caused by the format of picture books that contains two narrative systems that are as complex as the ecosystems in nature, where there are no two identical leaves.

Understanding *The Velveteen Rabbit* as a miniature ecosystem requires locating words and pictures as two indispensable systems that affect each other. Williams writes many visual descriptions of objects and characters that enable the original story to stand alone without accompanying pictures. In the retelling, Sakai simplifies the verbal text without changing the plot, reducing the descriptive words to a minimal number while making more room for pictures. As a result, the verbal text can no longer suffice in the role of telling the whole story, entailing the reader to look at the images for appearance of things (and more). For example, Sakai verbally and pictorially leaves out the "spotted brown and white" coat (Williams 1926, 1) from the Rabbit and instead draws a toy rabbit wearing only a blue ribbon around its neck. The verbal text never mentions the ribbon, which gradually wears out in the following pictures, conveying the passage of time and showing the process of being "loved off" (Williams 1926, 22).

Perhaps the largest counterpoint between words and pictures in the story is the anthropomorphizing of "real" toy characters, such as the Skin Horse and the Velveteen Rabbit. According to Nikolajeva and Scott, picture books can contain a "counterpoint in genre or modality" when "words and images tell different stories" in terms of genre and viewpoint (24). Sakai creates several counterpoints in modality by telling a fantasy story about talking toys with words while showing pictures of realistic depictions of inanimate toys. In the verbal text, the toys are sentient and can communicate with other toys and wild rabbits; yet the pictures always show a static moment, and the toys look like realistic playthings without implications of movement or ability to talk. Reading the words without Sakai's pictures, the reader cannot visualize the characters due to lack of descriptions; looking at the pictures alone, the reader will lose the conversations and thoughts of characters that are only available through words. As a result, the pictures complete the appearance of characters introduced by words, and the words in turn give life to the toys depicted on the page.

By limiting the words to dialogue and exposition of inner feelings and the pictures to the texture of toys in the setting, Sakai combines the realistic images of inanimate toys with a fantasy tale of talking and loving animals living inside the toy body. This ecosystem creates a strong impression of her characters. Consider the Skin Horse, who only appears in the beginning of the story. In this thirty-two-page book, Sakai spends two full pages on this character: a page of picture followed by a page of text. On the recto, Williams's original passage introducing the Skin Horse is reduced into a single sentence: "He was the oldest in the nursery and looked shabby and frayed, but his eyes gleamed wisely" (2012). The brevity of the text leads the reader to investigate the picture for further information. On the verso, a full-page illustration (figure 7.1) depicts the toys, in which Sakai's rendition of the Skin Horse emphasizes the texture of animal skin and hair, reminding readers of the real animal that existed before the toy animal.

In the illustration of the Skin Horse and the Velveteen Rabbit conversing, Sakai manipulates light and color to direct the viewers' focus to the Skin Horse and dismiss the background. Layered colors on the toy's torso create a sense of shabby skin; the outmost layer is white, resulting in strong contrast against the dim

Figure 7.1 The Skin Horse and the Velveteen Rabbit converse. © Komako Sakai.

background. This contrast calls for attention, as the dark-colored background seems to withdraw, and the light-colored toys appear to stand out more. In discussing how pictures/picture books evoke emotions, Molly Bang says, "contrast enables us to see" (100). The color contrast of the horse and the background enables the viewer to examine the toy in detail. Red stripes over the white body of the horse provide another contrast, evoking reins, the real constraint we impose on real horses.

Bang's statement only pertains to pictures, but if we apply the methodology of Lewis's miniature ecosystem, we cannot separate the words and pictures entirely. Therefore, the contrast in pictures not only enables us to discover the details in images, but it also echoes the inherent counterpoints between words and pictures, making the reader go back to the words once more. The text on the recto gives the short introduction of the Skin Horse and his famous lecture of "what is REAL?" But the picture on the verso entices the viewer to examine the contents closely and not to turn the page in haste. Bearing the question of, "what is REAL?" in mind, the viewer will look at the horse from a new angle. The coarse hair and the body shape of the horse could fool the viewer that this is just like a real horse, but the unmissable sewing marks across the front of the horse body and over its face challenge this illusion of realness. The horse toy is sewed up from pieces of calfskin, wood, and glass, restrained by more leather and metal.³ It is the opposite of Real since real, live creatures (a calf and a tree) were killed to make this toy. The picture of the Skin Horse faithfully shows what the toy looks like, embodying the material truth the verbal story understates and thus adds a sense of irony. Unlike the verbal text that assures the reader a toy "can become Real," this image of the Skin Horse offers an opposite view: that what appears to be real can be fake or even the deprivation of "Real," if Real equals being alive.

This microecosystem contains only two pages depicting the Skin Horse, yet by looking at words and pictures as separate ecosystems that deeply engage each other, the reader is obliged to examine the two counterpoints back and forth, each time with new information from the other medium. The understanding of the character from this reading thus evolves from a talking horse toy to a horse object that appears to be real to a toy that is made from real animal skin to the real animals that were killed for inanimate toys—and each signifies a different level of realness. This process of immersing oneself in the ecosystems of the picture book ultimately enables the reader to suspend our human self-interest, making room for appreciation and care about the other-than-human interests that Buell proposes.

J. Allen Williams Jr. et al. survey Caldecott-winning picture books from 1938 to 2008 and find "significant declines in depictions of natural environments and animals while built environments have become much more common" (145). Their definition of natural environments is "those that appeared relatively unchanged by humans, such as a forest area" (Williams et al. 150). The result leads to concerns about the lack of "understanding and appreciation of the natural world and the place of humans within it" from the current generation of young readers of picture books (156). Citing their research, Nathalie op de Beeck advocates the importance of engaging the readers of environmental picture books with "actual flora and fauna" (116). Although op de Beeck is aware of the "twenty-first century urban development" that affects animals and the environment, the emphasis on wild (or natural) lives and places still implies nature as separate from humans. This human isolation from nature is portrayed in Sakai's *The Velveteen Rabbit* as the drastic difference between natural and built environments. If the definition of Real from the Skin Horse is gaining human love by endurance, the wild rabbits exhibit a counterview on Realness as a living status that does not rely on humans at all. William Cronon argues that nature "is a profoundly human construction" (25). Nature in both Williams's original version and Sakai's *The Velveteen Rabbit* is defined in relation to humans: the wild rabbits are naturally reproduced and can live (better) without the care from humans, so they are real; the toys, made by humans to serve humans, are against the ways of nature, so they are artificial and therefore unreal. Just like the implication that wild rabbits are superior to toy rabbits, Sakai constructs nature as more desirable than a built environment. Her pictures of the garden and the wood scenes contain minimal human objects but are abundant in plants that seem to expand beyond the page boundary. Even when the playmates' indoor time is depicted in the pictures, their play is about nature: the Boy makes burrows with his comforter for the Rabbit, and they read a picture book showing a boat sailing in the sea. The verbal text supports nature over the home setting as the Rabbit comforts the bedridden Boy by planning "wonderful days . . . in the garden" for after the Boy recovers.

Sakai's *The Velveteen Rabbit* celebrates outdoor space through contrasting the lack of detail and color in the indoor environment with elaborated depictions of the natural environment. The indoor environment is dim and minimized, showing only the necessary physical clues such as a fraction of the bed and the flat surface where the toys are left. As in the picture of the Skin Horse, most indoor backgrounds are in low-saturated colors, without further depiction of tangible things. The viewer is given little perspective about the setting, such as where the bed is located, what other furniture the house contains, what's the shape of the toy cupboard, or whether the room has windows. The exclusion of architectural and interior design elements results in a sense of uncertainty and liminality. This reduction becomes evident when compared with picture books that have the indoor space as the only setting. A familiar example is Margaret Wise Brown's *Goodnight Moon*, illustrated by Clement Hurd. In *Goodnight Moon*, the bunny-child's room has green walls, a red floor, red and yellow furniture, and striped curtains of yellow and green. The pictures repeatedly show an overview of the room, followed by close-ups of each item in the room. Although the bunny-child character does not leave the bed, the illustrations take the child and readers on a visual tour around the room.

In Sakai's *Mad at Mommy* (2010), a picture book that also depicts the bedroom (which is also the dining room), light blue and cream yellow dominate the home, giving a tender and welcoming feeling that ultimately lures the mad runaway bunny-child back to home and mother. A third example is Sakai's *Hannah's Night* (2013), in which a girl wakes up at night and explores the house. Even though the events happen at night and the child does not use any electric light, the overall color palette of this book is not dark brown or black as one might expect. Instead, Sakai uses indigo to fill the background and connects the color of the home with the color of the sky before dawn. Clearly, Sakai knows how to depict indoor settings and nighttime with colors. Yet in *The Velveteen Rabbit*, when the characters are inside the house, they are almost always given close-up shots with dark backgrounds, leaving no space for the viewer to wonder about other aspects. The Boy is squeezed inside the room with no windows to look out of, just like his toys that are in total darkness due to being kept inside the closed toy cupboard. The room is uninteresting in itself. In contrast, Sakai depicts nature as open space with rich colors and perspectives. While Sakai shortens the verbal story, nature in the pictures becomes more colorful and inviting. Things not described in words are added: a white butterfly, white and yellow flowers, leaves in different shades of green, and the orange afternoon sky. Showing the details of wild space is an acknowledgment that there is much in nature for the Boy and readers to observe and explore and that nature is real, not imagined. The Boy in Sakai's *The Velveteen Rabbit* communes with nature: he plays more with animal toys than with mechanical toys; he imitates natural habitat by making a "rabbit's burrow" for the Velveteen Rabbit and placing it carefully on the grass, the place where wild rabbits live; he plays in the garden and the wood "for hours"; and he goes to the seaside to tend his health (Williams 2012).

The playtime in Sakai's richly embellished nature depicts the Boy as biophilic, a trait that is simultaneously desirable for children and the colonizing of nature. E. O. Wilson defines biophilia as "the urge to affiliate with other forms of life" (85). Marion W. Copeland and Heidi O'Brien expand this affiliation to include nature as a living being and define biophilia as "an affinity for all forms of life and the living earth" (51). In Sakai's *The Velveteen Rabbit*, both the Boy and the Rabbit show an affinity for nature. Cronon refers to the worship of nature as a "moral imperative" that "always implies a very particular vision of what ideal nature is supposed to be . . . as the mirror onto which societies project the ideal reflections they wish to see" (36). Aside from the fact that the wood in *The Velveteen Rabbit* is a fictional place that only exists on paper and in our imagination, what appears to be a human-free nature is deeply constructed by humans: the wood is located near the house so the Boy can go play in it; the wild rabbits are preserved as "free" while dangerous carnivores, such as wolves and coyotes, are omitted (both in the story and in our real life). The wild animals in this idealized nature are always healthy and happy; only humans ever get sick, and sick children are forced to stay indoors until they become well enough to re-enter nature. The nature in picture books is always wonderful and enticing, but like the toy Skin Horse, this ideal nature is not real because stories cannot provide the whole picture. We understand picture books in part by noticing what is not there. Uri Shulevitz notes that "what you don't see affects what you do see. It is this relationship between the seen and the unseen that contributes to a good picture book ... for the unshown elements can be just as significant as those that are shown" (59). Nature in Sakai's *The Velveteen Rabbit* does not appear in closed space and poor lighting; therefore, it does not connote danger or negative feelings. In the sense of pretending to offer reality, this picture book is analogous to toys that mimic wild animals for children to "play" with.

Relative Sizes and Hierarchies of Power

Scholars of picture books have noted the positive relationship between the size of an element in the picture and its psychological and social importance. Bang concludes, "The larger an object is in a picture, the stronger it feels" (90). In theorizing animal and toy fantasy for children, Nikolajeva observes that "the use of [animal and toy] characters empowers the [child] readers since a child is usually bigger and stronger than a toy..." (55). Perry Nodelman and Mavis Reimer even suggest that compared with miniature nonhuman characters, "greater size" compels "the normal-size child ... into the role of an adult" (197). While the power hierarchy of adults above children and humans above nonhumans is embedded in Sakai's verbal stories, her paintings reveal this hidden structure by bringing the relative size of characters into plain view. Many of Sakai's picture books are about parent and child relationships. Often the child is smaller than the parent, giving a sense of the child as vulnerable and in need of adult protection. In *Mad at Mommy*, however, Sakai reverses the relative size to convey the bunny-child's anger and destructive power. In one full-bleed double-spread, the bunny-child appears to be larger than skyscrapers as his temper grows to a peak; the bunny-child's body is tilted across the gutter, with one hand on top of a building, as if he is about to push it. It should be noted that the character has his back toward the viewers, yet Sakai successfully shows his emotion without depicting any facial expressions.

The relative size difference between adult characters, the Boy, and the Velveteen Rabbit in Sakai's pictures conveys a conventional power structure. Throughout the book, Sakai never depicts the faces of adult characters, and more than once the pictures of adult figures do not include their heads. Even though only parts of their bodies are shown, the big size of Nana and the doctor indicate that they are the persons who have control of everything inside the house, including the Boy. Likewise, the Boy is always larger than the Velveteen Rabbit when they are in the same picture, indicating that the Boy is in charge. The only time when the toy Rabbit is shown as large in size is on the cover, where the Boy is not present or mentioned and the picture serves as a close-up image echoing the title.

Moreover, Sakai's pictures reiterate a preference of real/wild animals over toy animals by always depicting the wild rabbits larger than the Velveteen Rabbit

Illustrations and the Eco-Reality of *The Velveteen Rabbit* 123

Figure 7.2 A wild rabbit sniffs at the Velveteen Rabbit. © Komako Sakai.

until after he changes into a wild rabbit. The verbal texts, both Williams's original tale and Sakai's retelling, never mention the size of the Velveteen Rabbit in relation to wild rabbits, so the relative size difference is open to the illustrator's interpretation. The narrated interaction between the Velveteen Rabbit and the wild rabbits is more or less the same in both versions, yet the illustrations of different editions give this scene various interpretations by assigning different sizes to the rabbits. In Nicholson's original illustration, the wild rabbits are slightly larger than the Velveteen Rabbit, so they seem stronger and more powerful than the Velveteen Rabbit. Sakai follows Nicholson's convention but amplifies the size contrast by making the wild rabbits twice the size of the Velveteen Rabbit (figure 7.2).

Naturally, the first thing the viewer will notice in this picture is the two brownish rabbits, one huge and the other small. The wild rabbit looks threatening, as the combined length of its head and ears equals the entire size of the Velveteen Rabbit. Because the verbal text of this book (in both English and Japanese) is read from left to right, readers will move their eyes from left to right. By making the wild rabbit face to the right, Sakai invites the viewer to follow its gaze to the Velveteen Rabbit, placed vertically. Seeing that the Velveteen Rabbit is small, stiff, and grounded, while the wild rabbit is large, agile, and active, the viewer absorbs the idea that a wild rabbit is better and more desirable than a toy.

Nodelman notes that "our understanding of pictures starts with wholes and breaks down into details" (202). In pictures, the overall shape and positioning of chunks of color get viewers' attention before they can examine small areas and identify individual characteristics. As a result, pictures directly show how the characters look in relation to other elements around them, including other characters. Bang's statement about contrast enabling us to see still stands true, as contrast exists only when two or more elements are presented together as a whole. The details of the Velveteen Rabbit's legs disappear outside of the picture frame and behind the green plants, yet the size and positioning of the characters still convey truth. Comparing Sakai's retelling to the original mockery at not having hind legs in Williams's story, *Publishers Weekly* (in a review of *The Velveteen Rabbit*) comments that "cruel truths are considerably softened and pared down." Sakai softens this scene by both omitting the verbal revelation about the rabbit's hind legs and hiding the bottom of the animals in the pictures.

Throughout the book, the Velveteen Rabbit is always shown in small size except in the double-spread where he becomes alive ("real") and joins other wild rabbits. The Velveteen Rabbit is smaller than the Boy, smaller than the wild rabbits, and smaller than other toys such as the Skin Horse and the mechanical toys, and even smaller than a book of the Boy's. The small size confirms the toy as powerless and in need of protection, while the enlarged real Rabbit gives an impression of him finally feeling at home in a community. The change of size celebrates the Rabbit's growing up as he becomes alive, once again implying real animals are preferable despite the Boy's affection for the toy.

Despite the evident celebration of real animals in a natural environment, the Boy's relationship with the animals is intricate. The Boy loves to play with animal toys and treats the Velveteen Rabbit as an organic rabbit who sleeps in a burrow and plays in the grass. Sakai frequently situates the Velveteen Rabbit close to the Boy, showing the emotional intimacy between the two characters. Imagining the Velveteen Rabbit as real, the Boy practices how to treat animals in his games, which may prepare him to appreciate wildlife and to ultimately reenter nature and encounter real animals. But can the love of an imagined animal really transform into the love of real animals? Can the practice of love in the built environment and a constructed nature apply to the actual natural environment? In the case of the Skin Horse, the life of a slaughtered animal can never be restored by loving a toy, and the toy teaches the children nothing about wild horses or the natural environment. In the case of the Velveteen Rabbit, the Boy brings the toy into nature and loses it for a time in the garden, and upon the Boy's recovery from homebound illness, the toy is discarded into a sack of garbage to be burned. Moreover, wild rabbits do not play with humans—they in reality would run away at the sound of the Boy's footsteps. As a book about how wild rabbits are "Real to all," Sakai's *The Velveteen Rabbit* suggests that Real is wild, and wild rabbits are unreachable. Filling the gap of relative sizes between the Velveteen Rabbit and wild rabbits, the pictures advocate a moral preference for real life that is not explicit in the words; but at the same time, the image relegates the nonhuman environment to what Buell calls "a framing device" (7) by keeping the real wildness outside.

Distance and Framing Perspectives

Sakai's paintings frequently focus on the distance between parent (usually the mother) and child characters as well as the distance between objects and people (Miyuki). In *The Velveteen Rabbit*, Sakai's pictures separate the Boy from the toy after his health starts to improve. The gutter separates the Boy and the Rabbit into two pages, with one side depicting the Boy preparing to go to the seaside and the other showing the Rabbit lying down on the empty bed before going to be burned. This separation creates a sense of loneliness and independence that foreshadows the Rabbit's abandonment. From here the Boy stops appearing in the pictures, and the Rabbit starts to take more space on the page. The size of the Rabbit grows larger as the pictures move on until the climactic double-spread of the real Rabbit among wild rabbits, where he takes up half the width and two-thirds the height of the page. Sakai omits the entire verbal description from Williams about how the Fairy changes the Velveteen Rabbit into a real rabbit, how she introduces the Rabbit to other wild rabbits, and how the Rabbit realizes its realness by feeling its hind legs, leaving only the picture of him with the big fluffy wild rabbits to show the physical change and inner growth of the Rabbit. A big yellow moon lights the space, so nature is still green and blue despite being night. Colors fill every corner of the wordless double-spread, so the space seems expanding and unlimited. Nature in this picture is undisturbed and pure as the rabbits live free on their own away from humans and language.

Just as pristine nature is an illusion, Sakai's celebration of wild animals in nature does not conclude this story. The uplifting effect the double-spread conveys is challenged by the last page (figure 7.3), where Sakai returns the animals to small size and within a single small frame. On the last page of the story, the words focus on the Boy, while the pictures show the rabbits. The picture of two real/wild rabbits is framed in a small rectangular shape. Surrounding the picture, the verbal text is divided into two parts. On the upper half, the text describes the change of seasons and how the Boy goes to the wood and meets the rabbits; on the lower half is the Boy's reflection that the rabbit looks like his old toy. The words also act as a frame that detaches the picture from the viewer, adding distance between the animals and the human reader. Nature is triple contained, first in the imagination of a fictional boy, then in the small picture framed by verbal texts, and, finally, all this is contained within a page of a book.

The alignment of words in the Japanese version interacts with the picture by surrounding it and condensing shapes into the center of the page. The lines of text are centered on the last page while aligned to the left in the rest of the book, which unfortunately is not kept in the design of the English translation. Having the text centered helps direct the viewer's attention to the middle of the page,

秋がさり、冬がさり、春がきて……
きせつは めぐって いきました。
あるとき ぼうやは 森で
こちらのほうを じっと みている
ふしぎな野うさぎと であったことが あります。

「どうしてかしら あの うさぎ。
そっくりだよ、病気のときに なくしてしまった
ぼくのあの ふるいうさぎに……」

Figure 7.3 The rabbits gaze out. © Komako Sakai.

where the two rabbits sit. Here the picture disturbs the rhythm of the verbal narrative. Two transformations happen. First, the reader of the text turns into the viewer of the picture as the verbal narrative halts before the picture. While the text says that the Boy "came upon an odd wild rabbit that seemed to be staring at him" (Williams 2012), the picture shows two rabbits of the same size standing side by side. Upon further examination, the reader will identify the rabbit on the right side as the "odd" one, for it is looking out toward the audience. Since the Boy is not illustrated on the page but the words say that "the Boy was in the wood" and he noticed the Rabbit's gaze (36), the audience adopts the Boy's perspective through the act of locating the Rabbit. This is the second transformation, where the omniscient reader of the story adopts the Boy's viewpoint. This last image echoes the opening scene of the toy rabbit inside a hanging stocking, looking slightly downward and outward from the page. The next picture shows the stocking on the floor and the toy held in the Boy's hand, suggesting the previous picture is from the perspective of the Boy within the book. Both the opening and ending pictures portray what the Boy sees without including him, making the reader adopt his viewpoint and focus on the Rabbit. The title suggests the Rabbit is the protagonist, while both images encourage the reader to align with the Boy, making which of the two is the real protagonist an arguable question. The counterpoint of protagonists and the imbalance between an omniscient verbal story and a homodiegetic visual perspective enable us to understand the Rabbit, to treat him as important, and to empathize with him. Nikolajeva and Scott observe that "the convention of visual communication . . . creates in us the expectation of seeing the protagonist in the picture" (125). The search for a protagonist is based on the belief in its importance. What Sakai unconventionally depicts, or rather what she chooses to not depict, hints at the significance of the Rabbit: to see the Boy is less important than to see the Rabbit, and to empathize with the Boy means to empathize with the Rabbit.

While the visual frame of words encourages the reader to focus on the center, punctuation slows down the rhythm of the story and signals an expansion of events and feelings. In the Japanese version, the first and last sentences on this page both end with ellipses. Although the story ends with the Boy's words/thoughts, the ellipses add a sense of a voice trailing off, suggesting a continuation. Both the Rabbit's gaze and the ellipses contribute to a sense of wonder. From the perspective of the Boy, the viewer identifies the rabbit as special and familiar. The real Rabbit is small in comparison to humans, as the small size on the page shows. Real animals are not overly friendly to human children, so the rabbits keep a distance from us, which makes them appear even smaller. Sakai makes readers look at the animals as if we are the Boy standing at a distance from the rabbits and feeling their gaze. The Boy always has the Rabbit in his mind, even though he is not presented in the pictures. The latter half of the story, from the moment the Velveteen Rabbit leaves the house to be destroyed, can be seen as happening in the Boy's imagination. Upon understanding the nature of wild rabbits and their difference from toy animals, the distance between the Boy and wild animals can also be read as a new way of love, of true *philia*, where the "love aiming to possess" matures to the "love between friends," the love that asks nothing in return and thrives upon mutual respect (Orr 142). Comparing the opening and ending scenes, the Rabbit transforms, in the Boy's eye and mind, from a toy to be taken from a stocking and played with into a living being to be observed in nature and not disturbed.

On this last page, the systems of words and pictures interrupt and literally frame each other. The words and pictures form a miniature ecosystem that simultaneously suggests the separation of humans from nature and the longing for their reunion, inviting us to read the story as an environmental text and to reflect on our relationship with nature in real life. Reading the picture book is like immersing oneself in this miniature ecosystem. Counterpoints within and between words and pictures allow the reader to experience the story in a dynamic way through which meaning develops. By acknowledging the interests of animal others (even toy animals) and identifying whether the natural environment is implicated in the story, such reading engages us in the ethics of human relationships with built and natural environments as well as nonhuman beings.

Notes

1. The Japanese picture book showcase site, *EhonNavi*, categorizes picture books by age from zero to twelve and has adults as a separate category. According to *EhonNavi*, children aged six to seven are supposed to be able to read the book by themselves, but adult company is recommended.

2. The two awards were originally announced in the January 2008 issue of *MOE* published by 白泉社 (Hakusensha) and the 2008 edition of この絵本が好き！(I Like This Picture Book!) published by 平凡社 (Heibonsha).

3. The Skin Horse appeals to readers because of its resemblance to real toys that epitomize real animals. Sakai's picture of the Skin Horse is highly accurate in the appearance of the toy. Williams used a real skin horse toy as her inspiration for the character and admitted that the Skin Horse was a toy that she "had loved as a little girl" (Moore 15). Explaining the popularity of skin horse toys, Assistant Curator Margaret Simpson comments: "Compared to timber, metal or plastic toy animals, those with a furry texture have long appealed to children, not only because of their feel but also because of their convincing portrayal of live animals. They closely resemble living animals yet withstand cuddling and torment without protest."

Works Cited

Bang, Molly. *Picture This: How Pictures Work*. Chronicle Books, 2016.
Bronze Publishing Inc. "ビロードのうさぎ [The Velveteen Rabbit]." www.bronze.co.jp/books/9784893094087/. Accessed 20 Jan. 2021.
Brown, Margaret Wise. *Goodnight Moon*. Illustrated by Clement Hurd, Harper Trophy, 1947.
Buell, Lawrence. *The Environmental Imagination: Thoreau, Nature Writing, and the Formation of American Culture*. Harvard UP, 1995.
Copeland, Marion W., and Heidi O'Brien. "Toward Biophilia: The Role of Children's Literature in the Development of Empathy and Compassion." *The State of the Animals II*, edited by Deborah J. Salem and Andrew N. Rowan, Humane Society Press, 2003, pp. 51–65.
Cronon, William. "Introduction: In Search of Nature." *Uncommon Ground: Rethinking the Human Place in Nature*, edited by William Cronon, W. W. Norton & Company, 1996, pp. 23–68.
Danielson, Jules. "A Bowl of Rice, Miso Soup, and Pickled Vegetables with Komako Sakai." *Seven Impossible Things before Breakfast*, 14 Aug. 2012, www.blaine.org/sevenimpossiblethings/?p=2402. Accessed 10 Oct. 2022.

EhonNavi. "ビロードのうさぎ [The Velveteen Rabbit]." www.ehonnavi.net/ehon/13437/ビロードのうさぎ/. Accessed 13 May 2020.

Gussan ぐっさん. "大人が好きな絵本作家 — 酒井駒子さんの世界観 [Adult Picture Book Writer—Komako Sakai's Worldview]." *Note*, 17 Jan. 2019, www.note.com/life_design/n/nc83b0762005f. Accessed 3 May 2020.

Lewis, David. *Reading Contemporary Picturebooks: Picturing Text*. Psychology Press, 2001.

Miyuki マヅメ ミユキ. "人気の絵本作家・酒井駒子さんのプロフィールと絵本を徹底紹介 [A Thorough Introduction to the Profile and Picture Books of Popular Picture Book Author, Komako Sakai]." *Mama-ehon* ママえほん, 21 Nov. 2017, www.mama-ehon.com/writer-117. Accessed 18 June 2020.

Moore, Anne Carroll. "Margery Williams Bianco." *Writing and Criticism: A Book for Margery Bianco*, edited by Anne Carroll Moore and Bertha E. Mahony Miller, Horn Book, 1951, pp. 3–20.

Nikolajeva, Maria. "The Development of Children's Fantasy." *The Cambridge Companion to Fantasy Literature*, edited by Edward James and Farah Mendlesohn, Cambridge UP, 2012, pp. 50–61.

Nikolajeva, Maria, and Carole Scott. *How Picturebooks Work*. Routledge, 2013.

Nodelman, Perry. *Words about Pictures: The Narrative Art of Children's Picture Books*. Georgia UP, 1988.

Nodelman, Perry, and Mavis Reimer. *The Pleasures of Children's Literature*. 3rd ed., Allyn and Bacon, 2003.

op de Beeck, Nathalie. "Environmental Picture Books: Cultivating Conservationists." *More Words about Pictures: Current Research on Picturebooks and Visual/Verbal Texts for Young People*, edited by Naomi Hamer et al., Routledge, 2017, pp. 116–26.

Orr, David W. *Earth in Mind: On Education, Environment, and the Human Prospect*. Island Press, 2004.

Publishers Weekly. Review of *The Velveteen Rabbit*, by Komako Sakai, translated by Yuki Kaneko. 1 Nov. 2012, www.publishersweekly.com/978-1-59270-128-5. Accessed 1 Mar. 2020.

Sakai, Komako. *Hannah's Night*. Illustrated by Komako Sakai, Gecko Press, 2013.

Sakai, Komako. *Mad at Mommy*. Illustrated by Komako Sakai, Scholastic Inc., 2010.

Shulevitz, Uri. *Writing with Pictures: How to Write and Illustrate Children's Books*. Watson-Guptill Publications, 1985.

Simpson, Margaret. "Pull Along Toy Horse." *Museum of Applied Arts & Sciences*, www.collection.maas.museum/object/169139. Accessed 3 May 2020.

Williams, J. Allen, Jr., et al. "The Human-Environment Dialog in Award-Winning Children's Picture Books." *Sociological Inquiry*, vol. 82, no. 1, 2012, pp. 145–59.

Wilson, E. O. *Biophilia*. Harvard UP, 1984.

Editions of Margery Williams's *The Velveteen Rabbit*

Williams, Margery. 1926. *The Velveteen Rabbit*. Illustrated by William Nicholson, Doubleday.

Williams, Margery. 2007. ビロードのうさぎ [The Velveteen Rabbit]. Adapted and illustrated by Komako Sakai, Bronze Publishing.

Williams, Margery. 2012. *The Velveteen Rabbit*. Adapted and illustrated by Komako Sakai, translated by Yuki Kaneko, Enchanted Lion Books.

Chapter 8

The Velveteen Rabbit in Italy

—Claudia Camicia and Elena Paruolo

Our chapter tackles Italian versions of *The Velveteen Rabbit: Or How Toys Become Real* (1922; in Italian, *Il Coniglietto di Velluto*) from the earliest 1987 published translation to this day. Our research shows that initially there were only abridged versions, simplified and even at times wholly adapted versions of the original text, possibly because *The Velveteen Rabbit* was considered too complex for children stylistically, linguistically, and intellectually. We also point out how translations, adaptations, and reductions of *The Velveteen Rabbit* were not particularly sought after, as verified by the absence of reviews, essays, or comments concerning these publications. Over a long period of time, only scant references of any critical value appear concerning *The Velveteen Rabbit*: just some excerpts from Toni Raiten-D'Antonio's essay attached to the Macro edition published in 2007. Nevertheless, any given text in translation and/or its adaptations can themselves be considered critical contributions to gaining an understanding of the original work. This essay aims to provide evidence of translation strategies adopted for *The Velveteen Rabbit* from 1987 until 2007—the year of the first unabridged translation by Macro—and to study their impact on *The Velveteen Rabbit*'s significance in terms of young readers and the publishing industry as well as their connection to the need to modernize national children's literature and the educational field in Italy, with a view to improving early literacy.

This essay also demonstrates how the reception of *The Velveteen Rabbit* in Italy since 2007 changed drastically as interest in this text became more prominent. Since 2007, an ever-increasing number of teachers and librarians have sponsored reading *The Velveteen Rabbit* by acknowledging its touching engagement with a child's emotions. In response to this, a range of reviews has been published on cultural and literary blogs. The movie *Il Coniglietto magico* (The Magic Rabbit) appeared on the market in 2009 as a translation of the American film directed by Michael Landon, Jr. In 2014, as the focus in Italy was on new technologies, an Italian app based on Williams's original edition was developed by Yvonne Sciò, a professional storyteller. There were, furthermore, three theater plays based on *The Velveteen Rabbit*, namely at Stabile Theater in Grosseto in 2004, at Teatro della Pergola in Florence in 2010, and at Teatro Barbieri in Vercelli in 2016. *The Velveteen Rabbit* became increasingly relevant as an educational instrument, mainly through being reevaluated in pedagogical terms. Its themes fitted well in the Italian context of those years when new topics—such as disability,[1] new family structures, encounters between cultures, and integration of immigrants—became more mainstream, and fairy tales were approached in a different way thanks to the publication of several critical essays that contributed to their reevaluation.

Therefore, this essay outlines a brief history of editions and adaptations of *The Velveteen Rabbit* in Italy, tracing the ascending popularity curve that *The Velveteen Rabbit* has obtained since 2007 and illustrating how, since 2009, these editions and adaptations have worked as fairy tales to help children heal mentally, emotionally, and physically and to uphold children's rights. Structurally, the chapter is comprised of three sections. The first section considers Margery Williams's literary editions and one rewriting of her story and focuses on translation problems as a cross-cultural transfer that weaves together diverse cultures. The second section tackles video, app, and theater adaptations of *The Velveteen Rabbit* and focuses on the pedagogical purposes developed since 2009 by professional educators, amateurs, and artists. The third section closes in on Williams, suggesting that she may have read Carlo Collodi's *Le avventure di Pinocchio* (1881–83) in the original Italian or in translation and that she may have been influenced by it. It also speculates that Gianni Rodari may have been influenced by *The Velveteen Rabbit* in the writing of *La freccia azzurra* (1964).[2] As a matter of fact, both *Pinocchio* and *La freccia azzurra* could be said to share some traits with *The Velveteen Rabbit*.

Italian Editions of *The Velveteen Rabbit*: Considerations Concerning Literary and Aesthetical Adaptations

The first extant Italian unabridged translation of *The Velveteen Rabbit* (for six- to eight-year-olds) was published in 2007 by Macro,[3] eighty-five years after the story's original publication in 1922. Prior to 2007, and after this first translation, several picture books appeared (for three- to six-year-olds). The first one, in 1987, was an Italian translation of an American abridged version of the original text. Additionally, in 1991, Malipiero published a translation of a rewriting of *The Velveteen Rabbit* by Flavia Weedn and Lisa Weedn (*Flavia and the Velveteen Rabbit*) originally entitled *Flavia e il Coniglietto di Velluto*, which was reprinted in 1999 for children aged six or above. Two more Italian adaptations of *The Velveteen Rabbit* were conceived by Italian editors, published by Panini in 1993 and Gribaudo in 2017. The first focuses on gender. In 2009, Macro published a translation of Raiten D'Antonio's essay, *I Principi del Coniglietto di Velluto* (originally, *The Velveteen Principles: A Guide to Becoming Real*, 2004), for teaching trainers, teachers, and educators. Macro presented that volume in a box with a reprint of *Il Coniglietto di Velluto*, which had appeared previously in 2007.

We will examine these editions chronologically from the point of view of translating strategies. A translator working on children's books will either adapt their translation to the linguistic and cultural norms of the target reader (*domestication*), or maintain some foreign, different, exotic elements from the original work (*foreignization*). Thus, the translator will opt for an interpretation of the original work by establishing a dialogue with it, engaging in a kind of conversation involving both adults and children. There are two theoretical approaches at the heart of these two ways of approaching translations. The proponent of the first modality (domestication) is the Finnish literary critic Riitta Oittinen, who developed the method of adapting the culturally specific givens of the source culture—food, proper names, furnishings, flora, fauna—to the target culture. Oittinen suggests that children (taking into account their limited understanding of the world) should not be exposed to aspects of a foreign culture that they are not capable of understanding. The second modality (foreignization) is represented by Göte Klingberg, who theorizes in favor of preserving in the translated text the culturally specific givens of the original—those of food and drink, for example. This theory emphasizes the idea of a child's capacity to absorb stimuli coming from another culture, thanks to which they can later widen their awareness of the world.

In simplifying the vocabulary and syntax of the original text, making cuts, and adding familiar names and comments that were not present in the original, some of *The Velveteen Rabbit* editions show how the translation/adaptation of texts for children is influenced also by educational, pedagogical, and editorial forces that can push the translator to modify the original text through domestication. Some other editions analyzed here, on the contrary, do not seem to be part of the new reader's own language and culture as they keep the feeling of "otherness" that comes with reading a book by a writer from another country.

The same process, as we shall see, happens with illustrations. There are some that replicate their originals, keeping foreign cultural data, and others that domesticate them. It is important to note that there are also at times inconsistences between the written text and illustrations. Below we explore the Italian editions in the light of the two translation modalities mentioned above, highlighting peculiarities and differences.

Figure 8.1 Margery Williams, *La storia di Emilio il Coniglio*, adapted by Karen Aspy, translated by Melissa Corbidge, illustrated by Robert Blake, Mondadori, 1987.

La storia di Emilio il Coniglio (1987)

The first edition of *The Velveteen Rabbit* in Italy—appearing sixty years after the original publication—is the translation of Karen Aspy's adaptation (Williams 1985), entitled *The Velveteen Rabbit*, illustrated by Robert Blake. This translation was printed by the prestigious publisher Arnoldo Mondadori in 1987 with the title *La storia di Emilio il Coniglio* (figure 8.1) only two years after its American edition.

This edition is coherent with the Italian agenda of the times, which sought to translate foreign literature, in particular fairy tales complete with illustrations, within a framework aimed at modernizing national children's literature. Among the picture books translated in the eighties, Jean De Brunhoff's *Babar* and Eric G. Hill's *Spot* are quite prominent. *La storia di Emilio il Coniglio* is to be added to these. It is a hardbound cardboard picture book with rounded corners (19×22 cm). It holds a central frame with a furry rabbit inside, which children can extract and play with while they read. It is targeted for children between three and six years of age, as is also made evident by the incipit "Once upon a time," a clear reference to fairy tales, a genre that Italian publishers considered suitable for children mainly in adaptations. The font is round, quite big, and very neat so that primary school children in their first year are able to read it autonomously.

The translation on the whole retains what is foreign, different, or exotic in the source text, respecting cultural differences and suggesting that small children can be exposed to aspects of a foreign culture even if they are not capable of understanding it. For example, the stocking where the Boy finds his gifts is maintained, although Italian children are used to getting presents on Christmas Day under the Christmas tree. They find their presents in the stocking on January sixth, the day of the "Befana."[4] As far as Blake's illustrations are concerned, in this case, too, culture-specific data is preserved. For example, in one illustration, a bag appears filled with old books as well as the rag rabbit, and the books' titles remain in their original English.

It must also be noted, however, that translator Melissa Corbidge and editor Francesca Lazzarato gave the Rabbit a name: Emilio. A widespread name in Italy, it has a double meaning. It derives from the prominent and powerful Aemilii family in ancient Rome, which is thought of as being the progeny of Mamercus who was given the name Aemilius because of his soft speech (αιμυλια λόγου). The name Aemilius may derive from the Greek word *aimylios* (αιμυλιος), meaning "sweet, gentle, persuasive, wily." The name Aemilius may also derive from the Latin verb *aemulor*, which means "to rival, to endeavor to equal or to excel one, to emulate."[5] The Velveteen Rabbit is doubtlessly gentle and well-mannered and also shows his will to emulate the Skin Horse and to become Real. Choosing the name Emilio for the Rabbit therefore seems appropriate. One should add that this name is also harking back to Jean-Jacques Rousseau's *Émile, ou de l'éducation* (Emile, or On Education, 1762). The Italian choice to give a name to the Rabbit accords with the editorial policies at the time because successful picture books translated into Italian (such as *Spot* and *Babar*) demonstrated that individualizing the animal with a name induces a greater empathy between the protagonist and the child reader.

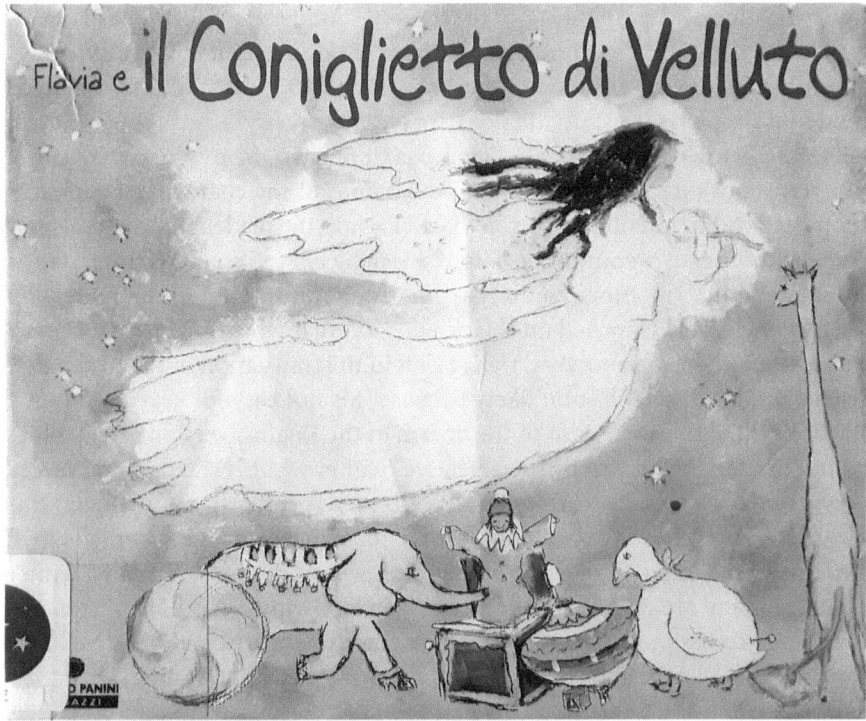

Figure 8.2 Flavia Weedn and Lisa Weedn, *Flavia e il Coniglietto di Velluto*, translated by Auretta Atzeni, illustrated by F. Weedn and L. Weedn, Malipiero, 1991.

Flavia e il Coniglietto di Velluto (1991)

A rewriting of *The Velveteen Rabbit* in which the Boy becomes a girl named Flavia—illustrated by F. Weedn and L. Weedn, edited by Applause Inc., and entitled *Flavia and the Velveteen Rabbit*—appeared in America in 1990. This adaptation was published in Italy with the title *Flavia e il Coniglietto di Velluto* by Malipiero (a small publishing house) in 1991 and then reprinted by Panini (a publisher devoted only to children's literature) in 1999. The translation is by Auretta Atzeni (figure 8.2). The illustrations replicate the originals. This picture book comprises forty-eight pages and comes in a large format (24×26 cm) for children aged six onwards. It is consistent with what appeared in Italy from many publishing companies in those days, all focused on fairy tales as suitable reading to induce young readers (especially girls) to draw valid suggestions for their growth from these stories.

Between the original version of *Flavia and the Velveteen Rabbit* and the Italian version, there are affinities and differences. The written text presents some domestication and simplification: the Rabbit is "under the adorned Christmas tree," as in the Italian tradition, rather than "inside a bright colored stocking" (Weedn and Weedn, *Flavia and the Velveteen Rabbit*). "Childhood magic" is rendered simply as "l'evento magico" (magic event; Weedn and Weedn, *Flavia e il Coniglietto di Velluto* 5) or as "qualcosa di magico" (something magic; 18). The translator's decision of changing the names of the characters is possibly motivated by her intention to bring them closer to the reader and create a sympathetic feeling, so Mammo (the name chosen by Flavia Weedn) is translated as "Mammanonna" (mommy-nanny; passim), and more intriguing, the expression "Magic uncle Jack" is turned into "Jack, suo zio, era un mago" (Uncle Jack was a magician; 12). Furthermore, no trace is left in the translation of the ocean that Flavia dreams of seeing soon likely because it is not easy for sea-surrounded Italians to imagine the width of the ocean. In the English version, the Rabbit's white fur is characterized by the adjective "winter white" (Weedn and Weedn, *Flavia and the Velveteen Rabbit*), which calls for a specific idea of a snowy winter. The Italian "bianco candido" (Weedn and Weedn, *Flavia e il Coniglietto di Velluto* 42) meaning "very white" or "whitest white," does not refer to a winter white as many areas in Italy don't have a snowy winter. Also of importance are some expressions open to the reader's emotional participation: "She knew for certain" (Weedn and Weedn, *Flavia and the Velveteen Rabbit*), referring to Flavia when she recognized the real rabbit as her own Velveteen Rabbit, is translated as "fu quasi sicura" (she was nearly sure; Weedn and Weedn, *Flavia e il Coniglietto di Velluto* 42). Another simplification is that the sentence "it's not always the understanding of life that's really important" (Weedn and Weedn, *Flavia and the Velveteen Rabbit*) is missing, and only "quello che è importante è credere nella meraviglia della vita" (what's really important is believing in the wonder of life; Weedn and Weedn, *Flavia e il Coniglietto di Velluto* 46) is kept in the translation.

As far as the illustrations are concerned, they replicate their originals and keep foreign cultural data: namely, the word "toys" appears on the game box, and the girl sits in the armchair and holds a book titled *The Story of Fairy*. However, while the cover in the original version presents the Rabbit as centered in the middle of the page—his ears are low as if to indicate sadness—Malipiero's cover, conversely, prefers presenting the Fairy holding the Rabbit in her arms as they fly out, past some other toys. This editorial decision emphasizes the magical element to the story and its status as a fairy tale. Another difference regarding the book cover concerns the title itself. While in the American edition "Flavia" and "Velveteen Rabbit" share the same font and graphic rendering, in the Italian edition, "Coniglietto di Velluto" stands out in comparison as its font is much bigger than "Flavia"—possibly to point out that the Rabbit is more pertinent to the story than the girl.

Figure 8.3 Margery Williams, *Il Coniglietto di Velluto*, adapted by Cosimo Baldari and Sandro Mazzari, illustrated by Renata Giannelli, Panini, 1993.

Il Coniglietto di Velluto (1993)

In 1993, *Il Coniglietto di Velluto* was published by Panini in Italy as an adaptation by Cosimo Baldari and Sandro Mazzari, illustrated by Renata Giannelli (figure 8.3). The picture book is quite small (12×16 cm), with a hardbound cover and thirty-two glossy pages designed for a five- or six-year-old reader with well-spaced text and rounded font. Williams's original story is rewritten quite freely, showing a domestication of the original culture, even though some important moments are maintained: the Velveteen Rabbit's lengthy chat with the Skin Horse, his encounter with real rabbits, and a final meeting with the child. In this version, there is a gender transformation, which apparently hints at the translation of *Flavia e il Coniglietto di Velluto* (1991). As in that American version, here too the Boy is a girl. Her name is Elisa, a popular name in Italy just as Eliza, short for Elizabeth, the Queen's name, is in England. Publishers preferred a girl as their protagonist given awareness that statistics for reading targets in terms of age and gender showed higher results for girls, who acquire better literacy, reading comprehension, and ability for concentration. They do not abandon reading and are more inclined to fairy tales (Liverani). It is not by chance that the china dog, which the Boy takes with him to sleep in Williams's version, is turned here into a rag doll (as in *Flavia e il Coniglietto di Velluto*).

There are more passages from this adaptation that seemingly echo *Flavia e il Coniglietto di Velluto*. Elisa is not an only child like the Boy; she plays with a younger brother and several friends. Furthermore, she comes down with a fever but not with scarlet fever, and her grandmother works, just like Nana. When the Rabbit ends up in a bag with old toys to go to the junk dealer, it is because the grandmother, as in *Flavia e il Coniglietto di Velluto*, decides he is too worn-out. At the end, Elisa understands her rag Rabbit has turned into a real one: "[L]o salutò da lontano e fu allora che entrambi capirono che se ami qualcuno, e lo ami davvero, quell'amore non finirà mai!" (She said hello from a distance, and at that point, both understood that if you love somebody and you love them truly, love will never end!; Williams 1993, 30). The message is clear: as we can read also on the book's sleeve, "this is a sweet fairytale . . . about love and friendship" (front matter).

The illustrations that accompany the text are particularly original in that the illustrator applies bits of lace and frills so as to create a real collage in a bright, lightly girlish style, projecting happiness and serenity. On the foreground of the cover, the reader can perceive a smiling *coniglietto* among the other toys, next to a Skin Horse—which is translated in the text as "rag horse," just like in the Mondadori edition, and at the back, there is a Christmas tree. There is no stocking with presents, but as the text also recites, "It was Christmas day and there was a Velveteen Rabbit under the Christmas tree" (1). Not one, but two illustrations show a drawing of the Rabbit with his hind legs and not in a seated position. This choice symbolizes the necessity to edit out the Rabbit's sense of frustration at not being able to jump like real rabbits. We also want to point out an inconsistency between the text and its illustrations: in one illustration, the girl is portrayed as a toddler of about three with a pacifier, even as she chats with her Nanny as though she were five or six years old.

These first editorial projects demonstrate the national interest in publishing fairy-tale stories to address the preference of young readers (five to eight years old) for this genre, confirmed by the great number of copies sold.

Il Coniglietto di Velluto (2007)

Between the nineties and the first decade of the third millennium in Italy, new topics within children's literature—connected with new family styles, disability awareness, diffused pathologies, immigration, and integration—were represented in a wide range of publications, all of educational and social relevance. At the same time, publishing companies continued to focus on fairy tales. This period bears witness to a true proliferation of more or less traditional fairy tales, some of which were rewritten with humor or by following Rodari's techniques, which, according to his creative suggestions, overturn roles to create a mix of tales, and some fairy tales were even rewritten within a feminist framework. Wishing to focus on Williams's tale as a specific case, one can note that while by 2007 a number of adaptations and abridgments had appeared, we can consider 2007 a *terminus-post-quem* year, when the first unabridged translation of *The Velveteen Rabbit* appeared in Italy. This appearance was a consequence both of the expiration of the copyright and of the changes as regards the fairy-tale canon.

In this connection, it seems necessary to recall that, before 1980, only a few pioneering theoretical studies had centered on the fairy tale. Among these are Vladimir Propp's *Morphology of the Folktale* (1928), translated into Italian in 1949 and in 1966; and Max Lüthi's *The European Folktale: Form and Nature* (1947), translated in 1972 and in 1992. The fairy tale was a marginalized genre at best until the mid-1970s and early 1980s when a change of attitude toward the fairy tale can be perceived among scholars and critics—and, with it, an ampler and more diverse approach resulting in a better perception and reception of the fairy tale among the public.

Throughout the years, several essays on fairy tales in North America and in Europe were published as well-known international scholars aimed at a reevaluation of the genre. Previously "relegated to children's rooms," to quote J. R. R. Tolkien (195),[6] fairy tales are now being studied through a range of cross-disciplinary approaches. Scholars and educators have become more aware of the in-depth meaning of this literary genre as they also point out that "the true meaning and impact of a fairy-tale can be appreciated by children, its enchantment can be experienced by them, only from the story in its original form" (Bettelheim 19). This argument attempts to dissuade people from considering fairy tales as "particularly" associated with children—and not to utilize them in an abridged and sweetened form.

Dieter Richter, in his book *La luce azzurra* (1995), considers fairy tales the most appropriate literary form shared by children and adults. Bruno Bettelheim, an educator and therapist of children with emotional and behavioral disorders, shows in his book *The Uses of Enchantment: The Meaning and Importance of Fairy Tales* (1976)—translated into Italian for the first time in 1977, reaching its sixteenth edition in 1997—how fairy tales are very valuable in restoring meaning to children's lives. They take very seriously their own existential anxieties and dilemmas, such as the need to be loved or the fear that one is thought worthless. While the stories entertain the child, they enlighten her/him about her/himself and foster her/his personality development, offering solutions. Jack Zipes, in a number of essays,[7] examines fairy tales that are brought about by a range of adaptations, rewritings, and reinvention of other texts as a portion of the complicated process of civilization that children and adults alike are part of in the Western world. In this context of intense cultural debate about fairy tales—to which several Italian scholars also contributed—and as a consequence of the social relevance of educational publications of fairy tales, Macro, a minor publisher, decided to publish the first integral translation of Williams's *The Velveteen Rabbit* in 2007. The translation is entitled *Il Coniglietto di Velluto* (with no reference in the translated title to the original subtitle *How Toys Become Real*). The original 1922 illustrations by William Nicholson (figure 8.4) are kept, so the reader first meets the Rabbit hanging in the stocking adorned with holly. The translation is by Silvia Nerini. In contrast with the original edition, which counted fifty-six pages, this Italian translation is ninety-four-pages long and hardbound with a 14.5×19.5, trim size. Each page is framed with silver flowery patterns in Liberty style (the Italian variant of Art Nouveau), and each section begins with an embossed sepia letter. The text is written in large, rounded font: it can be read by children aged seven and above, but the graphic elements seem too elegant and serious for such a target.

The volume also includes an excerpt from *The Velveteen Principles*, and in brackets at the bottom of the last page, the reader is informed that an Italian translation of the whole volume is being published shortly by Macro. In this excerpt, the author contributes an interpretation of *The Velveteen Rabbit* and talks to educators and therapists, pointing out how much the wisdom she found in the story informed her ideals—or shall we say her principles—and how it gave her life and her work as a psychotherapist a new direction. She claims that, through reading *The Velveteen Rabbit*, we learn that we all have a place in this world and that we deserve love and respect, that our true value has nothing to do with the way we look, and that, indeed, this is a story for children, but it is also meant for whoever has an open mind and a receptive heart. Some notes on Williams's life are abridged in the appendix of this version. It is also notable that the illustrations do not represent any human character, not even the Boy, because attention in the text is focused on the world of toys. This translation specifically

Figure 8.4 Margery Williams, *Il Coniglietto di Velluto*, translated by Silvia Nerini, illustrated by William Nicholson, Macro, 2007.

states that the text has two different goals. It aims to facilitate reading and help readers' reflections on an in-depth meaning of what the Velveteen Rabbit is being told and what he says.

The translation overall adheres to the English text, but there are some cases where cultural data is adapted from the original text and some elements are added from the target culture. For example, the line "when the Boy was called away suddenly to go out to *tea*" (Williams 1922, 7, emphasis added throughout paragraph) is translated as "quando il Bambino fu chiamato improvvisamente per la *merenda*" (Williams 2007, 39). Further on, the sentence "the Boy liked to go there after *tea* to play" (Williams 1922, 8) is translated as "il Bambino ci andava volentieri a giocare dopo *cena*" (Williams 2007, 44). The foreign cultural datum here is *tea*, which is alternatively being translated as *merenda* (snack) or *cena* (dinner). Another case of adaptation concerns the translation of "nursery magic," which becomes in Italian "la Magia dei giocattoli" (the magic of toys; Williams 2007, 43). In the English text, the emphasis is on magic as pertaining to the magic of childhood; in the Italian version, the translator stresses the "magic of toys" because she looks at toys as a representation of childhood. Another point of interest is how Williams uses different names for the Velveteen Rabbit. She names the rabbit as just "Rabbit" or "the Velveteen Rabbit," "Bunny," or even "little Rabbit." We assume she intended these appellations to indicate the degree of affection among characters—as between the Rabbit and the Boy: "Why, he looks just like my old Bunny that was lost when I had scarlet fever" (Williams 1922, 19); the narrator and the Rabbit: "The Velveteen Rabbit slept in the Boy's bed" (6); Nana and the Rabbit: "Here, she said, take your old Bunny!" (5); and the Fairy and the Rabbit: "Little Rabbit, don't you know who I am?" (17). The translator simplifies this. She always and only uses the word "*coniglietto*." One more example of adaptation can be seen in the use of the Italian verb "*implorare*" (to beg). When the real rabbits run away after the meeting with coniglietto, in the original story we read, "'Come back and play with me!' *called* the little Rabbit" (11). The translator in this case decides to add a rather more dramatic tone to the text when she translates this: "'Tornate qui! Venite a giocare con me!,' *implorò* il Coniglietto" (Please come back here, let's play together! The rabbit *begged*; Williams 2007, 25). Here, perhaps the translator wishes to make it even clearer that the Rabbit feels inferior, shy, and inadequate in his condition; it is interesting to note that the verb *implorare*—to beg—occurs also in *Flavia e il Coniglietto di Velluto*.

Il Coniglietto di Velluto: I Principi del Coniglietto di Velluto (2009)

In 2009, Macro kept to their word and, as they had anticipated in the 2007 edition of *The Velveteen Rabbit*, they reprinted the translation and kept the same formatting and graphic rendering, locating it in a compact, hard box, which also contained the translation of the unabridged edition of Raiten-D'Antonio's essay *I Principi del Coniglietto di Velluto* (figure 8.5). In her introduction, the therapist declares that what rules and principles she offers are based on values represented

Figure 8.5 Toni Raiten-D'Antonio, *I principi del Coniglietto di Velluto*, translated by Silvia Nerini, Macro, 2009.

by Williams's characters. Their objective is to propose a reliable pathway to peacefulness that would lead the readers to accept themselves as they are. This edition marks the real turning point in *The Velveteen Rabbit*'s reception in Italy because the story became ever more relevant as an educational instrument, mainly reevaluated in pedagogical terms.

Figure 8.6 *La magia del Natale: Storie sotto la neve*, adapted by Paola Parazzoli, illustrated by Giulia Rossi, Gribaudo, 2017, in which Margery Williams, *Il Coniglietto di Velluto*, can be found.

Il Coniglietto di Velluto (2017)

In 2017, the solidly established publishing house Gribaudo published *Il Coniglietto di Velluto* within a collection entitled *La magia del Natale: Storie sotto la neve* (Christmas Magic: Tales under the Snow; figure 8.6), a hardbound book (15×20 cm) made up of eight stories set at Christmas, with Giulia Rossi's cheerful illustrations in computer graphic format. *Il Coniglietto di Velluto* is the last story and is forty-three pages long, printed in a round and wide font well suited for primary school children. The editing of these texts, as well as the translations, are by Paola Parazzoli.

Overall, the only cultural datum of a foreign nature is the stocking containing presents that the child receives on Christmas Day. The remaining part of the plot is domesticated through and through. Parazzoli simplifies the story and proceeds by subtraction because she does not want hers to be a philological translation— and it is not. Rather, it is an adaptation made of rhythms and language closer to how children speak nowadays. She does edit out some significant portions of the text. For example, sentences that in the original tend to underscore the Rabbit's personality and his thoughtful and reflective character—such as "the little Rabbit lay tangled up among the bedclothes, thinking" and "all sorts of delightful things he planned" (Williams 1922, 13)—are missing from her version. The sentences that present the Rabbit as suffering for his lack of freedom since the child is too possessive with him are missing too. Rossi's illustrations are both adequate and expressive, yet an inconsistency emerges near the end of the translation. In the story we read, "Prese Coniglietto . . . lo posò sull'erba e volò via" (The Fairy took the Rabbit in her arms . . . put him on the grass and flew away; Williams 2017, 217). On the contrary, the illustration shows the Fairy and the Rabbit flying separately from each other. Hence, there is no correspondence between the text and illustration, and the consequence is that the young reader's understanding of the text may be partial since the two narrative levels do not coincide. Nevertheless, Parazzoli correctly notes how "written text and images do not always overlap wholly. . . . There are times when illustrations manage to shift the story, anticipating or postponing it, filling its silence and leaving some space for readers and illustrators to use their imagination."[8]

This volume is a Christmas edition. *Il Coniglietto di Velluto* is considered a long and sweet tale that provides readers with the enchanted mood of Christmas and leaves them with a consoling, good flair. This publication does not reflect what was happening in terms of education and children's rights around Williams's text in the multimedia circle after the 2007 *The Velveteen Rabbit* unabridged translation and the translation of *The Principles* were released.

Multimedia Editions and Web Publications

The publication of *The Velveteen Rabbit* together with the essay by Raiten-D'Antonio in 2007 and 2009 has had a significant impact on educators, therapists, staff-training personnel, and artists. Many have identified some pedagogical qualities in *Il Coniglietto di Velluto*, as well as a very strong stimulus for children—and those with psychophysical difficulties too—to speak about themselves, their dreams, and desires through the mediation of a symbolic-fantastic dimension. The story, they believe, can help heal children psychologically, emotionally, and physically, verifying theoretical claims that fairy tales and their content are not irrelevant as they in fact leave an impression in the receptive developing subject. Teachers and librarians in Italy are now presenting readings from *The Velveteen Rabbit* in classrooms and workshops. Within the context of primary schooling, children are stimulated by the theme of love and relationships and how potentially relevant interpersonal relationships are. In the workshops, the young audience can notice a remarkable correspondence between the Rabbit's and their own wishes for love and their desire for protection and friendship. Several reviews of *Il Coniglietto di Velluto* have appeared on cultural and literary blogs (Ishtar). In a 2014 column entitled *Capire i conflitti, praticare la pace* (Understanding Conflicts, Practicing Peacefulness), one reads that *Il Coniglietto di Velluto* "contains potentialities that are gradually perceived at different levels of reading. They allow the reader to contemplate even the most dramatic of events through the protective filter of storytelling; hence, it is considered an adequate reading tool promoting a peaceful and non-violent culture" (Department of Culture of Vicenza). In 2018, on the occasion of the ninety-fifth anniversary of the Declaration of the Rights of the Child, the journalist Maria D'Amico, glancing through various texts of international literature, added *Il Coniglietto di Velluto* to a list of compelling books for the well-being, protection, and education of children, "books which assume the shape of small bricks paving the way for the road that every child has a right to follow as he or she grows aware of his or her abilities ... feeling free to rejoice in life." D'Amico emphasizes how children reading *Il Coniglietto di Velluto* are taught about the importance of values—embodied by the protagonist—that adults, subjugated by the harshness of reality, have forgotten: solidarity, well-being, honesty of mind, and peace.[9]

Meanwhile, the publishing industry in Italy was faced with a complex competitiveness from the media and entertainment channels. The traditional method of reading a book falters because of this challenge. The market for young adult and children's books gained an enhanced awareness of book-related selling strategies and successfully employed them. New interactive modalities appeared through e-books, apps, and video games, paving the way for a new approach to reading, all of which impacted the reach of *The Velveteen Rabbit*, amply disseminated through various media to target child readers.

In 2009, the translation of the film *The Velveteen Rabbit*[10] was launched on the market, with the title *Il Coniglietto magico* (The Magic Rabbit), underlining the fantastic element of the protagonist. An exhaustive review of the movie reads: "This is one of the most beautiful and relevant movies of these years not simply for teenagers, nor just to promote intellectual and creative development; rather, it provides young readers with an emotional education" (elgatoloco). In 2014,

Sciò, a professional storyteller, developed an app for *Il Coniglietto di Velluto* that brings together illustrations and narration, reminiscent of fairy tales of yore but presented through touch-screen technology.[11] The app stimulates readers' understanding that love can give intense moments of joy and sweetness if only you declare your most secret wishes.

The theater world also paid attention to *The Velveteen Rabbit*. Already in 2004 to 2005, an emotional and poetic performance by the Stabile Theater (in Grosseto, Tuscany) was choreographed with the technique of acting theater,[12] offering reflections about a desire for consumerism, on the one hand, and dismissed, worn-out toys, never-fading evergreens, keeping their original role as a child's trustworthy friends, on the other. A 2010 performance in Florence was based on the educational project carried out by the internationally renowned Meyer Hospital. In an interview, production director David Ballerini comments: "*Il Coniglietto di Velluto* (2007) is a rebirth story and therefore we thought it would be perfect for a performance sponsored by the Meyer foundation . . . as it aimed at suggesting good practices for well-being; among them being mind-stimulating techniques achieved by getting children to read and listen to adequately selected texts in order to help them develop both physically and psychologically" (Rifelli 17–19). At the Teatro Barbieri in Vercelli (Piedmont) in 2016, a performance presented by Perdincibacco Aiutiamoci Onlus, entitled *Io sono vero . . . perdincibacco!* (I Am Real . . . Good Gracious!), shows disabled actors and volunteers setting up the stage, demonstrating how functional research allows improved communication (social, cognitive, and creative) and stimulates the unlimited expressiveness of children.

Affinities and Differences between *Le avventure di Pinocchio*, *The Velveteen Rabbit*, and *La freccia azzurra*

This chapter closes with a reflection on the similarities and differences between *The Velveteen Rabbit* and *Le avventure di Pinocchio* (figure 8.7) by Collodi as well as *La freccia azzurra* (figure 8.8) by Rodari. Indeed, the prospect that Williams might have read Collodi's novel in the English translation (1892) or in Italian before she wrote her story or that Rodari read *The Velveteen Rabbit*, before he wrote *La freccia azzurra*, is very evocative; however, there is no certainty in such consideration. In Williams's case, although there is no confirmation of her specific readings in her biography, we know by way of Laurel Davis Huber that she was very well-read and could speak French and Italian.[13] She had married Francesco Bianco, an Italian, in 1904, and had lived in Italy for a time, so her family spoke Italian at home. Many of her works for children have protagonists that start out as toys and then become animated, and in *Poor Cecco* (1925), the wooden character, Jensina, reminds us of Pinocchio. In Rodari's case, we know,

Figure 8.7 Carlo Collodi, *Le avventure di Pinocchio*, illustrated by Enrico Mazzanti, originally published by Felice Paggi Libraio-Editore, 1883.

Figure 8.8 Gianni Rodari, *La freccia azzurra*, illustrated by Simona Mulazzani, Editori Riuniti, 2003, originally illustrated by Maria Enrica Agostinelli, 1964.

by way of Ermanno Detti, his coworker for years, that the writer was moved by an omnivorous curiosity and possessed a bright, fervid intelligence. In order to read the classics pertaining to Anglo-Saxon young adult and children's literature, he taught himself English. It seems possible, therefore, that he may have read Williams's story.[14]

Both *Le avventure di Pinocchio* and *The Velveteen Rabbit* suggest an identification of children with nonhuman characters, sharing with toys an inferior condition and one of vulnerability. Both works have been read as bildungsromans with fairy-tale traits, and one of these is metamorphosis. As Lois Rostow Kuznets notes, both Pinocchio and the Rabbit show us "a young male at a level of human development where physical and emotional instability test his sense of being or becoming *real*; together they can constitute a survey of key points in the process called growing up" (60, emphasis original). To reinforce the concept of affinity between *Le avventure di Pinocchio* and *The Velveteen Rabbit*, we would like to single out some passages. For example, when Pinocchio is hanged from a branch of the Great Oak, alone while death is approaching, his thoughts turn to his poor father. Like Pinocchio, the Rabbit has a brush with death. When the Rabbit ends up in a bag ready to be burned, he is also alone. He thinks of the good times with the child and of his chats with the Skin Horse. In both cases, a fairy appears to save the protagonist, and then, by magic, the fairy also makes their final transformation possible. Another similarity occurs with bullying. It happens to Pinocchio at school with real boys: "You can imagine those schoolboy scamps when they saw a puppet walk into their schoolroom! There was such a roar of laughter that went on and on" (Collodi, *The Adventures* 93). When the Velveteen Rabbit meets real rabbits, he is laughed at: "He hasn't got any hind legs! He doesn't smell right.... He isn't a rabbit at all! He isn't real" (Williams 1922, 11). In *Pinocchio*, the puppet has contradictory feelings: on the one hand, he knows he has to go to school, but on the other hand, he lets himself be taken to the puppet show. He wants to be "a good boy," but he is attracted by life off the road. The Rabbit shares similar contradictory emotions: "he longs both to remain with the Boy and to go with the wild rabbits" (Kuznets 62). We could continue, but we shall not look any further for references as *Pinocchio* is well known to speakers of English too, and it is evident to most that many more such references may be found just by scrolling through the book.

La freccia azzurra (translated as *The Befana's Toyshop: A Twelfth Night Tale*, 1970), which is not well known to English-language readers, also contains echoes of Williams's story. Its major characters are toys, like the Velveteen Rabbit: the yellow bear, the dolls, a blue train, marionettes, a small rag dog, and others. These toys, all crowded inside a shop run by a human toy seller, the "Befana," are not simply alive and animated. They are characterized by ambitions and personalities that become more and more perceivable and concrete as the narrative proceeds. Moved by the boy, Francesco, who gazes at the blue train (the title [English: The

Blue Arrow] being a metaphoric rendering of the blue train) with longing eyes through the shop's glass window, they revolt against the Befana and decide to give toys to poor children. A rag dog named Spicciola sets them out on their journey—a series of episodic adventures that constitute *La freccia azzurra*. Spicciola exhorts the other toys to give Francesco the blue train and declares that, with his sense of smell, he will take them to Francesco. His love for Francesco will allow him to overcome all obstacles in his path and to get back to him. This love will turn him into a real dog.

Spicciola, it seems to us, echoes the Velveteen Rabbit through a range of differences and similarities, all the way through the metamorphic final process. Both the Rabbit and Spicciola are shy, and no one at the beginning is particularly looking after either of them, so they feel as though they are wholly insignificant and banal: "The little Rabbit lay tangled up among the bedclothes, thinking . . ." (Williams 1922, 39). Like him, Spicciola is capable of thinking, as another toy called Penna D'Argento rightly points out: "Cane avere parlato sempre poco e pensato molto" (The rag dog doesn't speak much but thinks a lot; Rodari 27). Both protagonists have a dream: they want to become real beings. The Rabbit "would have done anything in the world to be able to jump here and there like real rabbits" (Williams 1922, 34). Spicciola says, "Ah, quanto darei per riuscire a cacciar fuori un bel latrato" (Ah, what would I do if I could manage a real bark?; Rodari 46).

The Velveteen Rabbit—a comfort toy for the Boy and thus the *transitional object* as analyzed by D. W. Winnicott (1–25)—is transformed twice. The first transformation happens when he is no longer beautiful as he has been worn out by the kisses and tight hugs of the child. The second transformation takes place when the Fairy turns him into a real rabbit. After the Velveteen Rabbit meets with the Fairy, he acquires hind legs and "the joy of using those hind legs was so great that he went springing about the turf on them" (Williams 1922, 51). Differently from the Velveteen Rabbit, Spicciola does not benefit from a fairy's magical help. However, he is nonetheless transformed thanks to his love for the boy. When he finally reaches Francesco, he discovers he can bark: "Per la prima volta nella sua vita Spicciola si sentì uscire dalla gola un suono strano forte e vigoroso . . . abbaiava con tutte le sue forze" (For the first time he felt a strange sound come out of his throat, strong and vigorous . . . he barked with all his might; Rodari 141) and, by doing so, demonstrated his joy of being in the world.

The Velveteen Rabbit becomes a real rabbit, "at home with the other rabbits" (Williams 1922, 51). Spicciola becomes a real dog: "Un cuore vero batteva, nel punto giusto, entro il suo corpo vibrante" (A real heart was beating, in the right place, in his vibrant body; Rodari 141). His "real heart" immediately reminds us of the "little sawdust heart" of the Velveteen Rabbit! The rabbit keeps to his peers and will casually meet the Boy's eyes one last time when his soft nose and round eyes look somewhat familiar to the Boy, "who thought to himself: Why, he looks just like my old Bunny that was lost when I had scarlet fever" (Williams 1922, 51). At the same time, Spicciola, as a real dog, stays with the child, who is no longer attracted by the blue train or any other toy from the Befana's shop, which is where he finally ends up working. He plays only with Spicciola, never leaves him, even sleeps with him, and is helped by him in his job, where "Spicciola imparò a stare ritto sulle zampe posteriori, reggendo con i denti una ciotolina dove i clienti mettevano la mancia per Francesco" (Spicciola learned to be on his hind legs, holding in his mouth a little bowl where the customers used to leave a tip for Francesco; Rodari 145). The child does not recognize in the real dog the rag dog of the Befana's toyshop, but Befana's assistant notes that Francesco's dog "Assomiglia a quel cagnolino che avevamo in vetrina la settimana scorsa ... era più piccolo e non abbaiava" (looks like the one we had for sale last week ... but that was smaller, and it didn't bark; 145).

To conclude, we would like to underline that even if *Le avventure di Pinocchio*, *The Velveteen Rabbit*, and *La freccia azzurra* are all different expressions of how their authors position themselves vis-à-vis fantastic elements, they "are all concerned with metamorphosis, a defining dynamic of certain kinds of stories, myths, fairy stories," what Marina Warner calls "a kind of literature where metamorphosis is often brought about by magical operations" (12). They all adhere to the metamorphic tradition with some violations at the same time. All three present extraordinary transformations: a puppet is turned into an animal and then into a child, a stuffed animal turns into a real rabbit, and a rag dog turns into a real dog. Moreover, the three stories present similar themes. *Pinocchio* sets out to criticize and denounce misery, hunger, ignorance, violence, and abuses on children. Its character becomes a speaker for the rights of children to be themselves, respected as children, and testifies the power of love of a child for the father and vice versa. *La freccia azzurra* belongs to *Pinocchio*'s tradition as it contains a strong denunciation of injustice in the real world, attacking consumerism and its myth, supporting solidarity and peace, and emphasizing the power of love and children's right to see their dreams come true. *The Velveteen Rabbit* lends itself to becoming a sort of "manifesto" for upholding children—including those with disabilities—and their rights, underlining that we all deserve love and respect.

The presence of fairy-tale elements and the similar themes of these three stories show a trend in Italian storytelling, situating *The Velveteen Rabbit* within a history of this type of tale, and this is also partially why *The Velveteen Rabbit* has become so successful in Italy.

Notes

1. See Scott T. Pollard and Kara K. Keeling on the topic of disability in *The Velveteen Rabbit* in chapter 12 of this volume.

2. Gianni Rodari (1920–80) is arguably Italy's most important children's author of the twentieth century. He was awarded the Hans Christian Andersen Award in 1970. In 1973, he published *Grammatica della fantasia: Introduzione all'arte di inventare storie* (The Grammar of Fantasy: An Introduction to the Art of Inventing Stories, 1977), which focuses on the use of imagination, fairy tales, folk tales, children's stories, cognitive development, and compassionate education in creative writing. In 1954, he published *Il viaggio della freccia azzurra* and, in 1964, a revised and a definitive version entitled *La freccia azzurra* (The Blue Arrow). In 1996, the movie director Enzo D'Alò directed *La freccia azzurra*.

All translations from Italian to English in this essay are by the authors.

3. A second integral translation of *The Velveteen Rabbit* was published in November 2022, *Il Coniglietto di Velluto*, translated by Giuditta Campello, Edizioni Emme/Einaudi.

4. The "Befana" is an unmistakably Italian myth. According to the tradition, at night between January fifth and sixth, the Befana flies on her broom to bring all good children gifts.

5. See G. Gemoll (ed.), *Vocabolario greco-italiano*, Sandron, 1983; F. Lübker, *Lessico ragionato dell'antichità classica*, Zanichelli, 1989.

6. This essay, "Sulle fiabe," was first published in *Albero e Foglia* (1976), then reprinted in 2000 and 2003.

7. Books by Zipes available in Italian include *Breaking the Magic Spell: Radical Theories of Folk and Fairy Tales* (1979), translated in 2004; *Fairy Tales and the Art of Subversion* (1983), translated in 2006; *Sticks and Stones* (2001) translated in 2002 and *The Irresistible Fairy Tale: The Cultural and Social History of a Genre* (2012), translated in 2012 and reprinted in 2021.

8. From a personal correspondence with Parazzoli.

9. There are also other interesting pieces of evidence: In May 2018, Azzurra Bergamo wrote that *Il Coniglietto* "is a title worthy of entering the Olympus of children's books," adding, however, that "it risks being forgotten." *Rai Play Sound* reported that Williams's fairy tale will be held among the "never-to-be-forgotten" classics listed in Italian bibliographies for addressing educators in order to facilitate a harmoniously human education.

10. It appeared in the USA, directed by Michael Landon Jr. with the screenplay by Cindy Kelley. The story narrated in the film format is quite different from Williams's text. After his mother's death, the child protagonist, Toby, is left with his very stern paternal grandmother. To make the spectator perceive the two narrative levels of reality and imagination, the director utilizes both live actors and cartoon characters.

11. See also Elena Spadiliero's "Le migliori app dedicate ai bambini."

12. In fact, the director, Alessandro Gatto, chose to substitute the Skin Horse with a robot as well as including a tin puppet because their roles could be filled by real people. In this performance, he gave an amusing interpretation of various episodes of the story, removing the melancholy mood.

13. From a personal correspondence with Huber, Margery Williams's daughter and author of the romance biography *The Velveteen Daughter* (2017).

14. From a personal correspondence with Detti, chief editor of *Il Pepeverde*, a magazine about children's literature. He is also a literary critic and a visual art teacher at the Istituto Europeo di Design in Rome.

Works Cited

Bergamo, Azzurra. "Il Coniglietto di Velluto." *Frammentirivista*, 7 May 2018, https://www.frammentirivista.it/il-coniglietto-di-velluto-di-margery-williams-limportanza-di-essere-veri/. Accessed 12 May 2022.

Bettelheim, Bruno. *The Uses of Enchantment: The Meaning and Importance of Fairy Tales*. Penguin Books, 1976.

Collodi, Carlo. *The Adventures of Pinocchio*. 1892. Translated, introduced, and with notes by Ann Lawson Lucas, Oxford UP, 1996.

Collodi, Carlo. *Le avventure di Pinocchio*. Felice Paggi Editore, 1881–83.

D'Amico, Maria. "Diritti e libertà: I bambini e la letteratura." *CityNow*, 25 Nov. 2018, https://www.citynow.it/diritti-liberta-bambini-la-letteratura/. Accessed 12 May 2022.

De Brunhoff, Jean. *Babar*. Jardin des Modes, 1931.

Department of Culture of Vicenza. "Capire I conflitti: Praticare la pace." *Praticare la pace*, Feb. 2014, www.praticarelapace.altervista.org. Accessed 12 Feb. 2021.

Detti, Ermanno. Personal interview. 4 May 2020.

elgatoloco. "Il Coniglietto magico." *MYmovies*, 6 Jan. 2015, https://www.mymovies.it/film/2009/ilconigliettomagico. Accessed 12 May 2022.

Gatto, Alessandro. "Un Coniglio di Velluto." *Teatro Stabile di Grosseto*, 2004, www.stabilegrosseto.it/coniglio.html. Accessed 12 May 2022.

Hill, Eric G. *Where's Spot?* Frederick Warne & Co., 1980.

Huber, Laurel Davis. Personal correspondence. 10 Mar. 2020.

Il Coniglietto magico [The Magic Rabbit]. Directed by Michael Landon Jr., performances by Jane Seymour, Tom Skerritt, and Ellen Burstyn, Eagle Pictures, 2009.

Ishtar. "Il Coniglietto di Velluto." *Oltrelavergogna*, 30 Aug. 2013, https://oltrelavergogna.wordpress.com/?s=williams. Accessed 12 May 2022.

Klingberg, Göte. *Children's Fiction in the Hands of the Translator*. CWK Gleerup, 1986.

Kuznets, Lois Rostow. *When Toys Come Alive: Narratives of Animation, Metamorphosis, and Development*. Yale UP, 1994.

Liverani, Cristina. "Bambini, adolescenti e valore del libro." *Parlamento Italiano*, 29 Jan. 2008, https://www.parlamento.it/documenti/repository/commissioni/bicamerali/infanzia/290108/290108_bozza_stampa.pdf. Accessed 12 May 2022.

Lüthi, Max. *The European Folktale: Form and Nature*. Indiana UP, 1976.

Oittinen, Riitta. *Translating for Children*. Routledge, 2000.

Parazzoli, Paola. Personal interview. 5 May 2020.

Propp, Vladimir. *Morphology of the Folktale*. U of Texas P, 1958.

Rai Play Sound. "Tutti i libri cacciati in ordine alfabetico QZ," 21 Feb. 2022, www.raiplaysound.it/articoli/2022/02/Tutti-i-libri-cacciati-in-ordine-alfabetico-Q-Z-0c09517c-280f-44e4-9d43-f3450b7fc41e.html. Accessed 12 May 2022.

Raiten-D'Antonio, Toni. *I Principi del Coniglietto di Velluto*. Translated by Silvia Nerini, Macro, 2009.

Raiten-D'Antonio, Toni. *The Velveteen Principles: A Guide to Becoming Real*. Health Communications Inc., 2004.

Richter, Dieter. *La luce azzurra: Saggi sulla fiaba*. Mondadori, 1995.

Rifelli, Alice. "Dalla favola al teatro: *Il Coniglietto di Velluto* va in scena." *Libera il libro*, 6 May 2010, https://issuu.com/macroedizioni/docs/libera_il_libro_3_2010. Accessed 12 May 22.

Rodari, Gianni. *The Befana's Toyshop: A Twelfth Night Tale*. Translated by Patrick Creagh, Littlehampton, 1970.

Rodari, Gianni. *La freccia azzurra*. Editori Riuniti, 1964.
Rodari, Gianni. *The Grammar of Fantasy*. Translated by Jack Zipes, Teachers and Writers Collaborative, 1996.
Rodari, Gianni. *Grammatica della fantasia*. Einaudi, 1973.
Rousseau, Jean-Jacques. *Émile, ou de l'éducation*. Duchesne, 1762.
Sciò, Yvonne. *Il Coniglietto di Velluto*, app, 2014, https://apps.apple.com/it/app/velveteen-rabbit-by-yvonne/id581365215?affId=1507406. Accessed 12 May 2022.
Spadiliero, Elena. "Le migliori app dedicate ai bambini." *Sul Romanzo*, 23 Mar. 2015, https://www.sulromanzo.it/blog/le-migliori-app-dedicate-ai-bambini. Accessed 12 May 2022.
Tolkien, J. R. R. "On Fairy-Stories." *Essays Presented to Charles Williams*, edited by C. S. Lewis, Oxford UP, 1947, pp. 38–89.
Tolkien, J. R. R. "Sulle Fiabe." In *Il Medioevo fantastico*, by J. R. R. Tolkien, Bompiani, 2003, pp. 167–238.
Warner, Marina. *Fantastic Metamorphoses, Other Worlds: Ways of Telling the Self*. Oxford UP, 2002.
Weedn, Flavia, and Lisa Weedn. *Flavia and the Velveteen Rabbit*. Applause Inc., 1990.
Weedn, Flavia, and Lisa Weedn. *Flavia e il Coniglietto di Velluto*. Translated by Auretta Atzeni, Malipiero, 1991.
Williams, Margery. *Poor Cecco*. George Doran, 1925.
Winnicott, D. W. *Playing and Reality*, Routledge, 1989.
Zipes, Jack. *Breaking the Magic Spell: Radical Theories of Folk and Fairy Tales*. UP of Kentucky, 1979.
Zipes, Jack. *Fairy Tales and the Art of Subversion*. Routledge, 1995.
Zipes, Jack. *The Irresistible Fairy Tale: The Cultural and Social History of a Genre*. 2013. Princeton UP, 2021.
Zipes, Jack. *Sticks and Stones*. Routledge, 2001.

Editions of Margery Williams's *The Velveteen Rabbit*

Williams, Margery. 1922. *The Velveteen Rabbit: Or How Toys Become Real*. Illustrated by William Nicholson, Heinemann.
Williams, Margery. 1985. *The Velveteen Rabbit*. Adapted by Karen Aspy, illustrated by Robert Blake, Joshua Morris Publishing.
Williams, Margery. 1987. *La storia di Emilio il Coniglio*. Edited by Francesca Lazzarato, translated by Melissa Corbidge, Arnoldo Mondadori.
Williams, Margery. 1993. *Il Coniglietto di Velluto*. Adapted by Cosimo Baldari and Sandro Mazzari, Panini.
Williams, Margery. 2007. *Il Coniglietto di Velluto*. Translated by Silvia Nerini, Macro.
Williams, Margery. 2009. *Il Coniglietto di Velluto*. Translated by Silvia Nerini, Macro.
Williams, Margery. 2017. *Il Coniglietto di Velluto*. *La magia del Natale: Storie sotto la neve*, edited by Paola Parazzoli, illustrated by Giulia Rossi, Gribaudo, pp. 177–219.

Chapter 9

Boy Caretaking and Authority in a Twenty-First-Century Fairy Tale

—Paige Sammartino

Readers of all ages recognize talking animals, magic, and moral lessons as fairy-tale staples. As readers spot the signals and symbols of these narratives, they adjust their reading patterns and suspend their disbelief accordingly to match the genre of the work. Within the fairy-tale tradition, animals can speak, magic is real, and stories don't need a tremendous amount of setup to proceed. Characters don't need fully fleshed-out histories either as "there is only a minimum of information provided about characters.... At times the characters are not even given names" (Barchers 139). Simplicity in structure belies complexity in thought, however. Fairy tales, and particularly modern fairy tales, are capable of great observation and commentary in their fantastic elements and unnamed characters.

The reimagined fairy tales of the nineteenth century—the sanitized, happily-ever-after revisions most widely known today—have no shortage of female characters who cook, clean, and care their way to marrying a prince or otherwise being blessed or gifted with riches, authority, and happiness. The moral of these stories is clear: putting others' needs first and being selfless proves one worthy and deserving. Fairy tales privilege these female characters, but portrayals of male characters who earn their happy endings via caretaking are far less common. This chapter identifies Margery Williams's *The Velveteen Rabbit* (1922) as a modern fairy tale, with comparative discussion of Antoine de Saint-Exupéry's *The Little Prince* (1943). It examines how a male character disrupts expectations of gender and authority as a child—and, more specifically, as a boy—caretaker.

The Velveteen Rabbit celebrates its centennial while still in print, and a beloved classic proves its longevity; *The Little Prince* met its seventy-fifth anniversary in 2018 as one of the most translated literary works of all time. With their talking animals, hints of magic, and life lessons, both check the structural boxes of the fairy tale. Both emphasize how that which is loved, no matter how small or ordinary, has value and show boy characters who are simultaneously authority figures and caretakers. While *The Velveteen Rabbit* takes the perspective of the object of care, a toy who transforms into a real rabbit, *The Little Prince* reflects many of the same narrative themes and concerns from the perspective of the child caretaker. Each narrative plays with conventions of fairy tales, balancing traditional values with nontraditional gender roles and coding.

The Velveteen Rabbit and his Boy largely play in the gardens and woods beyond the playroom, and it is in this natural space where the Boy imagines his stuffed animal into Realness. The little prince cleans and cares for his asteroid, in particular a lone rose who boasts of her thorns but requires his aid for water and protection from storms. Williams and Saint-Exupéry both portray nature as, generally, a safe or suitable space for children. The tiny volcanoes on Asteroid B-612 "were convenient for warming his breakfast" and present no threat to the little prince's home; potential eruptions from the one dormant and two active volcanoes are as easily managed by the prince as caring for a small garden (Saint-Exupéry 105). The Boy runs about in the woods behind his home on "long June evenings" and hides in the trees with no one but "Bunny" to watch him, indicating little reason for an adult guardian to be concerned (Williams 21). The wood where the Boy takes the Rabbit is a place of play, and the prince's asteroid is a place of work and rest.

As Lisa Lebduska notes, "Nonhuman nature has always played a significant role in children's literature, particularly as a device for conveying social and political goals" (170). The inclusion of a flower and a toy-rabbit-turned-real rabbit as the objects of child caretaking does not complete the reversal of the child and adult roles. The Boy still reports to parents, a nanny, and a doctor, while the little prince depends on the pilot's care in the desert. Yet these boys are shown to have authoritative qualities, which the Rabbit and rose recognize. In placing children in charge, Williams and Saint-Exupéry dilute adult power. What these children do with authority contradicts the expected actions adults might take, and thus the Boy and the Little Prince convey their authors' viewpoints on what an adult authority figure should do or how they should behave.

The Velveteen Rabbit exhibits value in hierarchical stages: toy, Real toy, and living creature. The transition from toy to rabbit requires an interstage in which a child loves the toy into candidacy for animation. Prior to achieving the fantastic, the Rabbit must prove himself exemplary; he "quests" for his Realness much in the tradition of myths and legends (Blackford 80). He must grow and change to earn his transformation. Following in the tradition of animal characters in folk and fairy tales, toys like the Rabbit "stand for children when they embark on journeys to understand their relationship to their creators and develop their own sense of consciousness and agency" (Blackford 76). How he proves himself worthy of Realness adheres to fairy-tale parameters: through love.

Initially, the Velveteen Rabbit doesn't quite differentiate between living creature and toy, though he is aware that he is not a as nicely made toy as others in the nursery. In fact, "he didn't know that real rabbits existed; he thought they were all stuffed with sawdust like himself, and he understood that sawdust was quite out-of-date and should never be mentioned in modern circles" (Williams 4). He shyly compares himself to others with nascent self-awareness. The author's "anthropomorphic portrayal of the toy rabbit" thus "dramatizes the experience of a subject grappling with its own sense of itself—grappling with the question of what it is" (Jacobson 8). This developing sense of self is analogous to that of a child, so that the Rabbit is repositioned as the child-coded character of the story, while the Boy—"whose love endows [the Rabbit] with life"—is thus coded as a parent figure (Daniels 21). The Boy's treatment of the Rabbit and the importance it receives in the Rabbit's narration support this reading of coded agency and authority.

Saint-Exupéry empowers the child character more explicitly, in rank and title. The little prince is royal, positioning him over the pilot although the latter is an adult. Even in instances of which the prince is outranked, such as when he travels to the planet of the king, his childlike sensibilities give him an advantage. He is wiser than the many adults he meets across the universe, seeing through societal expectations and titles and questioning, as many times as necessary, why things are the way they are. The prince cares for his rose and dormant volcanoes, tending to their needs, while for himself only engaging in the humble hobby of watching sunsets. On Earth, the prince engages with sentient animals and plants as equals.

The boys' care for beings smaller than they, which might warrant a critical comparison to the perception of nature(/female) as smaller or more helpless than humans(/male) but for the subversion of their forms of caretaking. Neither of their alleged positions of power over flora or fauna demonstrate their domination. Rather, both boys invoke reciprocal relationships with the objects of their care. The role reversal in these stories of boy characters who act as caregivers rejects the binary that places adults above children (in terms of authority, capability, and responsibility) as well as the binary that equates gender and task, as caretaking in the domestic sense is frequently a female-coded action.

The Boy's relationship does not follow a strict binary in which he exclusively provides and the Rabbit is provided for. As a toy, the Rabbit is "vulnerable to the manipulations of others" and depends on the Boy to carry him and decide the action of their play, much as a child is subject to the care and schedule of their parent (Blackford 79). The Rabbit is unable to rebel or disobey the Boy's will as a stuffed animal, but at no point does he feel the need to resist accompanying the Boy. He is happy, and even in the Boy's illness, the Rabbit would prefer to stay in his bed, hidden under the covers, rather than leave his side. The child-coded Velveteen Rabbit earns his Realness; the Boy loves him, but the Rabbit also loves the Boy and cares for him as best a toy can.

The Boy's love bestows Realness, which is why he possesses comparable authority and transformative power in the narrative to the adult characters. The two most prominent adults are the Boy's nanny and doctor. The nanny often seems powerless and even silly in her alleged role of authority, going out to fetch the forgotten Rabbit after the Boy has gone to bed. The doctor, "a figure of peremptory authority," threatens the Rabbit in his demand that the toy be burned after the Boy's illness and lacks the warmth and comfort that the Rabbit displays by staying close to the Boy's side in his illness (Daniels 19). Barking orders without tenderness distracts from the doctor's professional role as a caretaker after pages of evidence of the Boy's gentler care of his Rabbit. Indeed, with the reader's insight into the Velveteen Rabbit's perspective, the actions of the adult characters, who do not see him as Real, separate those characters from the magic and lesson of the tale.

Williams creates an inversion in her characterization of the child and adult characters, highlighting the Boy's role as caretaker and position of authority versus the "imperfect" adult characters of children's books whose grown-up logic can't comprehend the magic that propels the story forward (Christensen 236). The little prince also exhibits parental qualities and frets often for his rose back on his home asteroid. As the narrative progresses, the story's narrator shares that concern. Even after the prince departs, what happens to the rose "is still of great consequence to [the pilot], because it is of great consequence to the little boy he has come to love" (Higgins 56–57). In *The Little Prince*, the adult character (and narrator) is more present to the reader, but his priorities and concerns revolve around the prince. The combination of placing the child in a position of authority while also relaying a child-centric narrative from the perspective of a nonchild character complicates our reading of both the Boy and the little prince.

Fairy tales often focus on select qualities or qualifiers in their characters, such as characters being identified by a title instead of a name. Yet even as these stories follow that structure, they subvert expectations. The Boy and the prince are simultaneously adult-coded authority figures and caretakers as well as child-coded dependents, and they are male-coded by name ("boy," "prince") but female-coded by action (the domestic tasks of fashioning a nest for a doll, sweeping dust, and watering plants). This binary-breaking characterization modernizes the fairy tales and questions what an authority figure looks like, what authority itself looks like, and how characters demonstrate authority.

The prince's view of his asteroid is certainly that of a home, and though he titles himself a prince, he positions himself as a homemaker and caretaker. Most of all, he is a steward, tending to his rose and raking out his little volcanoes, two active and one dormant (though he cares for all three, just in case). His title does not place him above his subjects but in a servile state in which he must tend to the needs of others. There is reciprocity in the prince's authority as well as he gains satisfaction from his work and enjoys how the rose perfumes his planet. The pilot marvels at the prince's dedication to his duties in caring for his asteroid, and the narration encourages the reader to do so as well. The prince himself considers this attention to be the duty of a royal and takes his responsibilities very seriously, and he is surprised to encounter adults who think that his royal role might situate him away from caretaking.

The importance of a child's undivided attention is equally pivotal to *The Velveteen Rabbit*. The Skin Horse, a toy that once belonged to the Boy's uncle, introduces the concept of a third state of being between a toy and a living creature: Realness. "'Real isn't how you are made,' said the Skin Horse. 'It's a thing that happens to you. When a child loves you for a long, long time, not just to play with, but REALLY loves you, then you become Real" (Williams 7). The Realness that the Skin Horse explains is not the full magical transformation that the Rabbit eventually undergoes, but rather a selective transformation in which a toy is so beloved that it possesses unique status and significance to its child owner. A toy that becomes Real is still a toy, as the Skin Horse is, but a child's love elevates it to a mezzanine state—like a half floor in between the ground (toy) floor and upper (Real) levels. It is precious compared to other toys; though not alive in all eyes, it is a toy in transition.

There is a performative aspect to Realness and the act of becoming Real. As the Skin Horse explains, "It doesn't happen all at once. . . . You become. It takes a long time" (7). By the Skin Horse's definition, Realness is an act of becoming that is the result of a meaningful relationship, as it was the Boy's uncle whose love made the Skin Horse Real. He also notes the difficulty that can go into this transformative process: "Generally, by the time you are Real, most of your hair has been loved off, and your eyes drop out and you get loose in the joints and very shabby. But these things don't matter at all, because once you are Real you can't be ugly, except to people who don't understand" (7). Having experienced the transformation of Realness himself lends itself to the Skin Horse's credibility of being "wiser than most of the present toys" (Jacobson 2). The act of becoming Real is the result of a reciprocal relationship between the Boy and the Rabbit. To be Real requires a second party that wills the original party into Realness.

Williams explicitly writes that a child must be part of this transformation and indicates that a child's love is the catalyst of the magic in her tale. Caretaking is action, but care itself is action as well. The transformation from toy to Real toy to Real requires the Boy's participation. He loves the Rabbit, much in the tradition of fairy tales demonstrating good and worthy characters through their caretaking, but the Rabbit is also a toy. The element of play or playacting might undermine the goal of showcasing the Boy's character, but because our "focalizer" is the Rabbit himself, the Boy's care is elevated even higher.

Gendered expectations of the early twentieth century were ingrained in the culture from a very young age. Regarding toys of the time, toy soldiers and dolls "symbolize most clearly the division society marks between girls and boys at play—as well as the gender separation assigned to nurturing and aggressive instincts. Toys thus become ideal tools for societal gender modeling" (Kuznets 16). Girls were introduced to caretaking as a form of play through the toys and games marketed toward them. Toys marketed toward boys were much less housed in the domestic. However, due to the rise in popularity of the teddy bear at the time of *The Velveteen Rabbit*'s publication, a boy in the early twentieth century might "be encouraged to develop his nurturing instincts or express his emotions through such cuddly bears" (Kuznets 17). The Boy's primary interactions with the Rabbit are outdoor play, perhaps more indicative of male-coded toy use at the time of publication. However, the Boy does exhibit consideration for his stuffed companion that perhaps would not have been part of his play with other "boy" toys of his era.

Though being a favored toy at first troubles the Rabbit—the Boy's hugs suffocate him, and he misses talking to the Skin Horse back in the nursery at night once the Boy takes him to bed as a sleeping companion, he soon comes around. The Boy makes "nice tunnels for him under the bedclothes that he said were like the burrows the real rabbits lived in," foreshadowing that the Boy will build the Rabbit's pathway to Realness (Williams 12). This moment also demonstrates playtime thoughtfulness on the Boy's part in that he creates an environment that, to the best of his knowledge, is suitable for rabbits, as opposed to, for example, placing the Rabbit in a toy castle or a boat as part of his play. The Boy's care for his toy is evident, both in the abstract sense of loving the Rabbit and in observable actions, such as making a tunnel for him out of bed sheets.

Williams details nearby woods where the Boy brings the Rabbit for play. While there, the boy "wander[s] off to pick flowers" or hide among the trees, but he makes an effort to fashion "a little nest somewhere among the bracken, where [the Rabbit] would be quite cosy, for he was a kind-hearted little boy and he liked Bunny to be comfortable" (21). In contrast to the action-play of a toy soldier or the explicit cuddling of a teddy bear, the Boy places the Rabbit in another mezzanine position: as passive observer to the boy's outdoor play. He is part of playtime but is neither the object of play (as a toy would be) nor the player (as a real being would be). Williams lists the Boy's activities side by side in a single sentence: picking flowers (girl-coded, passive) and playing cops and robbers (boy-coded, active). So, too, does his interaction with the Rabbit defy gendered coding.

Outside of the nursery, physically beyond the space where child behavior must follow rules or adhere to societal expectations, the Boy may do as *he* chooses and engage in activities pertinent to his interests. The Rabbit serves as his only witness in this play, and the Boy invites him to participate by embedding him into the natural environment where the Boy's imagination rules. In this space, only the Boy and his rabbit exist. As James Higgins observes, for children and child characters, "play is not frivolous escape" (84). Though "Bunny" takes a passive role in this outdoor play, the Boy places him with care and takes time to create a nest as a parent bird does for its eggs. Williams highlights the Boy's conscientious treatment of his stuffed animal to foreshadow his capacity for the transformative magic of a child's love. She details the environment in this scene, showing how the same natural space might lend itself to child activities across the spectrum of gender coding. She establishes a woodsy nest as an appropriate place for the Rabbit to be comfortable. The Boy does not bring a chair for the Rabbit or lay out a picnic blanket; instead, he nestles the Rabbit in the bracken, as a live rabbit would sit.

Admittedly, the Boy is not always so thoughtful, as his "rabbit is sometimes left behind . . . but is then searched for and found because the rabbit matters to the boy and it has become a part of how he does things" (Jacobson 2). Caretaking is a means for the Boy to show how he views his toy as Real, and it contributes to the performance of animation. By extension, caretaking tasks are built into the Boy's play or serve as prerequisites for play, such as his setting up a nest for the Rabbit to sit and watch him. The Rabbit plays his part as well in acting Real and participating in the Boy's games and activities.

Like the Rabbit's experience with the Skin Horse, the little prince too encounters a wise creature that educates him in the manner of recognizing value and Realness. He meets the fox, who encourages the prince to tame him so that they will always be unique to one another, even among other foxes and boys. It is in this way that the prince learns how meaningful his rose is to him, even though it is a common flower on Earth. The fox tells the prince: "Here is my secret. It's quite simple: One sees clearly only with the heart. Anything essential is invisible to the eyes" (Saint-Exupéry 143). Hearkening back to the concept of Realness, the fox helps the child prince to realize his love for his rose. Learning to appreciate the uniqueness of his relationships and the reciprocal nature of care, the prince undergoes a transformative experience of his own.

Reciprocity manifests in the love between the Boy and the Rabbit as well. The Rabbit enjoys spending time with the Boy and playing, particularly in the garden during springtime. Williams writes that "the little Rabbit was very happy—so happy that he never noticed how his beautiful velveteen fur was getting shabbier and shabbier, and his tail becoming unsewn, and all the pink rubbed off his nose where the Boy had kissed him" (Williams 12). The Boy's outdoor play impacts the quality of the toy with which he plays; as the Rabbit is shy to admit in his first moments in the nursery, he is not as well made as the other toys. Yet he is beloved, and the love shows in how he becomes dirty through play and hugs and use.

Even though the Rabbit becomes worn and ragged, to the Boy, "he was always beautiful, and that was all that the little Rabbit cared about" (27). Here, the reader sees the Boy's devotion through the eyes of the object of his care and how that care has impacted the Rabbit. Just as the prince is happy to care for his rose and loves her because of the time they've spent together, so too is the Rabbit unwaveringly devoted to his Boy as they have loved each other uniquely and specially.

Both books deal with potential dangers that threaten the protagonist's loved one. For the prince, many elements may threaten his fragile rose; for the Rabbit, it is illness that threatens his Boy, bringing their outdoor play to an end. As the Boy grows sicker with scarlet fever, the Rabbit remains under his bedsheets, watching and listening, and being very careful not to be discovered for the risk of an adult taking him away from the Boy. Williams writes that "he never stirred, for he was afraid that if they found him someone might take him away, and he knew that the Boy needed him" (27). Though the Rabbit is yet an inanimate toy, he feels a responsibility to stay with the Boy and care for him.

The Rabbit's care, much like his play, is a passive role, one of comfort and support. The text doesn't confirm what it means to the Boy to have the Rabbit nearby—and in his feverish state, he may not realize the Rabbit is with him—but the reader is privy to the Rabbit's determination to care for the Boy in whatever way is possible for him. This scene layers another complexity, in which the child-coded Rabbit acts as a caretaker to his adult-coded child owner. For a character who is both a toy and an animal figure to guard and heal the human child upends the Boy's role of caretaker as a stable position of authority. Instead, in his time of need, it is a small, simple facsimile of nature that cares for him. Much as the narrative puts forth that the Boy's love makes the Rabbit Real, it also implies that the Rabbit's love makes the Boy well.

The final fairy-tale shake-up is, appropriately, the happily-ever-after element. Both stories instead invoke a bittersweetly-ever-after ending. The prince and the pilot are separated, and whether or not the prince is able to return to his rose is left up to the reader's interpretation. The Boy and the Rabbit are separated as well. Long after he's recovered, the Boy sees the Velveteen Rabbit, now real, in the garden and marvels, "Why, he looks just like my old Bunny that was lost when I had scarlet fever!" (38). Though the Boy and his Rabbit no longer live and play together, a humble toy still remains in the Boy's memories and heart, and the Rabbit still watches over him from afar. This moment shows a transformative experience for the Boy as well, into an older and wiser self who looks back on a beloved toy with nostalgic fondness. This is the Boy who has undergone a life-threatening illness and come out a new person in a new chapter of life, just as his Rabbit is embarking on a new chapter of *real* life.

When the Rabbit does achieve animation, it is through the magic of a garden fairy who appears in the story's third act. When introducing him to the other rabbits, the garden fairy says, "I've brought you a new playfellow. . . . You must be very kind to him and teach him all he needs to know in Rabbit-land, for he is going to live with you for ever and ever!" (36). Though he has become a Real ("Real" by all and not just his Boy), living rabbit, these instructions fantasize the Rabbit's transformation. Rabbit-land, anthropomorphic in its very name, alludes to a fairy-tale space beyond the Boy's world, a community of rabbits to which the Rabbit now has access. In addition, the Fairy suggests that the Rabbit may now live forever as a real rabbit. Building off the Skin Horse's implication that a toy made Real lives forever, in a sense, the magical transformation solidifies that immortality.

The ending isn't sad but lacks the tidiness of a traditional happily-ever-after conclusion, leaving the reader with more to parse through when considering the meaning of the story. Perhaps the reader might return to the image of the Boy as a parental figure; the Rabbit has now become real and grown up, moved away from the playroom and into the woods of Rabbit-land, and the Boy too is growing beyond childhood and free play. Yet, though the central relationships of these texts are parted for now—the Boy and his Rabbit, the prince and his rose, the indelible impact they've had on each other and the care they've taken of one another remain.

Works Cited

Barchers, Suzanne. "Beyond Disney: Reading and Writing Traditional and Alternative Fairy Tales." *The Lion and the Unicorn*, vol. 12, no. 2, 1988, pp. 135–50.

Blackford [Humes], Holly. "PC Pinocchios: Parents, Children, and the Metamorphosis Tradition in Science Fiction." *Folklore/Cinema: Popular Film as Vernacular Culture*, edited by Sharon R. Sherman and Mikel J. Koven, Utah State UP, 2007, pp. 74–92.

Christensen, Nina. "Childhood Revisited: On the Relationship between Childhood Studies and Children's Literature." *Children's Literature Association Quarterly*, vol. 28, no. 4, 2003, pp. 230–39.

Daniels, Steven V. "*The Velveteen Rabbit*: A Kleinian Perspective." *Children's Literature*, vol. 18, 1990, pp. 17–30.

Higgins, James E. *The Little Prince: A Reverie of Substance*. Twayne Publishers, 1996.

Jacobson, Kirsten. "Heidegger, Winnicott, and *The Velveteen Rabbit*: Anxiety, Toys, and the Drama of Metaphysics." *Philosophy in Children's Literature*, edited by Peter R. Costello, Lexington Books, 2012, pp. 1–20.

Kuznets, Lois Rostow. *When Toys Come Alive*. Yale UP, 1994.

Lebduska, Lisa. "Rethinking Human Need: Seuss's *The Lorax*." *Children's Literature Association Quarterly*, vol. 19, no. 4, 1994, pp. 170–76.
Saint-Exupéry, Antoine de. *The Little Prince*. 1943. Edited by Alban Cerisier and Delphine Lacroix, translated by Vali Tamm, 75th Anniversary ed., Houghton Mifflin Harcourt, 2018.
Williams, Margery. *The Velveteen Rabbit: Or, How Toys Become Real*. 1922. Illustrated by Donna Green, Smithmark, 1995.

Chapter 10

Born-Again Bunnies: The Velveteen Rabbit, Edward Tulane, and Redemptive Love

—Maleeha Malik, Elisabeth Graves, and Lisa Rowe Fraustino

Kate DiCamillo's 2006 middle-grade novel, *The Miraculous Journey of Edward Tulane*, illustrated by Bagram Ibatoulline, tells the story of a vain and narcissistic china rabbit doll who embarks on a cruise with the girl who loves him, is lost overboard, and then experiences a decades-long journey through several keepers. Many similarities of detail suggest that DiCamillo's rabbit story is a reimagining of *The Velveteen Rabbit* (1922) by Margery Williams. Both are illustrated storybooks that begin with physical descriptions of toy rabbits given to privileged upper-class children as gifts. Both stories contain toys partially made with real animal parts (the Skin Horse and Edward).[1] Most of Edward's body is made of china though, and it is a china dog that the Velveteen Rabbit replaces in the Boy's bed. Children in both stories love their rabbits and consider them real. In fact, both stories build to their climactic turning points through the loss of their children, and thus their love, to illness or death. Both playthings experience physical wear and tear on their way to figurative rebirth, with the Velveteen Rabbit saved from a bonfire and transformed into a biological animal by the nursery magic Fairy and Edward Tulane saved through his resurrection by a doll mender who repairs his shattered head.

However, while an underlying question of both stories remains—"What does it mean to become Real?"—and the answer concerns being loved, DiCamillo provides a more nuanced and child-centric resolution through the developmental growth and change of Edward. Unlike the Velveteen Rabbit, the china rabbit, Edward Tulane, has a proper human moniker, sharing a family name with his girl Abilene as if he is a biological relative. He sits at the dining room table with the Tulanes rather than being *on* the table as rabbit pie, like Peter Rabbit's father.

His ego suffers when Abilene's mother "referred to him as 'it'" and he hates being called "bunny," finding that label "derogatory in the extreme" (DiCamillo 15). Thus, he comes across less as a toy and more as an anthropomorphized stand-in for a human child reader to identify with than his velveteen counterpart, who identifies with living rabbits. Edward cannot feel emotions necessary to connect to others, including empathy and love, and he is as lost spiritually as he is physically when he sinks to the bottom of the ocean. Ultimately, Edward is saved by learning to love, accept loss, and open his broken heart to hope. With multiple biblical allusions woven throughout the text and illustrations, both explicit and subtle, *The Miraculous Journey of Edward Tulane* can thus be read as an allegorical rewrite of *The Velveteen Rabbit* to replace becoming Real through "nursery magic" with the redeeming power of Christian love.

Two Rabbits of Privilege

According to Lois Rostow Kuznets in her 1994 monograph *When Toys Come Alive: Narratives of Animation, Metamorphosis, and Development,* "Class distinctions—often based on the origin of the doll and the material from which it was made—have always been exploited in doll books" (103). The same can be said of other kinds of toys. The Velveteen Rabbit and Edward Tulane begin their respective stories in the homes of privileged children, as evidenced by their expensive toys, the kinds of rooms and furnishings described, the presence of servants, and other class signifiers. The Velveteen Rabbit's Boy gets so many Christmas gifts that after a couple of hours he forgets the "splendid" plush toy from his stocking (Williams 1), and the Rabbit joins a nursery full of modern mechanical toys, a model boat, a wooden lion, and the Skin Horse, among others. But being among them doesn't mean the Rabbit is high-class: "He was naturally shy, and being only made of velveteen, some of the more expensive toys quite snubbed him" (2). They act "superior" and "put on airs" until "the poor little Rabbit was made to feel himself very insignificant and commonplace" (2).

The Boy's snobby toys share the superior attitude of Edward Tulane, a vain, custom-made china rabbit who "felt himself to be an exceptional specimen" (DiCamillo 4). Far from being clothed in humility, he was commissioned from France by Abilene's grandmother for her seventh birthday, complete with "an extraordinary wardrobe" fit for a little lord (5). While the "fat and bunchy" Velveteen Rabbit has a simple construction, with "real thread whiskers, and his ears were lined with pink sateen" (Williams 1), Edward has ears and a tail "made of real rabbit fur" (DiCamillo 3), and his "long and elegant whiskers" also come from a real animal "of uncertain origin" (4). The biological rabbits recognize that the Velveteen Rabbit cannot hop because he is "made all in one piece, like a pincushion" with "no hind legs at all" (Williams 10). In contrast, Edward has four limbs "jointed and joined by wire so that his china elbows and china knees could be bent, giving him much freedom of movement" (DiCamillo 3). Thus, these two rabbits, despite sharing surface similarities in their circumstances as toys belonging to privileged children, actually come from two different social classes, one of humble origins and the other highborn. This difference in character puts the two rabbits on different journeys to the same end of being saved by loving others—something that comes easily to the unpresuming Velveteen Rabbit but that the preening Edward must learn through humiliating trials. As Roni Natov states in an essay on empathy through "imagining the other" in novels by DiCamillo, Edward is "like the classical hero who begins as the son of nobility, and then is cast out so that he must experience what the ordinary person does, without the benefit of his name" (158). To his new owners, he becomes Susanna, Malone, Clyde, and Jangles; while hanging on a pole as a scarecrow, Edward bemoans: "Would the world never tire of calling him by the wrong name?" (117).

Servants enter into the privileged homes and plots of both tales, further highlighting the contrast between the two rabbit characters through how they respond to the help. "There was a person called Nana who ruled the nursery," we are told, and the Velveteen Rabbit is the only plaything who doesn't mind her "tidying up," during which she "went swooping around like a great wind and hustled them away in cupboards," because "wherever he was thrown he came down soft" (Williams 5)—a fitting metaphor for his pliant disposition. After Christmas, the Rabbit is long forgotten in the cupboard until one evening the Boy "couldn't find the china dog that always slept with him," and Nana "dragged the Rabbit out by one ear, and put him into the Boy's arms" (5). That night begins the inseparable relationship that eventually, after some time, leads Nana to say, "You must have your old Bunny! . . . Fancy all that fuss for a toy!" and the Boy to respond: "You mustn't say that. He isn't a toy. He's REAL!" (7). In contrast, Edward doesn't like the condescension of adults toward him or the "derogatory" treatment by the new maid who says, "What's this bunny doing here?" (DiCamillo 15) and proceeds "to shove him in among the dolls on a shelf in Abilene's bedroom," leaving him there "at a most awkward and inhuman angle" after vacuuming him "like every other thing in this house, something needing to be cleaned and dusted" (16). Unlike the Velveteen Rabbit, Edward doesn't come down soft but bristles at being "handled by the maid as cavalierly as an inanimate object" (18). Here we have a china rabbit doll with a grandiose sense of human self-importance, who feels he is owed admiration and entitled to special treatment, yet ironically does not recognize that he already possesses the highest level of respect that most toys never receive: being "real" to a child. From the very beginning of *Edward Tulane*, Abilene "thought almost as highly of Edward as Edward thought of himself" (4), and she treats him like another person, seating him "at the dining-room table with the other members of the family," and "Abilene's parents found it charming that Abilene considered Edward real" (6). Edward's pride leads him to take that for granted.

The Velveteen Rabbit has long wanted to become Real as described by the Skin Horse: "When a child loves you for a long, long time, not just to play with, but REALLY loves you, then you become Real" (Williams 3). The Rabbit's response to the Boy's proclamation "He's REAL!" is an inability to sleep due to happiness as "so much love stirred in his little sawdust heart that it almost burst" (8). In "Primary Narcissism and Primary Love" (1960), psychoanalytic theorist Michael Balint claims: "It is only when someone is completely in love that the main quantity of libido is transferred onto the object and the object to some extent takes the place of the ego" (11). The Velveteen Rabbit, possessing a healthy, maturing ego, is able to reciprocate a love relationship with an object outside of himself, the Boy. Hence, the Rabbit achieves the "aim of all human strivings," according to Balint, that is, "to be able to love in peace" (36)—unlike Edward. Each night Abilene tells him, "I love you, Edward," and listens for a response that doesn't come (DiCamillo 8). Upon finding him stuffed among the dolls on the shelf, she says: "Edward . . . oh, Edward. I love you. I never want you to be away from me" (17)—and indeed she keeps him close to her heart during their decades of separation by wearing his pocket watch "like a locket that hung around her neck" (210). Edward, though, doesn't reciprocate Abilene's feelings; to the contrary, he pushes away the very love that the Velveteen Rabbit longs for to become Real. Abilene's grandmother Pellegrina tells a cautionary tale that mirrors Edward's fatal flaw about "a princess who loved no one and cared nothing for love, even though there were many who loved her" (27). Like all narcissistic people, Edward has "very little love to give" and is "highly sensitive to any failure of the environment in treating them as they expect to be treated: they are easily hurt and offended, and the offenses rankle for a long time" (Balint 27). Edward's huge yet fragile narcissistic ego must be humbled before his story can have a forever Real happy ending, like its intertextual precursor *The Velveteen Rabbit*.

The Humbling of an Ego

Natov states of Edward, "The quest that he resists, at times consciously and at times unconsciously, is to become a listener, someone who feels for others" (156). We learn in the first chapter that "Edward pretended, out of courtesy to Abilene, to listen. But, in truth, he was not very interested in what people had to say" (DiCamillo 7). Later, we learn that "when Abilene talked to him, everything had seemed so boring, so pointless" (71). Without being able to "imagine what another feels, through listening and observing," Edward cannot love anyone but himself (Natov 156). Before his miraculous journey begins, Edward cannot imagine what another feels because he completely lacks the ability to feel emotions, as we learn after he is thrown off the Queen Mary by two boys who see no point in a china rabbit that does nothing and wears fancy clothes. Edward lands "on the ocean floor, face down; and there, with his head in the muck, he experienced his first genuine and true emotion. Edward Tulane was afraid" (DiCamillo 50). Thus, his humiliating fall from pride into fear commences the process of maturation toward empathy and compassion for others that will be necessary if Edward is to grow out of primary narcissism.

When we meet the Velveteen Rabbit, he already feels his emotions and knows how to listen, as we can intuit from his long talks with the "old and wise" Skin Horse, "the only person who was kind to him at all" (Williams 2)—conversations that the Velveteen Rabbit misses after he becomes the Boy's constant companion. It is from the Skin Horse that the Rabbit learns what it means to be Real from a child's love: "You become. It takes a long time. That's why it doesn't happen often to people who break easily, or have sharp edges, or who have to be carefully kept" (2). It doesn't happen often to people like Edward, that is—made of china, with an easily shattered ego and the inability to appreciate the love of a child that could make him Real. When Abilene weeps at saying "Goodbye" and "I love you" to her departing grandmother, Edward is annoyed to be dampened by her tears and "wished that she would not hold him so tight. To be clutched so fiercely often resulted in wrinkled clothing" (DiCamillo 38). Contrast this shallow response to the more mature Velveteen Rabbit who "at first found it rather uncomfortable" sleeping "in the Boy's bed . . . , for the Boy hugged him very tight, and sometimes he rolled over on him. . . . But very soon he grew to like it, for the Boy used to talk to him. . . . And they had splendid games together, in whispers" (Williams 6). In those whispers, the Boy experiences the mutuality with his Rabbit that Abilene wishes she could experience with Edward.

The journey of becoming Real, according to the Skin Horse, "takes a long time" and involves a great deal of wear and tear: "Generally, by the time you are Real, most of your hair has been loved off, and your eyes drop out and you get loose in the joints and very shabby" (4). Though at first the Rabbit finds this process "rather sad" and "wished that he could become [Real] without these uncomfortable things happening to him" (5), over time his relationship with the Boy makes him "so happy that he never noticed how his beautiful velveteen fur was getting shabbier and shabbier, and his tail coming unsewn, and all the pink rubbed off his nose where the Boy had kissed him" (6). Eventually, the Boy "loved all his whiskers off" and the Rabbit becomes so "old and shabby" that he "scarcely looked like a rabbit anymore," but to the Boy "he was always beautiful, and that was all that the little Rabbit cared about" (12). Edward will undergo wear and tear very similar to the Velveteen Rabbit's on his way to becoming, but his journey out of primary narcissism will be painful and humbling, with uncomfortable things happening to him not only from being loved to shreds but also from being exposed to the abuses of weathering and human cruelty.

Edward endures his "ordeal" on the bottom of the sea for 297 days (over ten months) until a ferocious storm "lifted him up and shoved him back down," "pummeled" him, "flung him all the way out of the sea," "tossed [him] back down into the depths. Up and down, back and forth" (DiCamillo 55)—and he winds up in the net of an old fisherman named Lawrence. With whiskers intact and "the little bit of fur left on his ears," Edward is recognized as "a rabbit toy" and, "glad to be alive," taken home to the fisherman's wife, Nellie (57). We can see his progression out of narcissism beginning now as Edward is "so happy to be back among the living that he did not even take umbrage at being referred to as "it" (58), though he vainly considers Nellie "a very discerning woman" when she looks him over and says, "Have you ever in your life seen anything so fine?" (65). Projecting her own gender expectations on the china doll lacking in genitalia, Nellie names her new rabbit Susanna and, along with giving him a new set of ears, "sewed several outfits for him" (69). "Stripped of his male privilege," writes Natov, "he is at first horrified" (157). Furthermore, the clothes "were so simple, so plain. They lacked the elegance and artistry of his real clothes" (DiCamillo 70). Remembering his ordeal in the ocean muck, though, Edward takes a step toward maturing out of egocentrism by deciding it doesn't make any difference if he wears a dress.

Nellie, old and wise like the Skin Horse, spends hours talking with Edward as she works in the kitchen, and "Edward was surprised to discover that he was listening" (71). Unlike when Abilene used to talk with him, "the stories Nellie told struck him as the most important thing in the world and he listened as if his life depended on what she said" (71). The reader may wonder here whether Edward's life really does depend on listening and, if so, how Nellie's stories may save him. This realization of Edward's is juxtaposed with Nellie's story of her son who died long ago at age five of pneumonia: "It is a horrible, terrible thing, the worst thing, to watch someone you love die right in front of you and not be able to do nothing about it" (71). Indeed, Nellie's story foreshadows the powerlessness and grievous loss Edward will later feel upon witnessing the death of Sarah Ruth, the first child he will actually be able to love back the way that Abilene loved him—a love that will redeem him at the end of his miraculous journey.

Lawrence and Nellie's daughter, Lolly, throws him in the trash after she finds out her parents have been talking to Edward "like a rabbit child" (79). Losing the love that he has just learned how to feel gives him "a sharp pain somewhere deep inside his china chest" (80). His rescue from the garbage heap comes from a dog named Lucy who digs him up, an echo of an incident back at the Tulane home. When their dog Rosie vigorously shook Edward, Abilene's mother shouted, "Drop it!" causing damage to his ego for being called "it" (15). In his comparative reaction to the two dogs, we can now see Edward's growth: "Who, having known him before, would have thought that he could be so happy now, crusted over with garbage, wearing a dress, held in the slobbery mouth of a dog...?" (90). During his seven years with Lucy and her hobo owner, Bull, Edward continues to grow in his ability to feel love: "To his surprise, he began to feel a deep tenderness for the dog [Lucy]," and at night he repeats "the names of people who loved him," going in circles, "Abilene, Nellie, Lawrence, Bull, Lucy, Abilene" (98). Part of Edward's growth out of primary narcissism is a "new and strange ability to sit very still and concentrate the whole of his being on the stories of another" (106) and "in his listening, his heart opened wide and then wider still" (107), developing empathy and love. But we see that he still has ego work to do when he "felt a surge of anger at being referred to as a dolly" by one of the hoboes (105). This work happens after his next heartbreaking loss.

A security guard finds Bull, Lucy, and Edward sleeping on a train and—with contempt—says, "No free rides for rabbits" (109) and literally kicks Edward off the railcar. He is found the next day by an old woman who says, "Looks like a rabbit.... Only he ain't real" (115). With echoes of both Peter Rabbit's clothes on a pole and Christ on the cross, Edward becomes a scarecrow: "She hung him from a pole in her vegetable garden," nailed up by his velvet ears (116). Ibatoulline's illustration presents a striking image of the crucifixion—an image that some, including *Horn Book* editor Roger Sutton, believe cost the book recognition by the Newbery Committee. Book-review blogger Janica Harayda, who shares that opinion, points out that rabbits are associated with Easter, making Edward's story "a Passion narrative" and "an allegory of Christian faith and resurrection."

In 1994, Kuznets placed *The Velveteen Rabbit* in the fairy-tale mythic tradition of "shape-changing enchantments," with "the whiff of paganism that such a metamorphosis brings with it," and (without documentation, unfortunately) she alluded to recent censorship attempts by Christian fundamentalists (59). Now, nearly thirty years later, a browser search turns up no trace of censorship attempts; in fact, the World Wide Web teems with articles and blog entries gleaning Christian messages from *The Velveteen Rabbit*.[2] The story is a favorite gift for a Christian's child "to help shape her heart and conscience" (Chapman). It is frequently used as a parable for spiritual lessons, such as "I don't want us to be those followers of Christ who break easily, have sharp edges, who need to be carefully kept" (Ciliberti). According to theologian Aaron Denlinger:

> The Velveteen Rabbit, true to the prophetic word of the Skin Horse..., achieves realness on a new level by virtue of the love bestowed upon him, even though that love... introduces, whether directly or indirectly, considerable pain and sorrow to the rabbit's life. God's love (and the realization of his love for us in the person and work of Christ) likewise leads to our own transformation (glorification). But,

as every Christian knows and numerous New Testament texts confirm, the path to glory is paved with pain and suffering.

Not long after Kuznets alluded to censorship, Oxford University Press, in 1998, published a monograph by theologian Vigen Guroian in which he reads *The Velveteen Rabbit* as a Christian allegory: "Real in the last analysis stands for immortality: the Velveteen Rabbit is an image and replica of a living rabbit just as every human being is an image and likeness of God" (69). In her rewrite of Williams, then, DiCamillo picks up on these themes and creates a stronger, more overt Christian allegory.

The opening lines of both *The Velveteen Rabbit* and *The Miraculous Journey of Edward Tulane* invite religious exegesis. "On Christmas morning," the holiday celebrating the birth of Jesus, the Boy finds in his stocking a Velveteen Rabbit "with a sprig of holly between his paws" (Williams 1). Holly, an evergreen plant associated with eternal life, is widely considered to be a Celtic Christian symbol of the crown of thorns on the head of Jesus during his crucifixion. The first line of *The Miraculous Journey of Edward Tulane* places him "in a house on Egypt Street" (DiCamillo 3), from which his long exodus begins. He leaves behind what Harayda calls "bondage to his inability to love" per the King James version of Exod. 13:13: "Remember this day, in which ye came out of Egypt, out of the house of bondage." This provides interesting circumstantial evidence of DiCamillo's allegorical intentionality. While Williams expresses Christian messages metaphorically through nursery magic culminating in the kiss of a fairy who makes the toy rabbit "Real" and able to live "for ever and ever" (18),[3] DiCamillo uses direct biblical references with enough ambiguity for plausible deniability, beginning with the book's title. "Miraculous" may denote either divine intervention or extraordinary improbability.

Edward Tulane's Miraculous Redemption

Not all readers will recognize DiCamillo's Christian allegory, and they do not need to in order to absorb the spiritual messages behind what it means for a china rabbit doll to learn to love others instead of only himself. Pat Pinsent argues that fantasy is probably the best form of fiction to explore themes like death and the nature of the universe (52). Modern fantasy writers are still interested in teaching children how to behave and live harmoniously in the world, "but references to church-going or religious belief as such are far fewer than in the past, reflecting the secular society inhabited by the authors and their characters, as well as by their implied readers" (Pinset 51). Weaving allegorical references within the larger question of love in a Christian context, in the realm of fantasy, allows DiCamillo to tell a moral tale in an engaging way. DiCamillo holds the reader's interest effectively by using an anthropomorphized character and by engaging with spiritual questions: What does it mean to love and is love possible after pain?

According to the evangelical theologian Andrew Messmer, the Christian faith can be captured in the words "faith," "hope," and "love" (276). Biblical support of these virtues is found in 1 Cor. 13:13, where Paul writes: "And now abide faith, hope, love, these three; but the greatest of these is love." What is generally referred to as "the Great Commandment" appears in several of the Gospels, summed up by 1 John 4:8—"God is love"—and stated fully in Matthew 22:35–39:

> And one of them, a lawyer, asked him a question to test him. "Teacher, which is the great commandment in the Law?" And he said to him, "You shall love the Lord your God with all your heart and with all your soul and with all your mind. This is the great and first commandment. And a second is like it: You shall love your neighbor as yourself."

Just as love is at the heart of Christianity, the theme of loving your neighbor as yourself is at the center of *The Miraculous Journey of Edward Tulane*. Edward spends the majority of his journey discovering what love is and feeling the heartbreak and pain that comes with it. When Pellegrina first tells the story of the princess "who loved no one and cared for nothing," Edward doesn't understand the significance (DiCamillo 27). But this little fairy tale becomes a metaphor for Edward's own experience. Having love taken from him forces him to be grateful for what he *does* have or else he would drown in despair. Over time, Edward finds himself caring less about what he is wearing and more about his companions and the stories they tell. It is love that teaches Edward to appreciate things beyond himself.

Illustrations that echo biblical scenes are strategically scattered among the pages of *Edward Tulane*; for instance, an illustration depicting Edward immersed in seawater (48) is reminiscent of the story of Jonah, a character full of pride and sin, who attempts to run away "from the presence of the Lord" (Jon. 1:2–3). When the Lord sends out "a great wind on the sea" (Jon. 1:4), Jonah admits to the other sailors that his sinful actions are to blame, and the tumultuous storm will stop if he is cast overboard. Edward is sinful in a similar way. His pride has made it impossible for him to appreciate Abilene's love much like Jonah's pride has made him reject the Lord's love. In the end, Edward cannot be saved by Abilene's love alone. He has to learn to love her as a Christian must love the Lord. When he is thrown overboard, it is simultaneously a punishment for his narcissistic attitude and the start to his journey to discover love.

Edward sinking to the bottom of the sea can also be read as his metaphoric baptism. He receives not the symbolic sprinkling of an infant christening but a full immersion in water symbolizing the purification of "born again" Christianity signaled by John the Baptist in John 3:5: "Jesus answered, 'Truly, truly, I say to you, unless one is born of water and the Spirit, he cannot enter the kingdom of God.'" In the ocean, Edward drifts farther and farther away from Abilene, his rightful owner. Up until this point, he has never taken time to appreciate Abilene, her family, or the privileged lifestyle he feels entitled to be given. We see Edward's downfall in Prov. 21:4: "Haughty eyes and a proud heart, the lamp of the wicked, are sin." But being baptized means that loyal Christians can be forgiven for their sins and receive the Holy Spirit (Acts 2:38). In the ocean, Edward is cleansed of those sins and can then experience a spiritual journey where love soon becomes more important to him than his narcissistic ego. It is no accident that "salvation arrived for Edward" when "miraculously" the dog Lucy brings him out of the darkness into the "light" (DiCamillo 86).

The most explicit visual reference to religion occurs when Edward is nailed to a wooden cross in order to scare off the crows (118). Christianity teaches that Jesus died on the cross for the sins of all humankind and gifted believers with eternal life. Given Edward's journey, he does not represent Jesus Christ himself, but rather the path he is following to Christianity by learning faith, hope, and love. Edward learns what suffering is as he is filled with a feeling of "hollowness and despair" while hanging limply from the cross (119). Rom. 6:6–7 says: "We know that our old self was crucified with him in order that the body of sin might be brought to nothing, so that we would no longer be enslaved to sin. For one who has died has been set free from sin." Thus, hanging on the cross not only suggests that Edward's sins led to his suffering but also signifies that his metaphorical death will free him from his sins. It has been frustrating for Edward to be powerless in his own movement: "He was bendable, though, only if he was in the hands of another. He could not move himself" (DiCamillo 108–9). He can only find solace in this horrifying thought by choosing to focus on his loved ones and the experiences around him rather than his lack of autonomy. As through Jesus's suffering, Christians believe they are healed of their sins (1 Pet. 2:24), Edward is healed of his sins through his own suffering. Edward is taken down from the metaphorical cross by Bryce, who works in the garden. Bryce takes him home to his dying four-year-old sister, Sarah Ruth, who cradles him like a baby. For the first time he is aware not just of being loved but of feeling love for another and puts words to those feelings after Sarah Ruth's death: "I loved her and now she is gone.... How could he bear to live in a world without Sarah Ruth?" (DiCamillo 150). This is a turning point for Edward. He realizes pain always follows the loss of someone you have loved. Only after experiencing this heartbreak does Edward learn what it feels like to love and live eternally in the memory of loved ones—and eventually in the seemingly endless state of what the mender calls "doll time" (181).

Bryce takes Edward with him and leaves home. Edward is made into a puppet so he can dance and earn money, but still they can't afford a meal ordered at a diner. The owner cracks Edward's head against a counter, smashing it into twenty-one pieces. Edward loses consciousness and has a near-death experience, reflected in the illustration of Edward walking toward an illuminated door (167). Back on Egypt Street and "wearing a fine suit made of red silk" (169), he sees everyone who has ever loved him, except for Sarah Ruth. She has become a star in the sky. DiCamillo could have had Edward awaken again right after his head is smashed but instead gives him "magnificent wings" (171). He attempts to fly like an angel "toward the stars, toward Sarah Ruth," who we know is already dead. His living loved ones beg Edward to stay with them. They pull him back toward the ground, protecting Edward's life with the power of their love (172).

Along the way, DiCamillo uses diction to draw other connections between biblical stories and Edward's journey. For example, Edward lies in the trash for exactly "forty days and nights" after being tossed away by the fisherman's daughter (84), an obvious reference to the biblical account of Jesus being led to the desert by the Holy Spirit to be tempted by Satan and test his faith in God. There, he fasts for "forty days and forty nights" (Matt. 4:2). In addition, it rains for "forty days and forty nights" in the book of Genesis (Gen. 7:12). Just as Jesus experiences the "forty days and nights" after his baptism, Edward experiences "forty days and nights" immersed in the ocean before his rescue by a fisherman (bringing to mind stories of Jesus being a fisher of men in Matt. 4:19). Perhaps for Edward, who begins to listen as if his life depends on it in the kitchen of Nellie and Lawrence, this is a test of his new faith. His days in the dump are spent thinking about Abilene and what he wishes he had done for her, not selfishly waiting for rescue and a new pair of clothes, but contemplating love and in some way facing the loss of Abilene, Nellie, and Lawrence. He has won his spiritual battle.

Throughout Edward's miraculous journey, DiCamillo uses language evocative of being saved or born again, a core principle of Christian faith. Bryce comes back to the garden (the location of humankind's fall) and removes Edward from the scarecrow cross, saying, Christ-like: "I bet you didn't think I'd come back. But here I am, I come to save you" (DiCamillo 126). At this point, Edward is totally humbled and feels he is "nothing but a hollow rabbit"—"only a doll made of china," but when the nails are out and Edward is in Bryce's arms, "Perhaps, he thought, it is not too late, after all, for me to be saved" (126). It is his savior Bryce who later delivers Edward to be born again in the hands of the doll mender. He tells Edward, "I brought you back from the world of the dead" (177). Just as the Christian God is said to have loved us so much that he sacrificed his own son to save human souls, the love of Bryce has saved Edward through sacrifice. Having no money, Bryce agrees to the doll mender's price of keeping Edward for himself. "He gave you up so that you could be healed," the doll mender tells Edward (180). In the Bible, salvation is achieved by being faithful to God (Eph. 2:8–9). By the grace of God, the believer will receive eternal life and be saved from the depths of hell and oblivion. For Edward, salvation is finding love. Every time Edward feels alone and full of despair, someone shows him love and renews his hope.

Two Forever Real Rabbits

A final argument in favor of reading *The Miraculous Journey of Edward Tulane* as a rewrite of *The Velveteen Rabbit* is the fact that so many points critics make about *The Velveteen Rabbit* could just as convincingly be said about *Edward Tulane*. For example, in "Heidegger, Winnicott, and *The Velveteen Rabbit*" (2012), Kirsten Jacobson makes a philosophical point that the rabbit survives after a near death in "a story of loss, of being torn away from previous forms of closeness and intimacy, of radical shifts in what counts as important, and of the often arbitrary happenings that can spark such changes." Allan Kellehear's "Death and Renewal in *The Velveteen Rabbit*: A Sociological Reading" (1993) applies equally to *The Miraculous Journey of Edward Tulane*: "The theme of renewal and survival in the face of death is a necessary narrative device for the support it gives to more important themes, at least for young readers. These broader themes speak to the mutual interdependence of relationships and the triumph of love in the face of change and transformation in life, particularly in the context of growing up" (36). Edward's transformative journey represents the child's maturational passage toward adulthood.

At the end of DiCamillo's novel, as "seasons turned into years" of sitting on the doll shelf, Edward feels hopeless (207). All his faith in love has gone. Then he meets an antique doll, at least a century old, who parallels the role of the wise Skin Horse. As he begins to tell her that he doesn't want to suffer from the heartbreak anymore, she corrects him: "There's no point in going on if you feel that way. No point at all. You must be filled with expectancy. You must be awash in hope. You must wonder who will love you, whom you will love next.... If you have no intention of loving or being loved, then the whole journey is pointless" (199). In this doll's words, we see the importance of having faith and hope during sad times and times of heartbreak—a message that we are also left with in *The Velveteen Rabbit*. Awaiting his death by hellish bonfire, the scarlet fever–infested plush toy wallows in despair, thinking, "Of what use was it to be loved and lose one's beauty and become Real if it all ended like this?" (Williams 16). The Rabbit's real tear turns into a flower from which the nursery magic Fairy emerges and turns him into a biological rabbit to live in the heaven of Rabbit-land "for ever and ever" (18)—his reward for Real love. Keeping our hearts open to love gives us a reason to live and to carry on.

The message of *The Velveteen Rabbit* and DiCamillo's more explicitly allegorical rewrite applies to the immortal rabbit characters within, but the target audience is the reader, who is "encouraged to realize that love and loss are constant riding companions in the rough and tumble of life's unpredictable splendor," according to Kellehear writing about *The Velveteen Rabbit* in a point equally applicable to *Edward Tulane*. "It is not loss that is triumphant but rather the love that can emerge from, and triumph over, the complex and unpredictable nature of life's changing fortunes" (Kellehear 43). For a child reader in the process of maturation from primary narcissism to healthy object relations, both rabbits provide developmental lessons that coincide with biblical teachings. Balint says of toys, "They are representatives or symbols of internal objects which, in their turn, derive from early contacts with the environment, satisfactory feedings, warm soft wrappings, safe holding or cuddling by the mother, rocking, and lullabies" (23). With the child Sarah Ruth standing in for a mother and the doll Edward standing in for a human child, we see this representation in action when Bryce gives Edward to Sarah Ruth as a replacement for the doll she has lost. "Baby," she says and then holds Edward "so gently and yet so fiercely," cradling him in her arms and gazing at him "with so much love" (DiCamillo 133–34). Like the Boy in *The Velveteen Rabbit*, Sarah Ruth is a sick child who loves her rabbit to shreds, "sucking on one or the other of Edward's ears. Normally, Edward would have found intrusive, clingy behavior of this sort very annoying, but there was something about Sarah Ruth. He wanted to take care of her. He wanted to protect her. He wanted to do more for her" (141). In other words, he wants to love her, as an action. Eventually, "Edward's ears became soggy and he did not care. His sweater had almost completely unraveled and it didn't bother him. He was hugged half to death and it felt good" (147). The Skin Horse would call this Real.

And since Real "lasts for always" according to the Skin Horse (Williams 20), Edward is ready to love the next child who "held him in the same ferocious, tender way Sarah Ruth had held him" (DiCamillo 208). That child is Abilene's daughter, and DiCamillo leaves us much as Williams does, with a moment of recognition from the one whose primary love made the reborn rabbit forever Real.

Notes

1. Edward's rabbit nature is treated with moral ambiguity toward real rabbits. Real rabbits, of course, live in completely different ways than their anthropomorphized versions. Edward's original ears and tail were made of real rabbit fur, and he has a flashback of his origins when Abilene's grandmother Pellegrina stares at him during dinner: "Perhaps the rabbit fur on Edward's ears and tail, and the whiskers on his nose had some dim memory of being hunted,

for a shiver went through him" (DiCamillo 25). Real rabbits are often hunted for their meat and fur; they can also be kept as pets. Perhaps his flesh was used for meat and his body parts were fashioned into a doll.

2. A few prominent examples include "The Velveteen Rabbit—Lessons on Love and Eternity" (2013; see Chapman), "Loving the Broken, or How the Church Becomes Real" (2013; see Duns), "The Velveteen Christian" (2017; see Ciliberti), "Being Real: The Gospel According to the Velveteen Rabbit" (2013; see Doyle), and "Identity and Inheritance in the Velveteen Rabbit" (2018; see Denlinger). Paul Weithman in "God's Velveteen Rabbit" (2009), published in the *Journal of Religious Ethics*, appears to focus on *The Velveteen Rabbit* but actually uses it as a springboard to discuss Nicholas Wolterstorff's ideas about love and attachment.

3. In the next chapter, Karlie Herndon also reads the "heavenlike reward" as typically Christian, although ironically in "approval for a life lived queerly" (195).

Works Cited

Balint, Michael. "Primary Narcissism and Primary Love." *The Psychoanalytic Quarterly*, vol. 29, no.1, 1960, pp. 6–43.

Chapman, Naomi. "The Velveteen Rabbit: Lessons on Love and Eternity." *Lighting the Lamp*, 15 Dec. 2013, https://aeon01.wordpress.com. Accessed 14 Jan. 2021.

Ciliberti, Suzi. "The Velveteen Christian." *Heartsprings*, 17 March 2017, https://blogs.bible.org. Accessed 14 Jan. 2021.

Denlinger, Aaron. "Identity and Inheritance in the Velveteen Rabbit." *Reformation21*, 5 Feb. 2018, https://www.reformation21.org/blogs/identity-and-inheritance-in-th.php. Accessed 14 Jan. 2021.

DiCamillo, Kate. *The Miraculous Journey of Edward Tulane*. 2006. Illustrated by Bagram Ibatoulline, Candlewick Press, 2015.

Doyle, Larry. "Being Real: The Gospel According to the Velveteen Rabbit." *Encourage: Inspiration for Christ Followers*, 11 July 2013, https://encourageyou.wordpress.com. Accessed 14 Jan. 2021.

Duns, Ryan. "Loving the Broken, or How the Church Becomes Real." *The Jesuit Post*, 28 Mar. 2013, https://thejesuitpost.org/. Accessed 14 Jan. 2021.

Guroian, Vigen. *Tending the Heart of Virtue: How Classic Stories Awaken a Child's Moral Imagination*. Oxford UP, 1998.

Harayda, Janice. "Kate DiCamillo's Allegory of Christian Faith and Resurrection." *One-Minute Book Reviews*, 27 Jan. 2007, www.oneminutebookreviews.wordpress.com. Accessed 16 April 2020.

The Holy Bible. English Standard Version. 2001. Crossway Bibles, 2018. *Bible Gateway*, https://www.biblegateway.com/. Accessed 1 Nov. 2021.

Jacobson, Kirsten. "Heidegger, Winnicott, and *The Velveteen Rabbit*: Anxiety, Toys, and the Drama of Metaphysics." *Philosophy in Children's Literature*, edited by Peter Costello, e-book ed., Lexington Books, 2012.

Kellehear, Allan. "Death and Renewal in *The Velveteen Rabbit*: A Sociological Reading." *Journal of Near-Death Studies*, vol. 12, no. 1, 1993, pp. 35–51.

Kuznets, Lois Rostow. *When Toys Come Alive: Narratives of Animation, Metamorphosis, and Development*. Yale UP, 1994.

Messmer, Andrew. "Faith, Hope, Love and Jesus' Lordship: A Simple Synthesis of Christianity." *Evangelical Review of Theology*, vol. 44, no. 3, 2020, pp. 276–81.

Natov, Roni. *The Courage to Imagine: The Child Hero in Children's Literature*. Bloomsbury, 2017.
Pinsent, Pat. *Towards or Back to Human Values? Spiritual and Moral Dimensions of Contemporary Fantasy*. Cambridge Scholars Press, 2006.
Sutton, Roger. "A Great Choice." *Read Roger: The Horn Book Editor's Rants and Raves*, 4 Jan. 2014. *The Horn Book*, https://www.hbook.com. Accessed 2 Feb. 2021.
Weithman, Paul. "God's Velveteen Rabbit." *Journal of Religious Ethics*, vol. 37, no. 2, 2009, pp. 243–60. *JSTOR*, https://www.jstor.org/stable/40378044. 13 Oct. 2019.
Williams, Margery. *The Velveteen Rabbit: Or How Toys Become Real*. Heinemann, 1922. *The Internet Archive*, 2007, https://archive.org/details/velveteenrabbitooobian. Accessed 14 Apr. 2020.

Chapter 11

"For Nursery Magic Is Very Strange and Wonderful": The Queer Space of the Nursery in *The Velveteen Rabbit*

—Karlie Herndon

In many a Victorian-era English home, the top floor was a bit different from the others: with one or two large rooms, bars on the windows, and an iron guard around the fireplace, the upper level was a stark contrast to the rest of the house. As Queen Victoria's reign progressed, this space—the space of the nursery—changed alongside shifting ideas about children, childhood, and the home. London grew as an industrialized city, and the middle classes expanded to unprecedented numbers; at the same time, middle-class parents, lawmakers, and educators also began to understand childhood as a distinct period of life in need of protection from the supposed chaos, filth, and depravity of the adult world outside of the home. In the midst of overcrowded, soot-filled London, the domestic sphere became a place of security and safety, and as those homes became increasingly child-centered, the nursery became a recognizable and necessary staple in middle- and upper-class British homes. By the final third of Queen Victoria's time on the throne, the Victorian nursery had become a highly specialized children's space, containing not only safety measures to protect small children from nasty falls and alluring fires but also furniture, cupboards, décor, and literature made just for children to use during their long hours in the nursery. The late Victorian nursery became a place in which adults attempted to control and protect children from the world of adults, a place of extended innocence, particularly sexual innocence. While the nursery was intended as a space of sexual innocence through adult control, many authors of Golden Age children's literature portray this space as a place of freedom, experimentation, and exploration of various pleasures, desires, and attachments. Thus, this chapter will examine the queer potential of the late Victorian nursery, specifically through its portrayal in one classic children's text.

Margery Williams and the Nursery

Margery Williams, author of *The Velveteen Rabbit: Or How Toys Become Real* (1922), was certainly no stranger to the late Victorian nursery. Born in 1881 to a "barrister and distinguished classical scholar," Williams lived in London until her father's death in 1888, when the family moved to the United States (Eiss 160). As a child of an upper middle-class British family, Williams would have spent her first seven years in a typical late Victorian nursery, most likely with a nurse to care for her and her sister. In her adulthood, she wrote several books, but none quite satisfied her in the way that the now-well-known and widely loved *The Velveteen Rabbit* would. In fact, Williams "claimed to have disliked everything she had written before this work" until she "happened to think of cherished toys from her childhood and toys that her children had loved" (Eiss 160). Thinking of her childhood toys inspired her most well-known children's book, in which a toy rabbit becomes real through the love of a child. Though Williams published this children's book in 1922, two decades after the end of the Victorian era, I will consider the space of the nursery in the book as a late Victorian space—a legacy space that inspired many authors of the early twentieth century to look back through the lens of nostalgia to write some of the most exemplary Golden Age children's books.

The late Victorian nursery was unique in terms of space: it was a space where a governing female adult created rules and order but where other adults generally did not spend a great deal of time, and male adults almost never entered. In contrast, a child spent the majority of his or her time in the nursery, learning through reading books, playing with toys, and spending time with a nanny or mother and often breaking or circumnavigating adult-imparted rules, particularly when no adult was present. Williams's nursery highlights the uniqueness of this space by imbuing it with "nursery magic" (16), a kind of magic that may allow the best-loved toys to become "Real" (17). In the end, this means that the titular Rabbit becomes a flesh-and-blood rabbit, while the magic keeps another "Real" toy, the Skin Horse, stuffed and sitting on rockers, sharing wisdom with new toys in the nursery. The nursery's magic seems to work differently in different situations, and a wide allowance for difference is, in fact, a welcoming mark for a queer reading of this narrative.

With these elements in mind, this space becomes a space of queer potentiality: a space in which heteronormative gender and sexual boundaries are blurred, transgressed, or altered. While there is no one definition of "queer," several critics outline an expansive set of possibilities for understanding the

Victorian nursery as a space of queer potentiality. First, various queer theorists—Steven Bruhm and Natasha Hurley in their edited collection *Curiouser: On the Queerness of Children*, and Duc Dau and Shale Preston in *Queer Victorian Families: Curious Relations in Literature*—emphasize Victorians' own definition of queer: anything unusual or strange or *curious*. Additionally, as Bruhm and Hurley explain, there is more to the definition of queer, as it "derives also from its association with specifically sexual alterity . . . the figure of the queer child is that which doesn't quite conform to the wished-for way that children are supposed to be in terms of gender and sexual roles" (x). As these and many other critics agree, queerness is related to sex, gender, and sexual identity. Eve Kosofsky Sedgwick also defines "queer" as "the open mesh of possibilities, gaps, overlaps, dissonances and resonances, lapses and excesses of meaning" (8) and "desires and identifications that move across gender lines" (9). In referring particularly to children, queer "is also the child who displays interest in sex generally, in same-sex erotic attachments, or in cross-generational attachments" (Bruhm and Hurley x). These definitions create a clear path for a close examination of the many ways in which the Boy's and the Rabbit's behaviors don't always "line up" with adult, heteronormative, reproductive ideals for gender and sexuality and how their experiences of bodily pleasures in bed together point to an interest in unsanctioned sexual pleasures.

With these connected and overlapping definitions of "queer" in mind, the nursery space transforms into a space of queer potential through a variety of performances, desires, and attachments that become possible in that space. Indeed, as Bruhm and Hurley note, the insistence on the sexual innocence of children, the dismissal of any "queer" behavior in a child, "actually opens up a *space* for childhood queerness—creating *space* for the figure of the child to be queer as long as the queerness can be rationalized as a series of mistakes or misplaced desires" (xiv, emphasis added). Though the authors are referring to more of an ideological space, their words will be no less useful in helping to show how ignoring queer behavior makes it possible for the nursery to be a physical space for such norm-blurring behavior, performances, identities, and desires to flourish.

This chapter will next examine the space of the Victorian nursery more generally, including the gendered lessons conducted in that space, before moving into a queer reading of the Boy and the Rabbit in the nursery spaces of *The Velveteen Rabbit*. As Lois Rostow Kuznets points out, Williams's "work concerns breaking down barriers between animate and inanimate, species and species" (148). In performing a queer reading that examines a new way in which *The Velveteen Rabbit* breaks down heteronormative barriers, this chapter continues the necessary work of recovery through identifying and celebrating the queerness of children in Golden Age children's literature classics, classics that children today still turn to for inspiration, comfort, and confirmation of their own behaviors and identities.

The Victorian Nursery: Lessons in Gender and Sexuality

As Judith Flanders explains, "In the eighteenth century and before, rooms had been multipurpose," but along with the focus on the domestic, the rise in the middle classes, and the increasingly prominent child-centered home, "segregation of each function of the house became as important as separation of home and work; both home and work contained an aspect of both a public and a private sphere, like a series of ever smaller Russian dolls" (8–9). Although many children in this period enjoyed a more leisurely, play-filled childhood than their predecessors, this childhood was spent, for the most part, confined to the nursery and separate from parents' spaces—perhaps the most interior of the aforementioned matryoshka. Many fathers left home for much of the day to work in the city, and their time at home was considered a refuge, a return to the "angel" of the house and her heavenly realm, which, of course, could not include children who had not yet learned the rules of adult manners, quiet interactions, and calm, low-pressure conversations. Many Victorians believed that the key to a happy family was assurance that children would be tucked away until they were well mannered, educated, and suitable for adult society.

These nurseries were spaces in which children learned what it meant to be a member of society without exposing their missteps on the path to becoming properly behaved—and properly gendered—adults. James R. Kincaid notes that "before the time of puberty or 'adolescence,' [the Victorians] did not take much official notice of gender" (107). Kincaid explains that advice manuals rarely mentioned difference in gender and often only in terms of sleeping and bathing arrangements. Children wore the same or similar clothing until boys were six or seven, at which point they donned trousers and, in families that could afford it, were sent off to school (Robson 4; Flanders 89). This moment "signaled the removal from the maternal or feminine care in the home into the masculine world of the school" (Robson 4). The nursery was, in a sense, a feminized space: controlled by adult women when children were small, with some of the responsibilities and care falling to older girls. For the most part, children interacted with their mother, nurse, or—in the wealthiest of families—a governess. Governesses were usually highly educated young women who took on the role of teacher in the nursery but who did much less of the lower-order servant duties of cleaning or preparing food. In *The Velveteen Rabbit*, the Boy has Nana, a woman who appears to be a nurse rather than a governess. In spite of the preponderance of female occupants in this specifically children's space, Kincaid emphasizes that gender was not a focal point: "We can assume that Victorians *saw* gender differences; but it does seem that they were far less eager than we to make them linchpins of an entire conceptual system" (107).

Even so, it seems that scholars who focus on the nursery itself find more evidence to the contrary: that children may not have been directly *instructed* in gender or sexuality, but the texts provided for their general educations often revealed the Victorians' ideas of what should make girls and boys different. In fact, one method of this gender-based "conditioning" was through the nursery bookshelves: "Girls were to read of 'duty,' 'trials,' 'perseverance,' which would make them 'Women of Worth.' Boys read of ambition, achievement, success—their 'nobility' would be in accomplishment, not abnegation" (Flanders 88–89). Adventure novels, like R. M. Ballantyne's *The Coral Island* (1857), and school stories, like Thomas Hughes's *Tom Brown's Schooldays* (1857), were aimed at boys, whereas books with domestic scenes, like Charlotte Yonge's *The Daisy Chain* (1856), were aimed at girls. This is not to say that children didn't read their siblings' books as well, but adult intentions and advertisements were fairly clear, with major publishers creating lists of books for boys and girls, even creating publications such as the *Boy's Own Paper* and the *Girl's Own Paper*. In 1879, the Religious Tract Society (RTS) began producing *Boy's Own Paper* in an attempt to draw young boys' attention away from the "blood and thunder" publications popular among boys (Hahn, "The Boy's Own Paper"). The next year, RTS began printing the companion magazine *Girl's Own Paper* with "much encouragement of duteous behavior and home-making skills" (Hahn, "The Girl's Own Paper"). In very wealthy families, girls were encouraged to stay home and remain in a state of childhood ignorance—namely sexual ignorance through the deferral of marriage—"as long as possible" (Flanders 89). While children were not receiving direct lessons in gender and sexuality, children's authors of the period made girls' and boys' acceptably gendered behaviors and attitudes clear. While children learned their ABCs, they also learned what it meant to be a girl or a boy, how their bodies experienced desire, pleasure, and excitement, and what divided child and adult.

Though the children were learning what caretakers' and authors' ideas were, the nursery was also a space to test out individual conceptions of gender, desire, or pleasure: the nursery became a veritable laboratory for queer performances of gender as well as queer constructions of sexuality and desire. As with other rules, the nursery was a place in which to safely test boundaries or break rules of gender and sexuality. Children could play at gender swapping, such as when a game calls for several police—a strictly male job at the time—and only girls reside in the nursery. They could test out activities like cooking or caretaking (for boys) and adventuring and giving orders (for girls) all in the safety of a space meant for protection and education. Particularly when adults were not in the room, children had a good deal of freedom to push the limits of gendered behavior, especially if no lasting evidence remained. But even with adults present, gender- or age-restricted sexual roles could be tested. For instance, in Juliana Horatia Ewing's *Flat Iron for a Farthing* (1872), the child Regie professes his intention to marry his much older nurse, displaying a "cross-generational attachment," as Bruhm and Hurley mention in their discussion of queer theory in children's literature (x). Similarly, Peter Pan—whose adventures with the Darling children begin and end in the nursery—could be read as a gay or asexual character, oblivious to the advances of several seemingly attractive girls in the story. The nursery, in other words, worked as a playground or testing space for these nonnormative gender or sexual performances, and this is no less true of the nursery in *The Velveteen Rabbit*.

In spite of its nascence in the 1920s, *The Velveteen Rabbit* is rooted firmly in the children's culture of the late Victorian era, and the lessons intended for the Boy seem as well to be those instilled in other Victorian boys. Though someone has placed the Rabbit in the Boy's Christmas stocking and though "[f]or at least two hours the Boy loved him" (Williams 13), the Rabbit is set aside in favor of other toys at the beginning of the story. According to *Miller's Antiques Encyclopedia* (2003), plush toys were first manufactured in Germany in the 1880s and were widely available in England by the turn of the twentieth century, but dolls and toy animals have been hand- or homemade for millennia (Miller). Though there is no indication in the story of the Rabbit's creation, we might assume it, like the other Christmas gift toys, was purchased for the Boy. Indeed, a toy rabbit from 1902, much like the Boy's as depicted in the book's illustrations, exists in storage at the Victoria & Albert Museum: the available online image of the toy could easily have served as the book's cover model ("Soft Toy").

While the Rabbit might be just as modern as the rest of the toys, the ones that soon take the Rabbit's place in the Boy's play on Christmas morning are modern as well as more clearly gendered: meant only for boys. Toys with clockwork and windup inner workings "were very superior, and looked down upon every one else; they were full of modern ideas, and pretended they were real" (Williams 15). Just as the industrialized, public spheres of business, government, and war were associated with masculinity, many mechanical toys, particularly those mimicking these masculine endeavors, were produced and purchased for boys. Mechanical toys, even as they rose in popularity among manufacturers, were still expensive and delicate, and boys would have been confined to the nursery to play with them—carefully (Barton and Somerville 50). Steam-driven toy fire engines and trains were available by the 1870s, and trackless, clockwork trains were popular throughout the second half of the nineteenth century (Fraser 152–53). Metal toy guns, steamboats, and even clockwork banks came into the hands of well-off Victorian boys (Fraser 156).

Indeed, the Boy's nursery seems to be populated by many mechanical toys, and the only other toy that is kind to the Rabbit is the Skin Horse, a toy that has "lived longer in the nursery than any of the others," and his age is the key to his understanding of "nursery magic" (Williams 16). As we later see in the case of the Rabbit, the Skin Horse has an advantage over the other toys: the Skin Horse began its toy life with a closer connection to living beings than other toys, with formerly living skin stretched over its manufactured horse body. The Skin Horse, with the softness of a real horse, has been fiercely loved, its skin now a patchy coat and its silky tail all but gone—a monument to past love from now-grown children. The Rabbit, as another of the few soft toys, is also a symbol of nostalgic forms of nursery play, a play steeped in the tradition of a somewhat genderless childhood. The prevalence of the modern windup toys, particularly gender-specific items, such as a toy engine, a model boat, and a jointed wooden lion, indicates adults' attempts to press more masculine play on the Boy, presenting him with items that he might encounter as a man, particularly a British citizen at the height of imperialism: a train and a boat will allow him to travel, and in his expeditions to British colonies, he may encounter a lion. Though these are my own guesses at the purpose of these toys' presence in the Boy's nursery, one thing is clear: there are no dolls or miniature cookware—no feminine "training" toys in the space. The Rabbit is one of the only soft, pliable items in the nursery and even displaces a china dog in the Boy's bed, replacing a hard figurine with something that can be cuddled and posed. While the windup toys practically demand a single type of (careful) play, the soft Rabbit allows for many kinds of play, adding to the queer possibilities of this toy in the Boy's nursery. He is not hemmed in by certain predetermined actions the toy can take, and instead, the Boy is free to manipulate the Rabbit in ways the other toys are incapable of. In other words, the Rabbit's physical body is more open to possibilities than the other toys', which will break if mis-/differently handled.

Bed-Play as Queer Performativity

After the Boy's initial two hours of Christmas-morning love for the Rabbit, the stuffed toy resurfaces as a last-ditch effort by Nana, the Boy's nurse, to comfort him to sleep one night. Nana "ruled the nursery," and though the other toys hate her "tidying up," the Rabbit doesn't mind because "wherever he was thrown he came down soft" (Williams 20): again, the Rabbit is able to change and adapt to new situations and is himself open to new positions in the nursery. As noted above, the nursery space was in itself feminized through the presence of female adults, though plenty of masculine items are present in this nursery. However, it is important to note the feminine influence of the choice of the Boy's "old Bunny" for a bedfellow. The nurse, always in a hurry, decides that the Boy's china dog is not worth looking for, and the Rabbit gets his chance to be part of the Boy's consciousness again. Nana does not choose another hard or mechanical object to give to the Boy; she chooses the softest item in reach. Softness has often been associated with femininity, and Nana's choice of a soft creature to join the Boy in bed may be her attempt to feminize the Boy's bedmate, to push him toward more heteronormative affection through a feminized item. However, the reader knows through the narrative that the Rabbit is a "he," and Nana essentially makes it possible for the Boy and his male Rabbit toy to become fast friends in the space of the nursery bed. As Jyotsna Kapur points out, "Unknown to the adults, the nursery is a secret enclave in which the boy and the rabbit share an intense friendship" (96), a friendship that reveals the "open mesh of possibilities" (Sedgwick 8), the queer potentiality of the Boy's play and love for the Rabbit in the space of the nursery bed.

Specifically, two things about this pairing of the Rabbit and the bed are striking in terms of queer interpretations. First, the bed has always been a symbolic space of both sleep and sex: two competing activities with different aims, both occurring in the same space. In the first night with the Boy in bed, the Rabbit "found it rather uncomfortable, for the Boy hugged him very tight, and sometimes rolled over on him, and sometimes pushed him so far under the pillow that the Rabbit could scarcely breathe" (Williams 21). At first, this physical encounter on the bed is one that is unpleasant for the Rabbit, though the Boy appears to enjoy having the Rabbit in bed with him since he continues to bring the Rabbit to bed "for many nights after" (21). Though children's literature rarely depicts scenes of actual sex, this scene of writhing embrace on the bed is one charged with bodily sensations, ones that are pleasurable, desirable, and comforting for the Boy and that come to be equally welcome by the Rabbit who "soon grew to like it" (21). The clasping embrace and position changes throughout the night are reminiscent of sexual couplings, perhaps even echoing the tentative entrance of new lovers into unfamiliar lovers' beds and new forms of bed-play.

The other striking element is the fact that the Rabbit is, after all, a rabbit. Though the text makes no mention of the Rabbit wishing for a mate or having sexual urges, the rabbit has symbolized a strong sexual appetite for centuries: even the classic *Alice's Adventures in Wonderland* (1865) includes a "March Hare," a reference to the seasonal libido of the quickly multiplying mammal. Although much of queer theory does not directly confront the possibilities of interspecies sexuality, queer does not rule out the exploratory nature of pleasurable relationships—for instance, the pleasure one might derive from a pet. This lack of confrontation is a testament to the malleability of sexual boundaries and the possibilities for physical pleasures beyond marital, heterosexual, reproductive bodily pleasures. Though Williams has based the Rabbit on a toy she remembers, "a toy rabbit named Tubby" (Eiss 160), the choice of pairing a sexually charged symbol with a Boy in his bed is revealing of the sexually charged relationship between the two male characters.

I point to these two striking elements in order to more clearly found my queer reading of the scene: a feminine authority figure gives the Boy a both feminine (soft) and masculine ("he") toy, one that is supposed to soothe the Boy to sleep. Even as Nana names the "old Bunny" a "he," she sees here only innocent cuddling:

the Rabbit might as well be a pillow or a fluffy blanket. Just as Bruhm and Hurley note, however, the adult-sanctioned innocence of childhood is exactly what makes queer performances so possible in children's literature: this scene of male Rabbit and Boy in bed together is one charged with subtle sexuality. As Kuznets points out, "Relationships between toy characters and human beings are themselves diversely complex" (142). In fact, once the Rabbit "grew to like it," we learn that, while they are in bed, "the Boy used to talk to him, and made nice tunnels for him under the bedclothes that he said were like the burrows the real rabbits live in" (Williams 21). The Boy speaks to the Rabbit as though he is a real, comprehending partner, and he attempts to replicate a natural surrounding for the Rabbit. Though the Rabbit has no experience of living outdoors among other rabbits, the Boy reveals to him what a natural rabbit would want, and he allows the Rabbit to learn about the future that awaits him when he becomes Real.

Additionally, many of the pair's interactions happen under cover of darkness and in unsanctioned playtimes. The narrator explains that "they had splendid games together, in whispers, when Nana had gone away to her supper and left the night-light burning on the mantlepiece" (21–22). These games that they have continue to occur in the space of the nursery bed, and they occur covertly. While we may assume that the Boy hides his play because it's after his bedtime, we might also read the bed-play as something the Boy knows is not, strictly speaking, allowed: something that adults would disapprove of—something queer. What games do they play in whispers? What games in the soft light of the lamp occur in the bed? Though this can, of course, be read as nonsexual fun, the whispers, darkness, the setting (a bed), and absence of a controlling adult make this a prime scene of queer potentiality, one that crosses heterosexual as well as species boundaries. This play happens in Sedgwick's "gaps and overlaps" between waking and sleeping, night and day, reality and fantasy, and play area and sleep area. The space of the bed is one rife with possibilities due to its many uses, and I read this bed-play as a scene of loving, affectionate bodily pleasure for both the Boy and the Rabbit. The Rabbit is "very happy—so happy that he noticed how his beautiful velveteen fur was getting shabbier and shabbier, and his tail coming unsewn, and all the pink rubbed off his nose where the Boy had kissed him" (Williams 22). The Boy's physical affection produces happiness in the Rabbit, and the loss of fur and "pink" come from a great deal of physical, pleasurable interaction between the two. The Rabbit has begun to resemble the much-loved, and Real, Skin Horse.

One might read the scene of bed-play like a sleepover scene between two children: they play after "lights out" because they're too excited to sleep and because the danger of getting caught always adds to the excitement of doing a forbidden thing. In fact, toys often represent children and children's development in stories, as Holly Blackford [Humes] explains: "As animals and folk heroes have traditionally functioned, toys are simultaneously child characters and more than children. They stand for children when they embark on journeys to understand their relationship to their creators and develop their own sense of consciousness and agency; characters undergo metamorphosis when they have explored and mastered what it means to be human" (76).

Add to the aforementioned sleepover between two boys the exchange of kisses and snuggles, and the scenes of the Boy and the Rabbit in bed become scenes of sexual exploration, particularly if the toy metaphorically stands in for another child, embarking on a journey of sexual discovery and identity formation. In the end, we also see the Rabbit undergo the metamorphosis Blackford [Humes] mentions. When the Boy proclaims to Nana that the Rabbit is "REAL!" (Williams 24), this further pushes the bed-play from a flight of fancy to a scene of true desire, enacted by a child on a child-like toy, not a scene of make-believe or forgettable play. The story explains, "The nursery magic had happened to him, and he was a toy no longer" (24). Although the Rabbit has not physically changed into a living, breathing rabbit at this point, the declaration of his Realness is enough to prove to the Rabbit that he is no longer *just* a toy, like the broken windup toys or the lost china dog. Instead, he has become a significant person to the Boy: the Rabbit has formed an identity through his attachment to the Boy and through their nightly play.

Sexuality and Disease: Crossing Healthy Boundaries in the Nursery

Concerns about health were top priorities in the Victorian nursery. For the most part, children were either kept indoors or allowed to go for walks or play in gardens under a nurse's supervision. Because of this, children were given a large space in the home to ensure they could partake in various forms of indoor exercise, and this space ensured that the air of the nursery was never trapped, stale, unhealthful air that might occur in a smaller, stuffier room. Marion Lochhead explains that advice manuals recommended that "the nursery itself should be one of the largest rooms in the house . . . it very often was a large attic or top-floor room" (14). Health was a major concern in every aspect of the nursery: windows were barred, fireplaces had high fireguards to keep little hands from burns, and walls were covered in whitewash rather than paper or paint, so that they could be redone (freshened; disease washed away) each year (Flanders 66–67). Even carpets needed to be small enough to be taken out and beaten once a week (67), and items that could collect dust were, particularly near the beginning of the Victorian era, not allowed (Lochhead 14). Lochhead notes that, by the beginning of the twentieth century, "comfort was to be more widely spread, treats were to be more frequent" in opposition to the early Victorians' strict focus on sterility and wholesomeness (236). The sterile nursery of the early years of Victoria's reign gave way to "a brighter place, furnished with an eye to the convenience and pleasure of its inhabitants, with little chairs, toy-cupboards conveniently placed, pictures and friezes of fairy-tale characters or of friendly animals, and gay colors" (236). However, even with a more child-centered vision of what a nursery should contain, the focus on health and safety remained, even as it does today in designated children's spaces. Bars remained on windows, children were allowed fresh air whenever possible, particularly in manicured gardens, and nurses supervised whenever possible.

As the Rabbit becomes more of a favorite with the Boy, their adventures also move outside the space of the bed and into a sanctioned satellite space of the nursery: the garden. Indeed, even the word "nursery" is one associated with a protected space in which to cultivate plants, and the Boy and the Rabbit are safely supervised here, getting plenty of exercise and fresh air for the Boy's health. However, near the end of the summer, the Boy becomes ill. As people come and go to check on the Boy, "the little Velveteen Rabbit lay there, hidden from sight under the bedclothes, and he never stirred, for he was afraid that if they found him some one might take him away, and he knew that the Boy needed him" (Williams 32–33). The Rabbit remains in the bed with the Boy throughout his sickness, thinking up adventures for them, but never abandoning him to his illness. In the reality of the narrative, the Rabbit can move on his own: "All sorts of delightful things he planned, and while the Boy lay half asleep he crept up close to the pillow and whispered them in his ear" (33). The Rabbit's whispered plans seem to be the loving cure the Boy needs, for in the next sentence, his "fever turned, and the Boy got better" (33). The narrative clearly portrays the Rabbit's presence as one of help and health for the Boy, his comfort and support helping to save the Boy's life.

However, the adults within the story do not see this Boy-Rabbit coupling as a healthy attachment. Just as the earlier bed scenes are coded for queer interpretation of same-sex, cross-species desire and pleasure, the scenes of disease are coded like those of interventions of queer childhood behavior: the Rabbit's expulsion from the nursery further indicates his status as something Other, something that is not appropriate for proper sexual and gender education in the confines of the nursery. Though these loving scenes most likely strike a reader as sentimental, charming, or sweet, we might consider a Victorian adult's reaction to finding two boys, kissing in bed together, to better understand the queer reading I present of the Rabbit's removal from the Boy's life. Michel Foucault has pointed out that the "homosexual" became a "species" in the Victorian era and that "species" was, for many years, interpreted as an aberration, particularly a medical aberration (passim). One might interpret the conscious toy as another "species," a Rabbit that is not quite Real: this species that hovers on the boundaries of toy and real rabbit would also appear to be an aberration, something that is unhealthy, that could have a damaging influence on the Boy. Doctors throughout the Victorian era and beyond sought to eradicate anti-heteronormative behavior whenever it appeared in children (childhood onanism in particular appeared to be a major problem to many doctors). Similarly, the Boy's doctor interprets any toy bedfellows as diseased as well.

The Boy's poor health appears, to his doctors and caretakers, to be tied to his reliance on the shabby bunny in his bed, and the adults move to eradicate what seems to be a cesspool of disease as soon as they come to this conclusion. While this does, in fact, have a logical explanation (we bleach and wash our children's toys after illnesses as well, of course), one can also see the metaphor of disease as sexual aberration and the need to remove any queer (read: diseased) influences from the nursery space. Once the Boy is well enough to get out of bed, the Boy and the Rabbit are separated: the Boy sits on the balcony while the Rabbit lays tangled in the bedclothes, and then the Boy is moved to another bedroom to sleep—it's important that the Boy is distanced from the space that previously allowed him to explore unsanctioned pleasures and attachments with the Rabbit, further indicating the significance of the nursery as a space of queer potentiality. With the many adults coming in and out of the nursery, the possibility for queer play (both in and out of bed) is eradicated when the Boy's doctor intervenes. The "doctor's orders" demand that the room "be disinfected, and all the books and toys that the Boy had played with in bed must be burnt," including the Rabbit, who, according to the doctor, is "a mass of scarlet fever germs" (Williams 34). While the disinfection of the room seems quite normal and precautionary for the child's recovered health and future safety from this deadly disease, the doctor's specific focus on the toys and books that the Boy *played with in bed* is revealing of the metaphorical sexual disease present in the Boy and Rabbit's attachment and play. Again, the space of the bed is the focal point of sexuality in the nursery, the space where the Boy performed the most explicitly sexual activities with the Rabbit through their bed-play and lamplight-softened games. The doctor makes no mention of other toys or items in the room but focuses specifically on the bed and the items that were part of the Boy's illicit bed-play.

In a way, the Boy's "summer fling," as we might call it, has left some of the adults in his life raising their eyebrows. Blackford [Humes] states that the Rabbit "stands for both child and parent developmental concerns. He is an object of competition between child and parents when the child becomes sick and the parents throw out the cherished toy for fear that he carries germs" (81). Building on her argument, it seems that developmental concerns also point to sexual development and the acquisition of sexual and gender identity in the Boy: the Rabbit not only carries germs, but he also carries the mark of anti-heteronormative, anti-reproductive sexuality that must be eradicated from the Boy's world. As Gayle S. Rubin explains: "sexuality that is 'good,' 'normal,' and 'natural' should ideally be heterosexual, marital, monogamous, reproductive.... It should not involve pornography, fetish objects, sex toys of any sort, or roles other than male and female. Any sex that violates these rules is 'bad,' 'abnormal,' or 'unnatural'" (144). The Boy's interactions with the Rabbit are in violation of "good" and "normal" sexuality, and the adults (everyone but Nana, it seems) scurry to remove the Rabbit before the Boy comes into maturity. In other words, the male sexualized (or sex?) toy must be removed before the Boy can use this as a learning experience for forming lasting attachments to living boys outside of the nursery.

Conclusion: Redemption in the Satellite Nursery

Once the Boy's room has been cleared of the items that must be burned, those items are taken out "to the end of the garden behind the fowl-house. That was a fine place to make a bonfire, only the gardener was too busy just then to attend to it" (Williams 36). It is important that the Rabbit remains in the space of the garden: as I mentioned above, the garden served as a sort of satellite space of the nursery, and many nursery-bound children found that their play could move outdoors but only into the space of the cultivated, hedged-in garden. This garden, where the Boy and the Rabbit played together all summer, should be the Rabbit's final resting place, and as Kuznets points out, "here the reader is asked to identify with a toy rather than with a human protagonist" (61). But this further implies the Rabbit's personhood, achieved through his homoerotic attachment to a living boy. As Claudia Mills argues in this collection, the Rabbit's personhood was achieved when he was no longer replaceable by some other thing, such as another toy, and his value—as a soothing object or a form of entertainment—is replaced by a dignity shared by other persons. The thing that makes the Rabbit Real—the personhood he acquires through loving and being loved by the Boy—is also what sends him out of the nursery. The Rabbit has essentially been sentenced to death because of his bed-play with the Boy, and even without a queer lens on this scene, readers suffer more with the discarded toy than with the child whose adult caretakers have removed the threat of anti-heteronormativity from the nursery. Many texts with queer child characters seek to "rehabilitate" their queer characters through eventual heteronormative couplings, such as stories of tomboys who fall in love with a boy. This story, which has focused on the Rabbit's perspective rather than the Boy's, does not ask us to follow the Boy into maturity or to see what happens with him. Instead, we follow the Rabbit to the end of his narrative, and whether or not the Boy is "rehabilitated" becomes less important—this allows for further queer readings of the attachment's outcomes.

By the story's end, the Rabbit is so "Real" now that he can shed actual tears. A tear drops from his eye to the ground, and "a flower grew out of the ground, a mysterious flower, not at all like any that grew in the garden" (Williams 37). In a queered scene of the birth of a fantastic flower, the tear produces the flower, which grows into a "blossom like a golden cup" (37), and out of this blossom "stepped a fairy" (38). It is in this extended space of the nursery where the tear can grow into a *curious* flower and create a fairy and where the fairy, "the nursery magic Fairy," can continue to hold sway over the inhabitants of the nursery. She changes the Rabbit into a completely real rabbit (flesh and blood with fully functioning back legs), and she sweeps him off into the wood to play with other living rabbits.

While this may seem like an unhappy ending for a queered character in a space of queer potentiality, I read it somewhat differently as a scene of queer redemption. The Rabbit, who first found the physical affection and attention of the Boy quite uncomfortable, came to reciprocate the love and pleasure the Boy found in him. When the Rabbit is removed from the nursery, another toy rabbit takes his place, but "the Boy was too excited [about a restorative trip to the seaside] to care very much about it" (36). The adults seem to believe a new bunny will be the necessary replacement for the attachment the Boy formed with the Rabbit, but this proves, at least for the moment, uncertain; we do not see whether the Boy grows to care for this new rabbit toy like he did for the Velveteen Rabbit.

However, the Rabbit does not forget his love for the Boy, and his tears in the garden are both for his miserable discomfort as well as his loss of the Boy's love: his steadfastness to the Boy is in turn rewarded, not only with a real body but also with a heavenlike everlasting life, as the Fairy promises that he will play with the other rabbits "forever and ever" (40). With his new body and a happiness that he can't contain, the Rabbit "gave one leap and the joy of using those hind legs was so great that he went springing about the turf on them, jumping sideways and whirling round as the others did" (41). Kuznets notes that "Christian fundamentalists, who have recently urged censorship of the *Velveteen Rabbit*, have perhaps rightly detected (if certainly unrightly banned) the whiff of paganism that such metamorphosis brings with it" (59). While the "whiff of paganism" might have to do with the lack of an angel or the lack of a human intervening in the scene, the scene instead reads very much like a Christian reward. In what may feel like a pagan ending of wild celebration, this is also a depiction of a typical Christian theme of reward through eternal life here at the end of this queer tale of love and devotion: both the Boy and the Rabbit are spared from death, and both have something rewarding to look forward to. In their essay in this collection, Maleeha Malik, Elisabeth Graves, and Lisa Rowe Fraustino argue that the Christian allegory of *The Velveteen Rabbit* becomes more overt in Kate DiCamillo's retelling of the story in *The Miraculous Journey of Edward Tulane*. Where Williams's Rabbit goes through the discomfort of being loved and becoming real, DiCamillo's reimagined rabbit suffers a great deal for his "sins" (as he begins his story with far more pride and self-interest than the Velveteen Rabbit) and must *learn* to love others in order to achieve a transformative redemption. Through depicting this scene of a heavenlike reward for the Rabbit, Williams subtly rewards his queer performances in the nursery with a widely accepted Christian reward: life everlasting and the ultimate stamp of approval for a life lived queerly.

With the one-hundredth anniversary of Williams's publication of this beloved book, it's important that we reexamine it for new readings as we expand our literary criticism toolset, celebrating the depth of meaning and variety of interpretations that a children's book can contain in its brief but powerful story. By applying the lens of queer theory to this story of a toy becoming real, we can better understand the myriad variations of the culture of childhood as well as discover new possibilities for reading children's books and understanding formative children's spaces. *The Velveteen Rabbit* raises a toy to the status of person, putting the Rabbit into a child position, and thus making him legible as another boy in the Boy's exploration of queer pleasures. The bed-play, loving embraces, and subsequent adult intervention serve as pinpoints of queer-child performance and adult resistance to nonnormative sexuality in the nursery space. Though the book has faced criticism and censorship for its "whiff of paganism" or the danger of making magic too real, the story's queer potentiality only adds to its magic and is a cause for celebration. In fact, the "whiff" Kuznets mentions that is off-putting to conservative ideals of love and redemption may be the idea that a queered toy should find a happy ending.

Works Cited

Barton, Christopher P., and Kyle Somerville. "Play Things: Children's Racialized Mechanical Banks and Toys, 1880–1930." *International Journal of Historical Archaeology*, vol. 16, no. 1, Mar. 2012, pp. 47–85, https://doi.org/10.1007/s10761-012-0169-y.

Blackford [Humes], Holly. "PC Pinocchios: Parents, Children, and the Metamorphosis Tradition in Science Fiction." *Folklore/Cinema: Popular Film as Vernacular Culture*, edited by Sharon R. Sherman and Mikel J. Koven, Utah State UP, 2007, pp. 74–92.

Bruhm, Steven, and Natasha Hurley. "Curiouser: On the Queerness of Children." *Curiouser: On the Queerness of Children*, edited by Steven Bruhm and Natasha Hurley, U of Minnesota P, 2004, pp. ix-xxxviii.

Dau, Duc, and Shale Preston, eds. *Queer Victorian Families: Curious Relations in Literature*. Routledge, 2015.

Eiss, Harry E. "Margery Williams Bianco (22 July 1881–4 September 1944)." *British Children's Writers, 1914–1960*, edited by Donald R. Hettinga and Gary D. Schmidt, Gale, 1996, pp. 45–49. Dictionary of Literary Biography 160. *Gale Literature: Dictionary of Literary Biography*, https://link.gale.com/apps/doc/KYOKDP063981956/DLBC?u=mag_u_usm&sid=DLBC&xid=07922272. Accessed 25 Apr. 2022.

Flanders, Judith. *Inside the Victorian Home: A Portrait of Domestic Life in Victorian England*. Norton, 2006.

Foucault, Michel. *The History of Sexuality: An Introduction*. Translated by Robert Hurley, Pantheon Books, 1978.

Fraser, Antonia. *A History of Toys*. Delacorte Press, 1966.

Hahn, Daniel, editor. "The Boy's Own Paper." *The Oxford Companion to Children's Literature*, 2nd ed., e-book ed., Oxford UP, 2015. *Credo Reference*, http://lynx.lib.usm.edu/login?url=https://search.credoreference.com/content/entry/oupocl/boy_s_own_paper_the/0?institutionId=3440. Accessed 25 Apr. 2022.

Hahn, Daniel, editor. "The Girl's Own Paper." *The Oxford Companion to Children's Literature*, 2nd ed., e-book ed., Oxford UP, 2015. *Credo Reference*, http://lynx.lib.usm.edu/login?url=https://search.credoreference.com/content/entry/oupocl/girl_s_own_paper_the/0?institutionId=3440. Accessed 25 Apr. 2022.

Kapur, Jyotsna. *Coining for Capital*. Rutgers UP, 2005.

Kincaid, James R. *Child-Loving: The Erotic Child and Victorian Culture*. Routledge, 1994.

Kuznets, Lois Rostow. *When Toys Come Alive: Narratives of Animation, Metamorphosis, and Development*. Yale UP, 1994.

Lochhead, Marion. *Their First Ten Years*. John Murray, 1956.

Miller, Judith, editor. "Soft Toys." *Miller's Antiques Encyclopedia*, 2nd ed., e-book ed., Mitchell Beazley, 2003. *Credo Reference*, http://lynx.lib.usm.edu/login?url=https://search.credoreference.com/content/entry/mae/soft_toys/0?institutionId=3440. Accessed 15 Jan. 2021.

Robson, Catherine. *Men in Wonderland: The Lost Girlhood of Victorian Gentlemen*. Princeton UP, 2003.

Rubin, Gayle S. "Thinking Sex: Notes for a Radical Theory of the Politics of Sexuality." 1984. *Culture, Society and Sexuality: A Reader*, edited by Richard Parker and Peter Aggleton, U College London P, 1999, pp. 143–78.

Sedgwick, Eve Kosofsky. *Tendencies*. Duke UP, 1993.

"Soft Toy." ca. 1902. *Victoria & Albert Museum*, 1 July 2009, http://collections.vam.ac.uk/item/O1127705/soft-toy/. Accessed 4 Apr. 2022.

Williams, Margery. *The Velveteen Rabbit: Or How Toys Become Real*. 1922. Avon Books, 1975.

Chapter 12

Metamorphosis: The Disabled Toy Made "Real" as an Eternally Abled Rabbit

—Scott T. Pollard and Kara K. Keeling

The Velveteen Rabbit (1922) is very much a story about bodies, and the issue of the "Real" body of the rabbit intersects with the theoretical issues that underlie the field of disability studies. These in turn also challenge the traditional objectifying views of the disabled body as not "Real," denying the subjectivity of those who possess such bodies. Thus, a reading of Margery Williams's story that is premised on disability studies and that examines the physical details of the Rabbit and the sick Boy makes sense. Such a study reveals that while Williams appears to take a conventional "cure" approach to the Rabbit's disabled body,[1] the ambiguities revealed in the text also enable a reading in which love makes the disabled body Real through that body's disability—that is, makes disability visible rather than invisible, included rather than excluded—unlike so many other disability narratives that cater to what Rosemarie Garland-Thomson calls "normate" assumptions.[2]

For over two decades in the humanities, the field of disability studies has developed a complex theoretical and aesthetic lexicon for the study of literature. This lexicon identifies and categorizes representations of disability, and more importantly, it inserts itself into the very concept of representation to challenge ableist hegemony and *cripple* the normative ideologies that have shaped and limited our understanding of representation. In her 2010 article "Roosevelt's Sister: Why We Need Disability Studies in the Humanities," Garland-Thomson writes, "it is literature ... [that] uncovers the richest tradition of disability" from which can be inferred its logical complement that disability uncovers the richest traditions of literature.[3]

Disability studies scholars regularly observe the profound presence of disability in culture and cultural productions. In *Claiming Disability* (1998), Simi

Linton notes that once we begin thinking about disability, its "pervasiveness ... in relation to literary representation, metaphor, ethical issues, symbolism, [and] subject matter in cultural products" is unavoidable (148). In *Narrative Prosthesis* (2000), David T. Mitchell and Sharon L. Snyder go further, claiming that "within literary narratives, disability serves as an interruptive force that confronts cultural truisms" (48). In *Feminist, Queer, Crip* (2013), echoing Mitchell and Snyder, Alison Kafer extends the possibilities of reading literature through a disability lens when she argues that intentionally "reading narratives ... as crip, even when they do not explicitly mention disability, might lead all of us to begin thinking disability" (24). In her final phrase, Kafer reveals that she perceives disability studies as a fully-fledged disciplinary approach that is useful for reading texts and the cultures that produce them, moving beyond foregrounding disability representation to thinking more deeply about how such representations reveal fundamental assumptions of social and narrative structure. In *The Secret Life of Stories* (2016), Michael Bérubé takes this claim one step further, agreeing with Linton that "representations of disability are ubiquitous, yes, even or especially when you are not looking for them," but then he goes on to claim: "narrative deployments of disability do not confine themselves to representation. They can also be narrative strategies, devices for exploring vast domains of human thought, experience, and action" (2). Bérubé's contention suggests that awareness of disability can shape the attention of the observer, who will then see the plentitude of disability signifiers in texts and how they function as markers of exclusion. Given the ethos of disability studies, the observer, however, will also then understand that such signifiers should be included in any textual analysis. Once past that threshold of critical inclusion, similarly to Mitchell and Snyder, Bérubé sees disability at the center of the narrative enterprise, where disabling is a troublesome creative act meant to undercut both writerly and readerly conventions and produce a new experience that has the potential to be the starting point for broader cultural analyses.

Such centrality of disability is signaled early on in *The Velveteen Rabbit*, when the Rabbit is getting to know the other toys in the nursery. Williams frames the introduction of the toys in terms that reflect Erving Goffman's concept of "stigma." He explores how society creates norms through the discrediting or disgracing of nonnormative traits, so that anything that is judged as "unusual or morally bad" may come to carry stigma (Goffman 1). Williams makes clear, as she introduces the toys, that the nursery society is structured as a hierarchy, with stigmatized toys on the bottom, rather than the toys all possessing equal value. The child as owner invisibly occupies the top of the pyramid. Although not mentioned since the opening paragraphs, the Boy possesses a real biological body; more generally, he represents the unmarked norm that the other toys wish to emulate. Although all the toys are marked by what Goffman might call "undesired differentness" from the norm that the Boy represents (2), the mechanical toys see themselves as "very superior" because they have some degree of mechanical animation that allows them to engage in a pretense that they too are real (Williams, *The Velveteen Rabbit* 3). Their need for pretense, however, shows their own "uneasiness" with their simulated bodies (Goffman 19); their need to deny their existence as simulacra indicates their need to avoid the stigma associated with a nonnormative body. Such uneasiness indicates that, as social beings, the mechanical toys understand that they lack equal ontological footing with the Boy to whom they belong. They deny stigma by claiming superiority and snubbing as inferior those with less mobility than themselves. The model boat follows their lead, ignoring his worn and damaged body, which has "lost most of his paint" through aging and use. He uses language to assert his likeness to the boats that his form simulates: the narrator notes that the boat "never missed an opportunity of referring to his rigging in technical terms" (Williams, *The Velveteen Rabbit* 3).

The Velveteen Rabbit, by contrast, feels no such pretense at realness or superiority. Instead, he acknowledges stigma to the point that he has internalized the others' judgment of his discredited body: "The Rabbit could not claim to be a model of anything, for he didn't know that real rabbits existed; he thought they were all stuffed with sawdust like himself, and he understood that sawdust was quite out-of-date and should never be mentioned in modern circles" (3). He does not realize that as a toy he is a simulacrum. As he compares himself to the other toys and absorbs their social attitudes about him, the Rabbit realizes that he is the least of them: "Between them all the poor little Rabbit was made to feel himself very insignificant and commonplace" (4). This differs from the Rabbit's original introduction in the story as a "splendid" toy that has an attractive body: "He was fat and bunchy, as a rabbit should be; his coat was spotted brown and white, he had real thread whiskers, and his ears were lined with pink sateen" (1). The narrator's introduction of the Rabbit creates an interesting tension between his simulated body and his verisimilitude in comparison with real rabbits: his shape and coloring are proclaimed to parallel those of rabbits, but his whiskers and ears are made of fabric—and yet, the narrator seems to try to undercut the artificial nature of the material from which he is constructed by paradoxically defining his whiskers as made with "*real* thread" (1, emphasis added). It is not until the Rabbit lives in the nursery with the other toys—not until he has a social milieu—that he learns to feel shame over his body's construction: "no one thought very much about him. He was naturally shy, and being only made of velveteen, some of the more expensive toys quite snubbed him" (3). The snooty other toys see him as made of second-rate materials: in addition to the unfashionable sawdust with which he is stuffed, the titular velveteen is itself a cheap material. It is made of cotton, has "a much shorter pile, is less expensive and more hardwearing" than velvet, a more highly esteemed fabric

(*The Guardian* 24). Williams thus uses the physical details of the Rabbit's body to underline his debased social status.

We find most interesting the tension between Williams's initial description of the Velveteen Rabbit as an aesthetically well-realized norm rabbit and the Rabbit's realization in this social context that his body is stigmatized.[4] This close linkage of norm and stigma creates an uneasiness that pervades the rest of the story and begins to resonate with Mitchell and Snyder's concept of "narrative prosthesis," which claims that disability pervades literary narrative "as a device of characterization" for its contrastive capacity to mark and illuminate conventionally invisible, unmarked norms (9). To put it simply, a "flawed" character (physically, emotionally, or intellectually) makes for a richer narrative and symbolic experience than a character built to fit social norms, and disability is a stock mechanism through which writers create their "flawed" characters: thus, norm values—unmarked—need to wear the prosthesis of disability to be visible. Although the Velveteen Rabbit has not been revealed as disabled yet (his back legs will later be shown as missing), his stigmatized body in the nursery-toy society foreshadows what is to come and telegraphs its prosthetic capacity within the story.

Still, it is not the Rabbit or the stigmatic organizing structure of this social scene that most obviously suggests disability as a useful analytical frame for *The Velveteen Rabbit*. That role instead goes to Timothy, the jointed wooden lion, who, although "he should have had broader views," will not admit that he was made by "disabled soldiers" and instead deflects attention to his vague connection with "Government" (Williams, *The Velveteen Rabbit* 3–4). So, in the lion's act to repress his origin, Williams inserts a detail that makes visible one of the realities of the post–World War I era that functions as a backdrop for the story. Many soldiers returned from the war disabled, and society felt the "culpability and moral obligation" to "repair, reestablish, [and] restore" these men. Thus, programs were created to rehabilitate disabled soldiers and give them productive—although often socially devalued—work (Stiker 123–27). In her article on picture books in the interwar years, Mary Galbraith points out the impact of World War I and the pervasiveness of trauma: "these picturebooks capture in uniquely effective ways the frightening predicaments children face and the unspeakable decisions they must make when adults behave strangely and dangerously" (339), that is, go to war and deal with war's aftermath. Although *The Velveteen Rabbit* is more storybook than picture book, Galbraith's claim rings true. While children's fiction of the interwar years most often celebrates the cause behind World War I as heroic and the soldiers as heroes (Paris 155–62), Williams, at the very beginning of the story, explicitly inserts two very different effects of the war: disability and rehabilitation. If stigma marks the Rabbit initially in the scene for his "undesired differentness," the introduction of rehabilitation through the mention of the "disabled soldiers" foreshadows the Rabbit's character arc, for a rehabilitated rabbit is what he becomes in the end.

Thus, a story that seems to be about a toy rabbit that lacks social standing becomes a story about disability for readers who have learned to see in ways that the field of disability studies promotes. The discipline offers glasses for those who choose to see through the lenses of disability theory. A good example of this shift in perspective is the disability theorist Ato Quayson, who in his book *Aesthetic Nervousness* recounts his own epiphany. Quayson says that he did not notice the disabled characters in the literature he assigned in his classes until a student asked him why he required so many works with disabled characters. Rereading what he had assigned, Quayson noticed that the books "were populated with disabled figures in casual and not-so-casual roles. Moreover, figures that did not initially appear as disabled suddenly took on a more significant hue when read through a prism of disability" (xii–xiii). Similarly, critic Bérubé notes: "Disability has a funny way of popping up everywhere without announcing itself as disability" (1). After seeing disability marked in a book, one reads that book differently.

Stigma and disability are also evident in the subsequent conversation between the Velveteen Rabbit and the Skin Horse. Here, however, Williams flips the disabled signifier, recrediting disability and empowering it with the narrative's central consideration: the nature of the Real. Motivated to overcome his stigmatized position at the bottom of the nursery hierarchy, the Velveteen Rabbit asks the Skin Horse, "What is REAL?" and the Skin Horse replies, "Real isn't how you are made. . . . It's a thing that happens to you. When a child loves you for a long, long time, not just to play with, but REALLY loves you, then you become Real" (Williams, *The Velveteen Rabbit* 5). For scholars like Kirsten Jacobson and Steven V. Daniels, this conversation functions as a catalyst for abstract philosophical and psychological discussions of the nature of reality and identity, and they mostly disregard the physical details of the Skin Horse and their impact on Williams's claim about the Real. Williams describes the toy's body in detail: "The Skin Horse had lived longer in the nursery than any of the others. He was so old that his brown coat was bald in patches and showed the seams underneath, and most of the hairs in his tail had been pulled out to string bead necklaces" (4). The horse could be read simply as an old, worn-out toy, but if a toy is an analogue for a human, and thus a human body, then the Skin Horse can be understood as not simply old but as damaged, injured, maimed, crippled, or lame—that is, as disabled.[5] Williams's narrative arc fits Mitchell and Snyder's formula for narrative prosthesis:

> First, a deviance or marked difference is exposed to a reader; second, a narrative consolidates the need for its own existence by calling for an explanation of the deviance's origins and formative consequences; third, the deviance is brought from the

periphery of concerns to the center of the story to come; and fourth, the remainder of the story rehabilitates or fixes the deviance in some manner. (53)

The Velveteen Rabbit, himself stigmatized and deviant, engages the Skin Horse in conversation, asking for an explanation of the Real. The disabled Skin Horse, now at the center of the scene because of his experience and wisdom, explains deviance to the Rabbit: he describes the rationale for deviance as the reason why certain toys transcend their existence as toys/simulacra to become real:

> He was wise, for he had seen a long succession of mechanical toys arrive to boast and swagger, and by-and-by break their mainsprings and pass away, and he knew that they were only toys, and would never turn into anything else. For nursery magic is very strange and wonderful, and only those playthings that are old and wise and experienced like the Skin Horse understand all about it. (Williams, *The Velveteen Rabbit* 4–5)

The love of a child makes a toy real, and only an old, worn-out, and damaged toy possesses the signs of love and a "real" existence.

The Skin Horse tells his own four-part story of narrative prosthesis, foreshadowing the Velveteen Rabbit's story, a story that develops out of the tension between the Rabbit's desire to be Real and his fear of becoming disabled: "He longed to become Real, to know what it felt like; and yet the idea of growing shabby and losing his eyes and whiskers was rather sad. He wished that he could become it without these uncomfortable things happening to him" (8). With this tension, Williams introduces the conventionally ableist fantasy of rehabilitation: to become without becoming disabled. Such a narrative arc is never smooth and unproblematic, though; it can never erase or fix disability. Rather, such narratives evince what Quayson calls "aesthetic nervousness . . . when the dominant protocols of representation within the text are short-circuited in relation to disability . . . a short-circuit triggered by the representation of disability" (15). Once a text like *The Velveteen Rabbit* is seen through the lens of disability, the dominant protocols of ableism cannot dominate and the attempts to enact them can only provoke uneasiness.

Initially, the story follows the Skin Horse's predictions. As the Rabbit become shabbier—as his body breaks down—he is more beloved by the Boy: "And so time went on, and the little Rabbit was very happy—so happy that he never noticed how his beautiful velveteen fur was getting shabbier and shabbier, and his tail becoming unsewn, and all the pink rubbed off his nose where the Boy had kissed him" (Williams, *The Velveteen Rabbit* 10–12). The Rabbit becomes Real by becoming disabled. He doesn't get the full ableist fantasy that there is no pain in his change, but he gets the Skin Horse's compensatory narrative. The Boy's authority confirms the Rabbit's transformed existence. When the nurse calls the worn bunny a toy, the Boy refutes her: "You mustn't say that. He isn't a toy. He's REAL!" (13). The Rabbit is happy with his new form, the entwined existence of being disabled and Real: "The nursery magic had happened to him, and he was a toy no longer. He was Real. The Boy himself had said it" (13). When the Rabbit is threatened by adult authority, diminishing his existence as a "toy," the Boy defends the Rabbit with a child's authority over his own space. The Rabbit's existence depends on the child. In the space of the nursery, the Skin Horse's narrative works.

The scenes of bonding between the toy and the Boy are disturbed by the Rabbit's eventual recognition that being real may not be real enough. Out in the woods, the Rabbit is in new and open territory—the world outside the hermetic space of the nursery, and the Boy's authority, his love, cannot protect the Rabbit as effectively as it did in the nursery, cannot offer him the same reassurance. As a result, the Rabbit must question and doubt himself again. When the Rabbit is confronted by the real rabbits and has to face ableist prejudice for the first time, he realizes that his prized "Real" is illusory. The Rabbit is a disabled child facing nondisabled children who do not understand him or his immobility: "Why don't you get up and play with us?" (17). The conversation centers on mobility and immobility. When the real rabbits hop to demonstrate their mobility and ask him if he can hop, the Velveteen Rabbit takes refuge defensively in his immobility, and when he is challenged to move, he realizes that the Boy is his mobility prosthesis: "'I can jump higher than anything!' He meant when the Boy threw him, but of course he didn't want to say so" (17). He feels shame and hopes that the rabbits do not notice that he cannot move autonomously, like them:

> "Can you hop on your hind legs?" asked the furry rabbit.
> That was a dreadful question, for the Velveteen Rabbit had no hind legs at all! The back of him was made all in one piece, like a pincushion. He sat still in the bracken, and hoped that the other rabbits wouldn't notice. (17–18)

But, of course, they do, and one of them reacts immediately: "'He hasn't got any hind legs!' he called out. 'Fancy a rabbit without any hind legs!' And he began to laugh." The derisive laughter forces the Rabbit to try to deny his immobility: "'I have!' cried the little Rabbit. 'I have got hind legs! I am sitting on them!'" (18). The wild rabbits nonetheless see his inability to perform the same way that they do as disability, a deviation from the norm they feel that they represent. Further, the stigmas build once they smell his velveteen and sawdust, and they reject him: "He isn't a rabbit at all! He isn't real!" (19). Read one way, this scene is simply about children encouraging another child to join in and play, but the scene also demonstrates how quickly such an innocent moment becomes cruel and exclusionary as ableist norms kick in. To invoke Goffman, "By definition, we believe the person with a stigma is not quite human" or, in this case, rabbit (3). This is the kind of conversation that disabled children too often have with nondisabled children, and Williams uses it to interrupt the scenes in which the Rabbit feels most secure and happy in his relationship with the Boy; thus, she explicitly cripples the narrative again. Although the Rabbit returns to the nursery with the Boy and can take solace in his earlier belief in his own Realness within the space protected by the Boy's authority, Williams causes him to doubt his Realness and to desire the mobility that the wild rabbits possess, for he "would give anything in the world to be able to jump about like these rabbits did" (*The Velveteen Rabbit* 18). Kafer's explanation of ableism in *Feminist, Queer, Crip* helps to explain Williams's narrative shift: "The presence of disability, then, signals something else: a future that bears too many traces of the ills of the present to be desirable. In this framework, a future with disability is a future no one wants, and the figure of the disabled person, especially the disabled fetus or child, becomes the symbol of this undesired future" (2). Rather than explore the possibilities of living with disabilities, Williams dismantles the Real-disabled link set up by the Skin Horse and inserts an ableist fantasy in its place.

In "Heidegger, Winnicott, and *The Velveteen Rabbit*: Anxiety, Toys, and the Drama of Metaphysics" (2012), Jacobson reinforces this ableist fantasy by grounding her understanding of the Rabbit's identity development in "self-movement" (5). She argues that this ability to move with self-direction defines the subject, its relation to the Real and others: that is, self-consciousness is created through autonomous movement, which also allows one to be recognized—"counted"—by others (Jacobson 6). Thus, for Jacobson, the self exists only insofar as others recognize it. Moreover, the existence of the self inherently hinges upon a particular form of social recognition, a kind of recognition that cannot occur unless others see the self moving independently: "Overall, then, we see in the story a progressive education into the way in which possession of the internal principle of motion is a significant element in a thing's character as a self-defined piece of reality, and, thus, as naturally *real* rather than as fabricated" (Jacobson 5–6). Jacobson offers this idea to explain the end point of the Rabbit's story arc—after he is transformed by the Fairy, he first moves on his own volition and realizes he is no longer a toy: "just then something ... tickled his nose, and before he thought what he was doing he lifted his hind toe to scratch it" (Williams, *The Velveteen Rabbit* 32). Hence, everything in the Rabbit's story preceding the first instance of that "internal principle" only "counts" if it is seen as leading to this moment of realization when the Rabbit moves on his own (Jacobson 6). In other words, the Rabbit's story is meaningful because it is plotted as a rehabilitation narrative. In Jacobson's interpretation, the Rabbit becomes "Real" only because he can move on his own. Reflecting back, then, the Rabbit earlier in the story arc has no autonomous existence because he cannot move himself and consequently cannot be "counted." Here is the dilemma of the disabled: to be dismissed as human, to not count as human, because of a lack of mobility. Like Williams, Jacobson follows a narrow path of normativity, devaluing the Rabbit's experiences of his disabled body. It is no wonder that the Rabbit is traumatized by his interactions with the real rabbits. In a world that is defined systematically by ableist prejudices, he has nowhere to hide from the gaze and judgment of the "real" rabbits, and he knows that as a nonmobile rabbit he "counts" for nothing. This is the experience of too many disabled people: to have their humanity disappeared or discounted because of a narrow ableist point of view and then be given a narrative resolution that is either untenable or unacceptable—unrealistic expectations of rehabilitation, divine intervention, or death. Jacobson offers a tidy theory of character development in *The Velveteen Rabbit*, but it depends on a highly exclusionary conception of humanity that demeans, degrades, and disregards human life and that cannot conform to a very particular and prejudicial apprehension of movement. One of the many functions Linton identifies for disability studies "is to mine the canons for the malignant, unsavory, or simply reductive representations of disability that insinuate themselves into our thinking" (130). So, although there are problems with the portrayal of disability in *The Velveteen Rabbit*, clearly the scholarship on the story has to be interrogated for its ableism as well.

To return to the story, disability in *The Velveteen Rabbit* might most obviously seem to refer to the Boy and his bout of scarlet fever. After all, this is the moment when sickness reigns in the book and the adult figure shifts from Nana to a doctor, who dispenses lots of medical advice to cure the Boy, including the destruction of the Rabbit. The momentary medicalization of the narrative signals the longtime ableist view of disability, which sees it primarily as a medical condition, a sick or flawed body in need of cure. As Linton notes, "Disability so defined is a medically derived term that assigns predominantly medical significance and meaning to certain types of human variation" (11).[6] But the Boy is not disabled; he is ill. Scarlet fever is dangerous, but as Williams plays it out, it is a temporary condition and not permanently incapacitating for the Boy.[7] The scene is important, though. The illness permanently separates the Boy and the Rabbit because, although the Boy recovers, the Rabbit becomes a medical object once the doctor sees him: "Why, it's a mass of scarlet fever germs!—Burn it at once" (Williams, *The Velveteen Rabbit* 24). Williams does not give the Boy a voice to countermand that order—he does not seem even to miss the Rabbit in the excitement of his upcoming trip to the seaside, especially when given a new toy rabbit to replace the old one—and so adult authority stands. Yet Williams also puts both characters on rehabilitative paths, and the Boy's return to wholeness and activity becomes the implicit model for the final stage of the Rabbit's story.

Faith McNulty finds the ending of the story poignant, as a "tragedy of lost love and betrayal" (180). Williams emphasizes the depth of the Boy's love in her description of the wearing effect it has had on the Rabbit's body—disabling that body through age:

> He loved him so hard that he loved all his whiskers off, and the pink lining to his ears turned grey, and his brown spots faded. He even began to lose his shape, and he scarcely looked like a rabbit any more, except to the Boy. To him he was always beautiful, and that was all that the little Rabbit cared about. He didn't mind how he looked to other people, because the nursery magic had made him Real, and when you are Real shabbiness doesn't matter. (*The Velveteen Rabbit* 20)

But by accepting a new toy bunny in place of the germ-ridden Velveteen Rabbit without a murmur, the Boy abandons the Rabbit that he has made "Real" with his love in a manner that Lois Rostow Kuznets terms "unfaithful and cavalier" (61). With the support of the Boy's love thus thrown into question by the child's emotional desertion, so is the Rabbit's Realness. When he is moved out of the nursery in the sack destined to be burned in the garden, he gets also moved out of the imaginary life made possible by the child in the nursery, where the Skin Horse still resides, who is still "real" from his loving child a generation earlier but who is also still in the space where childhood imagination reigns. It is worth noting that the questioning of the Rabbit's realness generally occurs when he has left the safety of the nursery sanctuary: Nana, the nurse, questions the Boy making a fuss over a toy when the Rabbit gets left behind on the lawn once the Boy goes in for tea, prompting the Boy's assertion of the Rabbit's "Realness" (Williams, *The Velveteen Rabbit* 12–13), and of course, the wild rabbits question his realness when they find him in the bracken, as discussed above (16–19). At the climax of the story, the Rabbit gets thrown out into the real world, where he faces a kind of death: the destruction of his toy body, and presumably his "Real" self with it, when all the sickbed paraphernalia is to be burned. This is the nadir: the Rabbit is abandoned, unloved, and his body has broken in his service as toy to the Boy.

Now, in the sack "among the old picture-books in the corner behind the fowl-house" (24), the Rabbit cannot be saved by the Real status that the Boy fixed on him. The reality of this abandonment elicits a paroxysm of nostalgia for his lost life, and consequently, "a tear, a real tear, trickled down his little shabby velvet nose and fell to the ground" (26). The Rabbit must save himself. The tear is magically real, and it is the perfect ableist vision of disability because it is a pity tear. The conventional emotion that the nondisabled world employs for the disabled is inevitably pity. In the normate world, much as the deviant body defines disability, so does pity, and so Williams invokes the pity trope as she saves her Rabbit protagonist from burning, given that the tear with which the Rabbit has watered the ground produces a flower from which comes the "nursery magic" Fairy, as she calls herself. She might as well be called the "pity Fairy," however, because it is the Rabbit's tear of self-pity that brings her out of the nursery to exercise her power in the larger natural world. Moreover, she produces a more powerful metamorphosis for him, to "be Real to every one" (28). Ironically, on the brink of destruction, the Rabbit can save himself through a conventional trope of disability. Williams could have simply had the Fairy transform the Rabbit through a generic exercise of magic power, but she chooses to ground the Rabbit's second transformation in the "Real" again through disability. Williams's choice reinforces Mitchell and Snyder's claim that narrative needs to be enabled by the prosthesis of disability to move forward, even at the last stage when "the remainder of the story rehabilitates or fixes the deviance in some manner" (53). Thus, the marks of the Rabbit's formerly disabled body remain stubbornly visible and powerful. Narratives are self-crippling artifacts. As the newly crip-empowered Fairy acts, she makes the Rabbit both real—he has a whole body and moves under his own power—and eternal, for, as she tells the other rabbits, "he is going to live with you for ever and ever!" (Williams, *The Velveteen Rabbit* 29). Williams's attempt to rehabilitate the Rabbit and make him normal thus "short-circuits" (to use Quayson's term) the ableist fantasy of rehabilitation because the Rabbit now ends the story in a far *more* powerful position than he occupied in the rest of the story. Even at the very end, Williams cannot erase the old Rabbit in the new hybrid real-eternal Rabbit. As the now-older Boy watches the rabbits in the forest the next spring, he finds one reminiscent of the Velveteen Rabbit that "had strange markings under his fur, as though long ago he had been spotted, and the spots still showed through" (33). The spots remind the Boy of the love that he still feels for his former, disabled rabbit toy. Thus, disability remains a powerful structural and motive force throughout the book, even as Williams would use ableist strategies to erase it. *The Velveteen Rabbit* is a book that rightly ends by leaving us uneasy and nervous, as both Goffman and Quayson would have it, because the happily-ever-after finish, like the rest of the book, is marked by stigma. To invoke the great tubercular poet John Keats's concept of "negative capability," *The Velveteen Rabbit* is "capable of being in uncertainties" (60).

In contrast, by 1927, Williams was no longer capable of "being in uncertainties" and produced *The Skin Horse*, a follow-up to *The Velveteen Rabbit* that is even more marked by disability than the first story but in far more conventional ways. It is darker, more sentimental, and oriented toward an adult audience, offering no hope of a cure or transformation in this world. The family donates the Skin Horse—older, more worn, now with a wobbly leg—as a gift to a children's hospital for its Christmas celebration. The Skin Horse finds its way to an unnamed child who is bedridden and cannot even sit up due to an unspecified back injury, which causes the child great pain. The Skin Horse and the child bond, love each other, and, per Williams's conceit, the Skin Horse remains Real. The Skin Horse is with the child for a year, and through the bond of their imagination, they talk of a bright mobile future when the child is cured and can travel the world. The child is not visited by parents, family, or friends. Before the next Christmas, an operation is performed which the nurse promises will "have you running all over the house soon" (Williams, *The Skin Horse* 35). But after the child returns to the ward, his condition does not improve. While the child is in surgery, the Skin Horse decides to exercise his wobbly leg in preparation for the child's recovery but falls out of the bed and onto the floor, where the ward nurse accidentally steps on him, separating the wobbly leg from the body and breaking the body as well. She throws the toy out, and when the child returns to the ward, she lies to him that "the horse galloped off somewhere by himself" (39). Feeling guilty, she buys the boy a brand-new toy horse, which he appreciates, but nonetheless he still pines after the Skin Horse. As Christmas approaches, the boy subsides into depression and confusion about the Skin Horse, "for . . . they had planned to go off together, when he was well, and see the world" (44). The boy is so sad that he does not want a Christmas gift, but on Christmas Eve, he dreams that he is visited by the Skin Horse, who is miraculously whole, full sized, and has wings. The boy gets out of bed and onto the back of the horse, and they fly out of the hospital room and high into the air, where the boy falls asleep, "knowing that wherever his friend should take him it would be well" (53). The Skin Horse functions as a mythic Christ figure escorting the innocent child to heaven. Mitchell and Snyder's template of narrative prosthesis is again applicable: disability is identified and brought to the center of the narrative. Although the reason for the boy's immobility is not identified, he is rehabilitated through the prosthesis of the Skin Horse, which allows the boy to finally move and then disappear into the afterlife.

The curtain on the story of the Skin Horse and his child comes down hard, for the implied deaths of the two disabled main characters disallows the possibility "that a life that includes impairment can also include positive change over time. It can include growth" (Michals and McTiernan). In *The Velveteen Rabbit*, Williams avoids this kind of closure, however, because the disability-enabled, transformed, marked, hybrid real-eternal rabbit continues to exist in this world, albeit in a new form. Williams abandons such an optimistic possibility in the later story for the Skin Horse and his child. Although Williams does not attempt to sketch out a possible future for the Rabbit, the story offers a future for readers to think about.

Notes

1. What Alison Kafer calls, in *Feminist, Queer, Crip* (2013), the "curative imaginary" (27).
2. Garland-Thomson defines "normate" as "the form, function, behaviors, and appearances that conform to all of the culturally valued traits in the social systems of gender, race, class, sexuality, and ability. The normate is medically and socially hypernormal, displaying the markers of that status and collecting resources and status from this embodied form of social capital" ("Eugenic World Building" 135).

3. For more comprehensive histories of disability studies, please see Simi Linton, Scott Pollard, and Ato Quayson (1–31).

4. In disability studies, "norm" is a term used as both an adjective and noun to indicate socially constructed ableist values.

5. See Lois Rostow Kuznets on how the story asks readers to identify with a toy protagonist (61).

6. One of the primary motives of disability rights activists and disability scholars is to transform disability into a broader, inclusive social category shaped by a network of discourses (political, cultural, environmental, educational, etc.) that recognizes the subjectivity of people with disabilities as social actors, rather than sees them as objects of medical practice.

7. The relationship between illness and disability is fascinating and complex—and far beyond the scope of this essay. For a useful overview, see Susan Wendell's discussion (19–22).

Works Cited

Bérubé, Michael. *The Secret Life of Stories: From Don Quixote to Harry Potter. How Understanding Intellectual Disability Transforms the Way We Read.* New York UP, 2016.

Daniels, Steven V. "*The Velveteen Rabbit*: A Kleinian Perspective." *Children's Literature*, vol. 18, 1990, pp. 17–30.

Galbraith, Mary. "What Must I Give Up in Order to Grow Up? The Great War and Childhood Survival Strategies in Transatlantic Picture Books." *The Lion and the Unicorn*, vol. 24, no. 3, Sept. 2000, pp. 337–59.

Garland-Thomson, Rosemarie. "Eugenic World Building and Disability: The Strange World of Kazuo Ishiguro's *Never Let Me Go.*" *Journal of Medical Humanities*, vol. 38, 2017, pp. 133–45, https://doi.org/10.1007/s10912-015-9368-y.

Garland-Thomson, Rosemarie. "Roosevelt's Sister: Why We Need Disability Studies in the Humanities." *Disability Studies Quarterly*, vol. 30, no. 3–4, 2010, http://dx.doi.org/10.18061/dsq.v30i3/4.1278.

Goffman, Erving. *Stigma: Notes on the Management of a Spoiled Identity.* Simon and Schuster, 1963.

The Guardian. "Get the Right Thing: An Expert Guide to Velvet." 11 Nov. 2005, p. 24.

Jacobson, Kirsten. "Heidegger, Winnicott, and *The Velveteen Rabbit*: Anxiety, Toys, and the Drama of Metaphysics." *Philosophy and Children's Literature*, edited by Peter R. Costello, Lexington Books, 2012, pp. 1–20.

Kafer, Alison. *Feminist, Queer, Crip.* Indiana UP, 2013.

Keats, John. *Selected Letters of John Keats.* Edited by Grant F. Scott, Harvard UP, 2005.

Kuznets, Lois Rostow. *When Toys Come Alive: Narratives of Animation, Metamorphosis, and Development.* Yale UP, 1994.

Linton, Simi. *Claiming Disability: Knowledge and Identity.* New York UP, 1998.

McNulty, Faith. "Children's Books for Christmas." *New Yorker*, 6 Dec. 1982, pp. 176–82.

Michals, Teresa, and Claire McTiernan. "'Oh, Why Can't You Remain Like This Forever!': Children's Literature, Growth, and Disability." *Disability Studies Quarterly*, vol. 38, no. 2, 2018, https://doi.org/10.18061/dsq.v38i2.6107.

Mitchell, David T., and Sharon L. Snyder. *Narrative Prosthesis: Disability and the Dependencies of Discourse.* U of Michigan P, 2000.

Paris, Michael. *Over the Top: The Great War and Juvenile Literature in Britain.* Praeger, 2004.

Pollard, Scott. "Introduction: The Art of Our Art, the Quirkiness of Our Forms." *Children's Literature Association Quarterly*, vol. 38, no. 3, 2013, pp. 263–66.

Quayson, Ato. *Aesthetic Nervousness: Disability and the Crisis of Representation*. Columbia UP, 2007.

Stiker, Henri-Jacques. *A History of Disability*. 1997. Translated by William Sayers, U of Michigan P, 1999.

Wendell, Susan. *The Rejected Body: Feminist Philosophical Reflections on Disability*. Routledge, 1996.

Williams, Margery. *The Skin Horse*. Illustrated by Pamela Bianco, Green Tiger Press, 1927.

Williams, Margery. *The Velveteen Rabbit: Or How Toys Become Real*. 1922. Illustrated by William Nicholson, Doubleday, 1991.

Chapter 13

Whiteness and the Selective Tradition in *The Velveteen Rabbit*

—KaaVonia Hinton

One of the first magazines for Black children, *The Brownies' Book*, published its twenty-fourth and final issue in 1921, the year before *The Velveteen Rabbit* was printed. The two one-hundred-year-old texts present ideas about race to children, though one, *The Brownies' Book*, does so overtly while the other, *The Velveteen Rabbit*, does so with stealth. Fern Kory argues that *The Brownies' Book* signifies on White American children's literature influenced by European folklore and fairy tales through its use of fairy stories that feature beautiful brown children and brown fairies. Thus, *The Brownies' Book* combats and revises standards of beauty, among other ideas, found in White children's literature (Kory 91). In *The Signifying Monkey: A Theory of African-American Literary Criticism* (1988), Henry Louis Gates Jr. describes signifying as a form of revision, a trope rooted in the Black American oral tradition and literature that appears as theme, rhetoric, and literary history (89). Gates goes on to explain, "Signifyin(g), then, is a metaphor for textual revision" (96). Leaning on Gates and others, I have posited that when signifying, "Authors read, revise, and (re)present Black experiences to illustrate the nuances of Black life in the United States" (Hinton, "Do You See" 52).

Signifying on, or revising, White American children's literature was necessary, in part, because Black characters were scarce in Eurocentric children's literature, and when included, they were depicted in racist ways. According to Violet Harris, *The Brownies' Book* set out to intervene by opposing the selective tradition of children's literature (192). The concept of the "selective tradition" derives from Raymond Williams, who defines it as "an intentionally selective version of a shaping past and a pre-shaped present, which is then powerfully operative in the process of social and cultural definition and identification" (115). R. Williams emphasizes that tradition or "the surviving past" is presented as neutral rather than as hegemonic, curated, and beneficial to "the interest of the dominance of a specific class" (115–16). Joel Taxel applies R. Williams's concept to children's literature and concludes historical fiction about the American Revolution presents a selective view of the Revolution that is "both simplistic and conservative because it omits significant dimensions of the conflict, as well as the concerns of the Black and lower-class ... population" (27). Drawing upon R. Williams's and Taxel's important work, V. Harris notes that the selective tradition is designed to portray the images, values, and beliefs of Whites, including "racial intolerance, institutionalized discrimination, and social inequity" (192). V. Harris also suggests the selective tradition is devoted to capitalism, colonialism, and domination (192). As Ebony Elizabeth Thomas reminds us, "Children's literature is a site for the origin of ideas about race and racism in the United States" (404). Of course, race and racism are not confined to the United States. White supremacy and colonization exceed US borders, and widely translated children's literature classics, such as *The Velveteen Rabbit*, are a site for other ideologies aligned with racism, too, including Whiteness.

On the surface, Margery Williams appears to offer a neutral story in which she avoids explicitly attaching racial identity to her characters in *The Velveteen Rabbit*. Similarly, at first glance, William Nicholson's seven lithographs support the author's raceless approach. Most of these illustrations depict the Velveteen Rabbit and are free of the four human characters the book refers to: the Boy, Nana, the doctor, and the gardener. However, in Nicholson's sixth illustration, "The Fairy Flower," a White fairy makes White racial identity undeniably visible for the first time in the storybook, firmly staking the book's claim in the selective tradition. Other than the fairy's obvious white skin, the ideology of Whiteness is almost imperceptible. However, a close reading suggests Whiteness, and how it intersects with gender and class is actually prominent throughout *The Velveteen Rabbit*. In this volume, Kelly Blewett and Alisa Clapp-Itnyre note that "there is undeniable power in [Nicholson's] illustrations," given that the original storybook has never been out of print in the United States or in England and prints of his lithographs continue to be sold today (39). Indeed, Nicholson's illustrations do "have staying power," and they "inspired late twentieth-century children's illustrators, who often echo his approaches to the story by illustrating the same key narrative moments" (Blewett and Clapp-Itnyre 39). Subsequent adaptations suggest that despite M. Williams's efforts to feature racelessness, adapters and illustrators, such as Michael Hague, Gennady Spirin, Charles Santore, and Steve Johnson and Lou Fancher, assumed Whiteness, preserve Nicholson's White fairy, and actually ascribe a White racial identity to the human characters.

Instead of maintaining the pretense that Whiteness is normal, universal, and natural or that it "embodies objectivity . . . truth, knowledge, merit, motivation, achievements, and trustworthiness," scholarship about Whiteness names it as racial identity, ideology, behavior, and power (Fine et al., viii). Michelle Fine et al. assert, "*Rarely . . . is it acknowledged that whiteness demands and constitutes hierarchy, exclusion, and deprivation*" (viii, emphasis original). The role of Whiteness in marginalization and destruction is seldom recognized because, as bell hooks writes, Blacks and Whites are socialized to believe "whiteness represents goodness and all that is benign and nonthreatening" (169). Cheryl Harris takes it a step further in "Whiteness as Property" (1993) and posits Whiteness not only has unearned privileges, including the power to define and exclude, but it also presents as material (e.g., landownership, buildings, and equipment) and intellectual property; this applies to children's literature and notions of the selective tradition as well. While examining US literature in *Playing in the Dark* (1992), Toni Morrison looks closely at how Whiteness uses Blackness to forge a US identity. Robin Bernstein's analysis in *Racial Innocence: Performing American Childhood from Slavery to Civil Rights* (2011) similarly involves literature and material culture and its participation in perpetuating ideas about White innocence and vulnerability while situating Black children as insensate. Critical Whiteness studies attempts to explore Whiteness as a racial identity and ideology imbued with power and privileges. Critical Whiteness scholars, such as Emily Lind, assert that Whiteness must be disrupted, and part of disrupting Whiteness includes illuminating it when it attempts to hide in plain view, "invisible" and silent (241). Tenets of Whiteness studies such as these are useful for examining Whiteness in *The Velveteen Rabbit*.

This chapter argues that Whiteness is positioned as normative, as a standard way of behaving, living, looking, and thinking in the original edition of M. Williams's book, and in later adaptations. Specifically, articulations of Whiteness are examined in the original 1922 version of *The Velveteen Rabbit* and four picturebook adaptations. Three—those illustrated by Hague (Henry Holt, 1983), Spirin (Marshall Cavendish Children, 2011), and Santore (Appleseed, 2012, published under the name Margery Williams Bianco)—adhere closely to the original text. The story has been simplified for very young readers in the fourth book considered, which is illustrated by S. Johnson and Fancher (Atheneum, 2002). All four versions read Whiteness in M. Williams's text and present the human characters *and* the fairy as White. In fact, on each of the four covers, a cherubic-looking, White boy with blond hair is shown embracing the toy rabbit (S. Johnson and Fancher; Santore; Spirin) or sitting near it (Hague), further cementing the classic as representative of children's literature in the selective tradition. I conclude by discussing the conflation of Whiteness and wealth and arguing that portraying the human characters as White helps convey the power these characters have over

Rabbit and support a selective tradition, which, V. Harris rightly points out, seeks to legitimate hierarchy and domination and enforce the image of childhood as White and upper class (192).

When *The Velveteen Rabbit* opens, Rabbit is a lovely Christmas present, among many, given to a raceless and nameless boy. Yet, the Boy quickly abandons the Rabbit, who finds himself neglected in the middle of a nursery where he observes the other toys and notices hierarchies exist around class—"Being only made of velveteen, some of the expensive toys quite snubbed him"; personality type—"He was naturally shy. . . ."; proximity in likeness to real objects—"The model boat . . ."; modernity—"The mechanical toys were very superior, and looked down upon every one else; they were full of modern ideas and pretended they were real"; and ability or function—"Even Timothy, the jointed wooden lion, who . . . should have had broader views, put on airs" (M. Williams 2014, 3). Hierarchical structures among the nursery's toys have parallels in society, just as humans set themselves apart from others and claim superiority. In this volume, Scott T. Pollard and Kara K. Keeling rightly assert, "The child as owner invisibly occupies the top of the pyramid" and "he represents the unmarked norm that the other toys wish to emulate" (198). Pollard and Keeling's reading of how M. Williams positions the Boy's physical body as normative and ideal is noteworthy, but it also alludes to how the author signals Whiteness when depicting the Boy, who is at "the top" and normative.

Other, subtler hierarchies exist as well. Paige Sammartino notes Rabbit's transformation can also be read as hierarchical, as he moves from "toy, Real toy, [to] living creature" (157). Nursery magic also seems to be hierarchical. Skin Horse tells Rabbit only certain toys are selected to be Real: "When a child loves you for a long, long time . . . REALLY loves you, then you become Real" (M. Williams 2014, 5). Even rarer are those few toys whom "the nursery magic Fairy" chooses to turn "into Real" (26). Confused by the Fairy's announcement that she will make him into Real because the Boy had already declared him so, Rabbit asks, "Wasn't I Real before?" The Fairy replies, "You were Real to the Boy. . . . Now you shall be Real to every one" (28). Only select toys become Real, and when Rabbit is transformed, he is allowed to live in nature with other rabbits "for ever and ever!" (28). Authority and power among the human characters—Nana, the doctor, the gardener, and the Boy—are also presented hierarchically, particularly concerning what is best for the Boy's health and well-being and determining Rabbit's fate. Hierarchies appear prominently throughout *The Velveteen Rabbit* and help fuel the tale. However, there is one hierarchy in society the book seems to be silent about: racial hierarchy. M. Williams might be performing what Bernstein calls innocence of or an "obliviousness" to racial hierarchies (8). Indeed, the text of *The Velveteen Rabbit* does not mention race at all. M. Williams appears to have written a largely colorblind or neutral story; however, Whiteness reveals itself.

Colorblindness and Whiteness Studies

In *Racial Innocence*, Bernstein maintains White conceptions of childhood exclude Black children and seek to manufacture White children as innocent, angelic, and deserving of protection (33). Henry A. Giroux calls the focus on Whiteness as innocent and benign "a mythic vision of whiteness" that needs to be disrupted (287). Whiteness scholars such as Giroux view Whiteness as a social construct that is underexamined (289). Whiteness studies stems from scholarship by W. E. B. Du Bois and others that is over a century old, particularly Du Bois's classic chapter, "The Souls of White Folk," published in 1920 in *Darkwater: Voices from Within the Veil*. For Du Bois, Whiteness is neither invisible nor neutral: "I see in and through [White folks]. . . . I know their thoughts and they know that I know. This knowledge makes them now embarrassed, now furious!" (923). Du Bois observes, analyzes, and evaluates Whiteness, making it both visible and knowable. "The Souls of White Folk" is a rich chapter, and in it, Du Bois argues that Whites are complicit in racism, European imperialism caused World War I, race is a social construct, and Whiteness relies on Blackness to manufacture an assemblance of status, of superiority. Further, Du Bois maintains Whiteness and its preoccupation with dehumanizing Blackness are insidious and ingrained: "This theory of human culture and its aims has worked itself through warp and woof of our daily thought with a thoroughness that few realize. Everything great, good, efficient, fair, and honorable is 'white,'" he claims, while "yellow," "brown," and "black" are the opposite, and "this theme [is] continually rung in picture and story, in newspaper heading and moving-picture, in sermon and school book" (933). The selective tradition Du Bois describes socializes members of society, emphasizes certain values, and influences behavior. Du Bois created *The Brownies' Book*, according to V. Harris, in response to letters he received from Black children requesting information about their history and culture that challenged what they were being exposed to in children's literature and textbooks. Though Whiteness is deemed beautiful, pure, innocent, and valuable, in "The Souls of White Folk," Du Bois illuminates the power and destructiveness of Whiteness and the selective tradition, and it lays the foundation for Whiteness studies.

Eduardo Bonilla-Silva maintains that "stories about whites become universal stories about all of us," and stories help maintain and convey a colorblind ideology (177). Scholars, such as Charles Gallagher, argue colorblindness is rooted in Whiteness, particularly ideas of what is natural, normal, and acceptable (25–26). In *The New Jim Crow* (2010), Michelle Alexander warns that colorblindness is dangerous and "has proved catastrophic for African Americans" (240). Further, as I have asserted elsewhere, "colorblindness masks, denies, and ignores structural racism, racist practices, and racial hierarchies" (Hinton, "What Are These" 245). One of the stories we tell ourselves, according to Bonilla-Silva, is that racial matters, particularly those involving Whiteness, are actually nonracial, natural, or just the way things are (54). As Morrison argues convincingly, ignoring race is nearly impossible; race seeps into the "writerly imagination" (xii). This seems true of M. Williams's imagination as well. There are articulations of Whiteness in *The Velveteen Rabbit*, that, like other literature in the selective tradition, as seen in Taxel's and V. Harris's studies, serve to shape and convey White beliefs and interests.

Racial Silences in *The Velveteen Rabbit*

There are several possible reasons why only a few characters are depicted in Nicholson's illustrations and M. Williams's text renders the humans raceless, providing no physical descriptions of the Boy, Nana, the gardener, or the doctor. M. Williams might have made this decision because as Lois Rostow Kuznets explains, "the reader is asked to identify with a toy rather than with a human protagonist" (61). Perhaps M. Williams concluded that descriptions of the human characters are unnecessary and could distract readers from focusing on the Rabbit. However, by ignoring race, M. Williams appears to follow a pattern of "silence and evasion" that has "historically ruled literary discourse" (Morrison 9). Morrison maintains that silence about race is "complicated by the fact that the habit of ignoring race is understood to be a graceful, even generous, liberal gesture" (9–10). Yet, Morrison goes on to note, "The act of enforcing racelessness in literary discourse is itself a racial act" (46). According to George Yancy, "Whiteness is deemed the 'One,' the axiomatic norm that defines racial 'difference,' which, by being so, maintains its status as the 'superior' race and yet, paradoxically, as unraced, human as such" (197). By making the human characters raceless in European culture they are deemed White, universal.

When *The Velveteen Rabbit* was written, the selective tradition of children's literature did not, according to V. Harris, depict the Black middle class, though *The Brownies' Book* set out to challenge this (194). In fact, though Black middle- and upper-class people existed during the late Victorian era, there were few, and it is unlikely M. Williams had a Black child in mind as the protagonist of her book, especially since she wrote the story based on family memories: "She happened to think of cherished toys from her childhood and toys that her children had loved. These memories led to *The Velveteen Rabbit* (inspired by a toy rabbit named Tubby) and formed the basis for all of Bianco's subsequent stories" (Eiss 160). Thus, it is not a stretch to read the Boy and his family as White. M. Williams was born in London in 1881, but after her father died in 1888, her family moved to the United States where Williams attended school in Pennsylvania and spent time in England (Eiss 160). Despite the author spending time and having lived in both England and the United States, critics often insist that *The Velveteen Rabbit* takes place in England and that the Boy is British. Perhaps this is because of the significance British literature has placed on the nursery, "a recognizable and necessary staple in middle- and upper-class British homes," as Karlie Herndon describes in detail in this volume (181).

The British nursery was an important place to socialize children. Herndon avers, "These nurseries were spaces in which children learned what it meant to be a member of society . . . and properly gendered—adults" (184). Not only were children taught to be "properly gendered," they were also taught to be properly raced and classed. When imagining the significance of the Boy's toys in the nursery, Herndon explains, "The prevalence of the modern windup toys, particularly gender-specific items . . . indicates adults' attempts to press more masculine play on the Boy, presenting him with items that he might encounter as a man, particularly a British citizen at the height of imperialism" (187). Placing the Boy in the future as a British man freely (both physically and financially) traveling to British colonies where he might battle wild animals (and maybe even indigenous peoples) is to read the Boy as White (and upper class). Herndon's interpretation seems sound, especially since George Lipsitz points out that colonization helps shape Whiteness (3). Herndon's is also a reasonable reading given what we know about M. Williams's personal inspiration for writing the story, which was influenced by her own background as the child of "a barrister and distinguished classical scholar" (Eiss 160). Herndon's reading is also sensible when Christopher P. Barton and Kyle Somerville's assertion about the uses of toys is taken into consideration, "Toys serve as medium of communication between children and adults, and suggest and reinforce norms of behavior. . . . Victorian toys were profoundly didactic objects, meant to reinforce notions of gender roles, moral values, and a strong sense of nationalistic pride" (50). While Barton and Somerville are referring to the US when they reference national pride, they could just as easily have been referencing England and how dominant notions of nationhood and citizenship in both countries connote Whiteness.

The family's disposable income, particularly the money spent on toys, further suggests Whiteness. Barton and Somerville posit many of the purchased toys during the Victorian era, particularly mechanical toys, were expensive, and they reason the toys might have been "highly curated objects. . . . received at special occasions and given a prominent place in the child's room as a visual reminder of the prosperity of the child's family" (50). The Boy's family does not appear to be concerned about the expense of the toys, and they do not require him to curate them or put his toys on display. Instead, the Boy plays with them, and some are even played with until they are worn, or worse, break: The Skin Horse "had seen a long succession of mechanical toys arrive to boast and swagger, and by-and-by break their mainsprings and pass away" (M. Williams 2014, 4). Similarly, "The model boat, who had lived through two seasons . . . lost most of his paint" (3). Besides, in order to become Real, a toy had to be loved so much, meaning it was played with extensively, which led to being worn out: Rabbit's "beautiful velveteen fur was getting shabbier and shabbier, and his tail coming unsewn, and all the pink rubbed off his nose where the Boy had kissed him" (10). According to Barton and Somerville, because of the cost of toys, they "would not have been brought outside where they might be damaged" (50). Perhaps the Rabbit was inexpensive, but he was considered "splendid" and "quite the best of all" of the items in the Boy's Christmas stocking (1). However, the Boy does play with Rabbit outside: "He had rides in the wheelbarrow, and picnics on the grass, and lovely fairy huts built for him under the raspberry canes behind the flower border" (11–12). The Boy even leaves Rabbit outdoors, putting him at risk of being damaged: "And once, when the Boy was called away suddenly to go out to tea, the Rabbit was left out on the lawn until long after dusk. . . . He was wet through with dew . . ." (12).

Rabbit and the other toys are also replaceable. On Christmas morning, the Boy plays with Rabbit for two hours before other toys capture his interest. Nana, too busy to hunt for the Boy's china dog, reunites him with Rabbit due to convenience. After Rabbit is sentenced to die by fire, someone buys the Boy a replacement bunny just in time for him to vacation to the seaside: "It was a splendid bunny, all white plush with real glass eyes" (24). The Boy's access to toys he can actually play with without regard to wear and tear or to whether they will be replaced not only suggests the family's wealth in nineteenth-century England but also its Whiteness.

According to C. Richard King et al., there are behaviors, beliefs, and practices that are "associated with whiteness" (161). For example, the lifestyle of comfort, leisure, and ease gained through others' toil featured in *The Velveteen Rabbit* suggests Whiteness and a stark contrast to the lives of most Black children in the 1920s. The Boy is free to play, take leisure, and use his imagination all day: "Near the house where they lived was a wood, and in the long June evenings the Boy liked to go there after tea to play. . . . [He] wandered off to pick flowers, or play at brigands among the trees" (M. Williams 2014, 13). The Boy is allowed the freedom to enjoy himself because his family is able to afford property, including a spacious garden, and employees, such as Nana, his nurse. The Boy's freedom and his family's wealth help make his innocence possible. According to Bernstein, "to invoke white childhood is to invoke innocence itself" (63). However, the Boy initiates a mixture of both innocent interactions and rough play with Rabbit: "The Boy hugged him very tight, and sometimes he rolled over on him, and sometimes he pushed him so far under the pillow that the Rabbit could scarcely breathe. . . ." (M. Williams 2014, 9). The Boy is also depicted as thoughtful, making a tunnel "under the bedclothes" to replicate "the burrows the real rabbits lived in" (10). Though the Boy exhibits "unfaithful and cavalier" behavior as Kuznets points out, his feelings for and interactions with Rabbit are both caring and neglectful (61). M. Williams writes that before the Boy went off to play, he left the Rabbit alone, but "he always made the Rabbit a little nest somewhere among the bracken, where he could be quite cosy" (M. Williams 2014, 13). Meanwhile, the Rabbit's appearance, because of how the Boy treats him, worsens to the point of being unrecognizable as "the little Rabbit grew very old and shabby.... He loved him so hard that he loved all his whiskers off, and the pink lining to his ears turned grey, and his brown spots faded. He even began to lose his shape, and he scarcely looked like a rabbit any more" (20). The Boy, who both loves and innocently destroys the Rabbit, is depicted as what Bernstein might call a "white angel-child," those children positioned in material culture to suggest purity (65). Due to class privilege, the Boy mis/handles Rabbit with the assurance that the toy is replaceable.

Whiteness in *The Velveteen Rabbit* is manifest most obviously through the image of the Fairy, a symbol of White purity, protection, safety, and security. It is quite likely M. Williams and Nicholson did not discuss how he would imagine the Fairy. M. Williams simply writes, "She was quite the loveliest fairy in the whole world. Her dress was of pearl and dewdrops, and there were flowers around her neck and in her hair, and her face was like the most perfect flower of all" (38). Nicholson's interpretation of the text is seen in his sixth illustration, "The Fairy Flower." A White, slim fairy with long, straight, silky-looking hair emerges from the center of a flower petal, reinscribing ideas about feminine beauty linked to Whiteness while simultaneously upholding the selective tradition. Beauty standards are established by the dominant culture and transmitted into society. Within the selective tradition, White women and girls embody beauty. Elsewhere, I discuss how white skin and light eye color, straight, long hair, preferably blond, and thinness are expressions of White beauty that all others are pressured to obtain/emulate (Hinton-Johnson 29). Nicholson's fairy, and those it has inspired in subsequent editions of the book, embodies a White-defined beauty aesthetic and helps standardize it.

Recent Adaptations of *The Velveteen Rabbit*: Whiteness Seeps Out

The four versions (S. Johnson and Fancher; Hague; Santore; Spirin) I explore here were published after *The Velveteen Rabbit*'s copyright expired in 1982. The text in the Hague, Santore, and Spirin editions echoes the original, while S. Johnson and Fancher's version was adapted for very young readers (i.e., toddlers). The illustrations in each book portray the Boy, other human characters, and the Fairy as White. For example, in Hague's 1983 book, the Boy is featured prominently on the cover, in a two-page spread opening and ending the book, and seven additional times throughout the book. Similarly, in Spirin's book published in 2011, in addition to the Boy being featured on the cover, he appears in eight more illustrations, though one is the cover image, which appears on page 17. Articulations of Whiteness are also evident in Santore's 2012 "heirloom" edition in which the Boy is shown nine times, including the image on the cover. The number of times the Boy is portrayed suggests these illustrators, in contrast to Nicholson, view the Boy's image, which is depicted as White, as pivotal, and it racializes the pseudo-colorblind original book.

Most of the illustrations in these books promote a narrative of White innocence and portray the Boy playing with Rabbit or in bed sleeping, reading, or embracing the toy. In Spirin's book, on Christmas morning, the Boy sits on the floor beside some gifts ("nuts and oranges and a toy engine, and chocolate almonds and a clockwork mouse"), holding Rabbit, one hand near his ears while the other touches Rabbit's paw (M. Williams 2011, 6). The cover image follows, showing the Boy sleeping soundly while holding Rabbit tightly (17). In these images, the Boy's innocence and angelic disposition are made clear. Conversely, in Hague's interpretation of the story, the Boy is depicted as innocent, but he has a rougher disposition than the little boys shown in the other adaptations. On the cover, for example, instead of being presented lovingly embracing the Rabbit the way the Boy is depicted on the other three covers, he is seated on the grass alongside the Rabbit, whom he has wrapped with a vine, an image that suggests imprisonment and the Boy's power and privilege as a human White male asserting authority. Hague's image also reinforces the hierarchical nature established in the text and the Boy's place at the top, as Pollard and Keeling describe it in this volume (198). Next, the Boy is shown standing pajama-clad on Christmas morning holding the Rabbit (whose bulging eyes show alarm) by the ears and smiling mischievously (M. Williams 1983, 2). Hague's decision to show the Boy's violent handling of the toy suggests a less obvious type of White innocence similar to what Bernstein finds in her study of material culture: a lack of awareness or acknowledgement of invoking pain (49). There are gentler, calmer, innocent interactions between the Boy and the Rabbit in the other depictions to be sure. For example, the Boy sleeps peacefully as Rabbit watches in one illustration, and in another, the Rabbit is seated while the Boy helpfully waters plants (M. Williams 1983, 7–8). And in still another painting, the Boy affectionately carries the Rabbit toward the wood (11). However, on the way back from the wooded area, the Boy holds the Rabbit carelessly once again, as Rabbit is suspended and held by one ear (18). Depictions of the Boy playing roughly with the Rabbit reflect a selective tradition that teaches Whites that they are dominant and that others, humans and possessions, are to be manipulated, positioned, and used as they see fit. In Santore's book, the Boy is first shown when the text states Nana has given him the Rabbit for the first time. To illustrate the Boy's immediate connection with the Rabbit, on two consecutive pages, small, boxed illustrations show him sleeping innocently with the Rabbit tucked in his arms (M. Williams 2012, 14–15). When the Boy is shown next, he is playing along the wood with a stick in his hand and his back to the Rabbit and two living rabbits (20). This image is juxtaposed against the next three illustrations of him subdued: first, in the picture from the cover that shows the blond Boy sitting in a rocking chair with his eyes closed, sweetly embracing the Rabbit (25); second, asleep in bed with the Rabbit by his side as he battles scarlet fever (26–27); and third, seated on the balcony swaddled in blankets marveling at a butterfly (28). Sitting out in nature, blue sky and lush green grass and trees surrounding him with a butterfly at his fingertips, signals Whiteness. Constructions of race (also class) and nature are intertwined. Whiteness has used nature to exclude, decimate, and dehumanize Black, Indigenous, and People of Color (BIPOC) while depicting nature as linked to healing and wellness for White people, notions that Cassandra Y. Johnson and J. M. Bowker argue stem from "European intellectualism and romanticism" (61).

Each version depicts the Boy as weak, suffering, and innocent—the epitome of White childhood as Bernstein describes it in her study (61). While sick, in Spirin's version, for instance, the Boy sits in bed reading a book about birds with Rabbit close by his side, continuing to suggest not only his love for and attention to Rabbit but also his innocence (M. Williams 2011, 28). Hague also portrays the Boy "able to sit up in bed and look at picture books" (M. Williams 1983, 20), though in Hague's book, the Boy is reading a book with a large picture of a White woman carrying a parasol, further centering Whiteness. The fictional book cover brings to mind Tyler Stovall's observations about White womanhood: "In both Europe and America, the proper lady was a white woman who not only kept her distance from subaltern classes and races, but whose presence could also foster the hegemony of white bourgeois civilization" (78). The book cover implicitly articulates an ideology that Whites are subjects and White womanhood, in particular, should be revered, appreciated, preserved (and emulated by women and girls).

Each adaptation concludes with a final illustration of the Boy, though he appears timider and more innocent in Hague's version, which portrays the Boy staring at the Rabbit with everlasting life from behind a tree (M. Williams 1983, 32). The image certainly contrasts with the cover image, which seems to show the Boy in control of Rabbit. Perhaps the Boy's cautiousness is due to encountering rabbits in the wild who are unpredictable and possibly dangerous, revealing his innocence one final time. The Boy positioned as one of the final characters depicted solidifies his significance. Spirin concludes the book with an illustration of the Boy wearing a sailor suit complete with knickerbockers, hands in pockets, and left foot propped on a rock, looking at two live rabbits, one of which is staring knowingly at him. The Boy looks serious and resolute as if he possesses power and has just conquered someone or something. Clothes and costumes help people consider who they are or imagine who they might become, and certain items of clothing, such as uniforms, connote power, privilege, and honor. The boy in the sailor suit is perhaps a gesture toward the prominence of imperialism and the British Royal Navy's role in it. The Royal Navy is an institution with a history of Whiteness, domination, colonization, and racism, including a "colour bar" that prevented "coloured men" from officially serving in the Royal Navy in 1940, discrimination that continued de facto after the bar was lifted, not just in the Royal Navy but also in "civilian life" (Costello 186–87, 199). Similarly, Santore's book closes with an illustration of the baby-faced Boy in a pirate costume, holding a wooden sword, and taking a moment from his imaginative play to peer at two live rabbits. The pirate outfit is likely a benign nod to the connection between pirates and British boyhood play and literature, especially children's books, but it also suggests Whiteness, imperialism, White notions of freedom, and even the slave trade (Stovall 37, 43). In S. Johnson and Fancher's interpretation of the final encounter with Rabbit, the Boy is outside playing with a ball and looks at Rabbit, who has his back to the Boy, with recognition. The prominent focus on the Boy and a sense of childhood as White and innocent remains, even in a book like S. Johnson and Fancher's that has been reimagined for a new, younger audience.

While Nana does not appear in the illustrations of the original book, and she only appears once in Hague's book, her presence is expanded in more recent editions, such as Spirin's, where she appears four times. In fact, Spirin replaces Hague's older, plain, efficient-looking Nana with another White woman who suggests idealized White beauty (M. Williams 2011, 10). This Nana has brown, long hair that sits on top of her head in a massive chignon and wears a grand, formal dress with puffy sleeves, rather than a uniform, as Hague's Nana does. Spirin's Nana connotes beauty, femininity, and opulence, which are all linked to Whiteness. In contrast, S. Johnson and Fancher depict a more matronly-looking Nana holding a contaminated Rabbit by the ear while looking at the doctor, a large White man dressed in dark clothes, who stands facing her with his hands on his hips. The doctor, in an attempt to protect the Boy, demands that Rabbit and other items exposed to scarlet fever be burned, as he does in the other adaptations, but S. Johnson and Fancher's is the only adaptation discussed here that depicts the doctor.

Similar to the Boy, the Fairy is shown multiple times in each of the books and appears as an innocent "white angel-child," to invoke Bernstein's phrase, who adores Rabbit (65). For example, Spirin's Fairy is shown three times. The frequency with which she is shown helps indicate her role as a symbol of beauty and goodness. In the first illustration, the Fairy, dressed in white, has blond hair braided into a bun sitting high on her head. Next, she flies while holding Rabbit tightly to her bosom, and then Spirin offers a closeup of the young and innocent Fairy with porcelain skin, blue eyes, and long eyelashes—staples of White beauty—kissing Rabbit (M. Williams 2011, 37–38). Nature is echoed in representations of the Fairy in each of the books, too. According to Sean Redmond, Whiteness can be made "symbolically visible" when connected to "purity, innocence, rationalism, naturalism and to the 'higher' motifs of Christianity, such as ascending angels. . . ." (92). The Fairy also appears three times in Santore's version of the tale. First, the White, long, straight, blond/yellow haired, winged Fairy springs from a flower, reminiscent of Nicholson's illustration (M. Williams 2012, 33). Second, she stares tenderly at the teary-eyed Rabbit she holds in her arms (34). And finally, in the last illustration of the Fairy, she stands angelic, complete with prayer hands, in the wood, watching the Rabbit interact with "wild rabbits" who dance about (36). Santore's Fairy (36) and Hague's (M. Williams 1983, 24–25), who stands with stars shining brilliantly in the beautiful sky behind her, particularly connote a connection to heaven and the ethereal. Interestingly, unlike the other books, S. Johnson and Fancher portray a Fairy who looks wooden or toy-like rather than lifelike. Yet, like the other versions, she appears to have white skin and reddish-brown hair, further confirming a focus on White innocence and beauty.

On Wealth and Whiteness

The selective tradition conflates wealth with Whiteness. Whiteness is grounded in exclusion and amassing opportunities, particularly those that lead to upward mobility. Slavery, segregation, and unjust policies, which have tended to help Whites financially, perpetuated a wealth gap that continues today. Bonilla-Silva maintains that "the effects of historic discrimination have limited blacks' capacity to accumulate wealth at the same rate as whites" and cites scholars who argue that "the 'accumulation of disadvantages' has 'sedimented' blacks economically so that, even if all forms of economic discrimination blacks face ended today, they would not catch up with whites for several hundred years!" (100). Blacks and other people of color have had fewer life chances in general and fewer opportunities to pursue education and lucrative careers. This has made it easier for wealth and other benefits to remain with Whites. The selective tradition depicts (and values) the upper class or wealthy and views them as White, and the adaptations discussed do this as well. Each book mentioned here shows the family's abundance and privilege through Nana's formal dress and mere presence and through the illustrations of the house, particularly the garden and nursery, the latter of which indicates the number of toys and books in the Boy's room. For example, a double-page spread in Spirin depicts the Rabbit surrounded by a huge rocking horse, White soldiers, a train, a horse-drawn carriage, and several other toys (M. Williams 2011, 10–11). Similarly, Hague has toys sprawled across the bottom of two pages, and unfortunately, one toy—with closed, slanted eyes, a round body, and wearing a large hat that looks like a sombrero—might be viewed as stereotypical or dangerously close to what Barton and Somerville call a racist toy (M. Williams 1983, 4–5). Santore's scene depicting Nana cleaning the nursery indicates wealth even more than the others, as the two-page spread shows a large room filled with books, toys, and two large doors that lead outside to the balcony (M. Williams 2012, 12–13). Spirin also suggests expansiveness of the rooms; there is an area for sleeping just behind the Boy seated in a rocker on the balcony (M. Williams 2011, 31).

If it is true that toys represent children, it is important to consider how the human/humanlike characters exert power and authority over Rabbit. Each human character shown in these adaptations is presented as White, has power, and helps shape Rabbit's fate. Authority and control are tropes of Whiteness (Giroux 304). "Nana who ruled the nursery" selects Rabbit, albeit randomly, to sleep with the Boy who becomes dependent on the toy (M. Williams 2014, 8). It is also Nana who rescues Rabbit when he is left outside and brings him in to the Boy so he can sleep. The Boy's power is more significant than Nana's, especially since she works for his family. The Boy, for example, uses a commanding tone at one point in the text and demands that Nana give him Rabbit, and because of her status, she obeys. He has the power to make Rabbit Real, and Rabbit's happiness depends on it, as he spends most of the book longing for this status. The Boy also controls Rabbit's movement: "I can jump higher than anything!" the Velveteen Rabbit tells his biological counterparts. "He meant when the Boy threw him, but of course he didn't want to say so" (17). Had he not abandoned Rabbit, the Boy would have likely had the power to interfere and prevent Rabbit's demise long before the Fairy was conjured to assist. Distracted by thoughts of the seaside, the Boy does not question where Rabbit is or protest when he is given a new toy rabbit, even though the Rabbit had practically cured the Boy: "All sorts of delightful things he planned, and while the Boy lay half asleep he crept up close to the pillow and whispered them in his ear. And presently the fever turned, and the Boy got better" (21). But when the Rabbit needs him most, the Boy engages in what Bernstein refers to in her study of racial innocence performed during childhood as "not-noticing" and in "obliviousness" (6), reminiscent of what M. Williams performed by not acknowledging racial hierarchies in her story. This seems odd coming from the same Boy who belligerently defended Rabbit's importance and declared him Real: "The Boy sat up in bed and stretched out his hands. 'Give me my Bunny!' he said. 'You mustn't say that. He isn't a toy. He's REAL!'" (M. Williams 2014, 12). The Boy's actions and tone betray his Whiteness through his sense of entitlement and his power over Nana and the Rabbit. Yet, interestingly, after his illness, the Boy relinquishes his authority over Rabbit and the adults, whom he surely could have tried to persuade, and turns his back on Rabbit, leaving Rabbit's fate in the hands of the doctor. Though only illustrated in S. Johnson and Fancher's adaptation, the doctor's power over Rabbit leads to his being sentenced to death. The doctor's authority, bolstered by his role as a physician, possibly would have rivaled the

Boy's authority, had he tried to use it, and it certainly supersedes Nana's, who questions the doctor only for the sake of clarity:

> "How about his old Bunny?" she asked.
> "*That?*" said the doctor. "Why, it's a mass of scarlet fever germs!—Burn it at once. What? Nonsense! Get him a new one. He mustn't have that any more!" (22)

The White, beautiful, powerful Fairy, consistently portrayed as such since the original via Nicholson's illustrations, has the ultimate power to make a difference for Rabbit—to free him. She treats him lovingly, saves him, and gives him eternal life. In these adaptations, powerful characters are ascribed Whiteness. V. Harris writes, "The selective tradition in children's literature also taught whites that they were the natural leaders of Blacks and to treat Blacks in paternalistic ways" (192). While there are no Native American, Black, or Asian characters in the book, the message to all about White superiority is implicit.

At first glance, *The Velveteen Rabbit* appears to be a colorblind story. Quite the contrary, *The Velveteen Rabbit* weaves what Giroux would call a narrative of Whiteness that complements the selective tradition, which implies how Whites should perceive themselves and others (290). This chapter suggests Williams's original book contains articulations of Whiteness via representations of characters such as the Fairy and the Boy. Later adaptations, particularly the four discussed here, make no attempts at colorblindness and, perhaps due to White domination and exclusion within society and the selective tradition, ascribe White racial identities to the Boy and other human characters portrayed in the illustrations. Remembering *The Velveteen Rabbit*, published a year after *The Brownies' Book*, invites us to consider the books we characterize as classics and the ways in which they might exclude and uphold the selective tradition.

Works Cited

Alexander, Michelle. *The New Jim Crow: Mass Incarceration in the Age of Colorblindness*. New Press, 2010.

Barton, Christopher P., and Kyle Somerville. "Play Things: Children's Racialized Mechanical Banks and Toys, 1880–1930." *International Journal of Historical Archaeology*, vol. 16, no. 1, Mar. 2012, pp. 47–85.

Bernstein, Robin. *Racial Innocence: Performing American Childhood from Slavery to Civil Rights*. New York UP, 2011.

Blewett, Kelly, and Alisa Clapp-Itnyre. "Visualizing Velveteen: Original Illustrations and Subsequent Adaptations." *The Velveteen Rabbit at 100*, edited by Lisa R. Fraustino, UP of Mississippi, 2023, pp. 38–61.

Bonilla-Silva, Eduardo. *Racism without Racists: Color-Blind Racism and the Persistence of Racial Inequality in America*. 5th ed., Rowman & Littlefield, 2018.

Costello, Ray. *Black Salt: Seafarers of African Descent on British Ships*. Liverpool UP, 2012.
Du Bois, W. E. B. "The Souls of White Folk." *W. E. B. Du Bois: Writings. The Suppression of the African Slave-Trade. The Souls of Black Folk. Dusk of Dawn. Essays*, edited by Nathan Huggins, Library of America, 1987, pp. 923–38. *Library of America*, https://loa-shared.s3.amazonaws.com/static/pdf/Du_Bois_White_Folk.pdf. Accessed 15 Oct. 2021.
Eiss, Harry E. "Margery Williams Bianco (22 July 1881–4 September 1944)." *British Children's Writers, 1914–1960*, edited by Donald R. Hettinga and Gary D. Schmidt, Gale, 1996, pp. 45–49. Dictionary of Literary Biography 160. *Gale Literature: Dictionary of Literary Biography*, https://link.gale.com/apps/doc/KYOKDP063981956/DLBC?u=mag_u_usm&sid=DLBC&xid=07922272. Accessed 18 Oct. 2021.
Fine, Michelle, et al. *Off White: Readings on Race, Power, and Society*. Routledge, 1997.
Gallagher, Charles. "Color-Blind Privilege: The Social and Political Functions of Erasing the Color Line in Post Race America." *Race, Gender & Class*, vol. 10, no. 4, 2003, pp. 22–37.
Gates, Henry Louis, Jr. *The Signifying Monkey: A Theory of African-American Literary Criticism*. Oxford UP, 1988.
Giroux, Henry A. "Rewriting the Discourse of Racial Identity: Towards a Pedagogy and Politics of Whiteness." *Harvard Educational Review*, vol. 67, no. 2, 1997, pp. 285–320.
Harris, Cheryl I. "Whiteness as Property." *Harvard Law Review*, vol. 106, no. 8, June 1993, pp. 1709–91.
Harris, Violet J. "Race Consciousness, Refinement, and Radicalism: Socialization in *The Brownies' Book*." *Children's Literature Association Quarterly*, vol. 14, no. 4, 1989, pp. 192–96.
Herndon, Karlie. "'For Nursery Magic Is Very Strange and Wonderful': The Queer Space of the Nursery in *The Velveteen Rabbit*." *The Velveteen Rabbit at 100*, edited by Lisa R. Fraustino, UP of Mississippi, 2023, pp. 181–96.
Hinton, KaaVonia. "'Do You See a [Hu]man Sitting Here?' Signifying in *Monster*." *Critical Explorations of Young Adult Literature: Identifying and Critiquing the Canon*, edited by Victor Malo-Juvera and Crag Hill, Routledge, 2020, pp. 51–66.
Hinton, KaaVonia. "What Are These Biographies *Not* Saying? Colorblindness in Biographies about Oprah Winfrey?" *Children's Literature Association Quarterly*, vol. 46, no. 3, 2021, pp. 244–62.
Hinton-Johnson, KaaVonia. "Subverting Beauty Aesthetics in African American Young Adult Literature (AAYA)." *MultiCultural Review*, vol. 14, no. 2, 2005, pp. 28–35.
hooks, bell. "Representing Whiteness in the Black Imagination." *Displacing Whiteness: Essays in Social and Cultural Criticism*, edited by Ruth Frankenberg, Duke UP, 1997, pp. 165–79.
Johnson, Cassandra Y., and J. M. Bowker. "African American Wild Land Memories." *Environmental Ethics*, vol. 26, no. 1, 2004, pp. 57–75.
King, C. Richard, et al. *Animating Difference: Race, Gender, and Sexuality in Contemporary Films for Children*. Rowman & Littlefield, 2010.
Kory, Fern. "Once Upon a Time in Aframerica: The 'Peculiar' Significance of Fairies in the *Brownies' Book*." *Children's Literature*, vol. 29, no. 1, 2001, pp. 91–112.
Kuznets, Lois Rostow. *When Toys Come Alive*. Yale UP, 1994.
Lind, Emily R. M. "I Once Was Lost but Now I'm Found: Exploring the White Feminist." *Unveiling Whiteness in the Twenty-First Century: Global Manifestations, Transdisciplinary Interventions*, edited by Veronica Watson et al., Lexington Books, 2014, pp. 229–46. *ProQuest*, http://ebookcentral.proquest.com/lib/odu/detail.action?docID=4694671. Accessed 17 Jan. 2022.
Lipsitz, George. *The Possessive Investment in Whiteness: How White People Profit from Identity Politics*. Temple UP, 2018. *ProQuest*, http://ebookcentral.proquest.com/lib/odu/detail.action?docID=5425334. Accessed 19 Oct. 2021.

Morrison, Toni. *Playing in the Dark: Whiteness and the Literary Imagination.* Harvard UP, 1992.
Pollard, Scott T., and Kara K. Keeling. "Metamorphosis: The Disabled Toy Made 'Real' as an Eternally Abled Rabbit." *The Velveteen Rabbit at 100,* edited by Lisa R. Fraustino, UP of Mississippi, 2023, pp. 197–210.
Redmond, Sean. "The Whiteness of the *Rings.*" *The Persistence of Whiteness: Race and Contemporary Hollywood Cinema,* edited by Daniel Bernardi, Routledge, 2008, pp. 91–102.
Sammartino, Paige. "Boy Caretakers in Twentieth-Century Fairy Tales: *The Velveteen Rabbit* and *The Little Prince.*" *The Velveteen Rabbit at 100,* edited by Lisa R. Fraustino, UP of Mississippi, 2023, pp. 156–65.
Stovall, Tyler. *White Freedom: The Racial History of an Idea.* Princeton UP, 2021.
Taxel, Joel. "The American Revolution in Children's Fiction: An Analysis of Historical Meaning and Narrative Structure." *Curriculum Inquiry,* vol. 14, no. 1, 1984, pp. 7–55.
Thomas, Ebony Elizabeth. "We Have Always Dreamed of (Afro)Futures: *The Brownies' Book* and the Black Fantastic Storytelling Tradition." *Journal of the History of Childhood and Youth,* vol. 14, no. 3, 2021, pp. 393–412.
Williams, Raymond. *Marxism and Literature.* Oxford UP, 1977.
Yancy, George. "When Heaven and Earth Are Shaken to Their Foundations." *Unveiling Whiteness in the Twenty-First Century: Global Manifestations, Transdisciplinary Interventions,* edited by Veronica Watson et al., Lexington Books, 2014, pp. 195–210. *ProQuest,* http://ebookcentral.proquest.com/lib/odu/detail.action?docID=4694671. Accessed 15 Oct. 2021.

Editions of Margery Williams's *The Velveteen Rabbit*

Williams, Margery. 1922. *The Velveteen Rabbit: Or How Toys Become Real.* Illustrated by William Nicholson, Heinemann.
Williams, Margery. 1983. *The Velveteen Rabbit: Or How Toys Become Real.* 1922. Illustrated by Michael Hague, Henry Holt.
Williams, Margery. 2002. *Margery Williams' The Velveteen Rabbit, Or How Toys Become Real.* Illustrated by Steve Johnson and Lou Fancher, adapted by Lou Fancher, Atheneum.
Williams, Margery. 2011. *The Velveteen Rabbit: Or How Toys Become Real.* Illustrated by Gennady Spirin, Marshall Cavendish Corporation.
Williams Bianco, Margery. 2012. *The Velveteen Rabbit: Or How Toys Become Real.* Illustrated by Charles Santore, classic ed., Appleseed.
Williams, Margery. 2014. *The Velveteen Rabbit: Or How Toys Become Real.* Illustrated by William Nicholson, Doubleday.

About the Contributors

Kelly Blewett is assistant professor of English at Indiana University East, where she also directs the writing program, teaches graduate courses in writing pedagogy, and researches what makes good teaching work. She's been interested in children's literature since she interned for the children's book publisher Philomel (an imprint of Penguin Books USA). Her scholarship on children's literature has appeared in *The Lion and the Unicorn*, the *Los Angeles Review of Books*, and in radio pieces for Cincinnati NPR-affiliate WVXU.

Claudia Camicia is the president of the national cultural association Service Group for Youth Literature (Gruppo di Servizio per la letteratura giovanile), which aims, since 1977, to promote and disseminate knowledge, literacy, and readings/animation in the field of youth literature with a critical psycho-pedagogical approach. She is a member of the editorial board of the magazine *Pagine Giovani*. Her research interests include multiculturalism, Italian authors of children's literature, and reading promotion/mediation. Some recent publications are *I giornalini del Terzo Millennio* (Youth Magazines in the Third Millennium; 2017) and *Cipro e il fascino dei suoi percorsi narrativi* (Cyprus and the Charm of Its Narrative Paths; 2017).

Alisa Clapp-Itnyre is professor of English at Indiana University East in Richmond, Indiana, where she teaches children's literature, young adult literature, a Harry Potter seminar, and Victorian literature. She is the author of *Angelic Airs, Subversive Songs: Music as Social Discourse in the Victorian Novel* (2002) and *British Hymn Books for Children, 1800–1900: Re-Tuning the History of Childhood* (2016) and maintains a website on nineteenth-century children's music, www.soundingchildhood.org. She has also published on young adult novels about the Civil War, the Nancy Drew and Hardy Boys series, and the Disney princesses. Her current research is on the children's Band of Mercy animal-welfare movement of the late nineteenth century and Victorian/Edwardian children's diaries. Clapp-Itnyre chaired ChLA's Phoenix Picture-Book Committee (2016–2018) and cohosted the 2019 ChLA conference in Indianapolis.

Lisa Rowe Fraustino, a professor emeritus in the English Department at Eastern Connecticut State University, is the director of graduate programs in children's literature at Hollins University. There, she teaches a range of literature and creative writing courses and edits the journal *Children's Literature.* Her article "The Rights and Wrongs of Anthropomorphism," published in the award-winning volume *Ethics and Children's Literature* (2014), edited by Claudia Mills, won the 2016 ChLA Article Award. A volume of essays she coedited with Karen Coats, *Mothers in Children's and Young Adult Literature: From the Eighteenth Century to Postfeminism,* won the 2018 ChLA Edited Book Award. She has published a number of articles taking various critical approaches to mothers in literature for young people. Her critically acclaimed work as a creative writer includes *The Hole in the Wall,* winner of the 2010 Milkweed Prize for Children's Literature.

Elisabeth Graves has recently completed her BA in English at Eastern Connecticut State University. She is passionate about learning foreign languages and, for her final project as a senior, she wrote her own fictional memoir. In a children's literature class with Dr. Lisa Rowe Fraustino, she wrote a paper on Christian undertones in *The Miraculous Journey of Edward Tulane* and was invited to contribute her ideas to a chapter in this volume.

Karlie Herndon is an English literature PhD candidate at the University of Southern Mississippi. Her chapter in this volume is part of her dissertation project on the late Victorian nursery in British children's literature, in which she examines this specialized children's space using feminist and queer critical lenses. She has written on themes of food and sexuality in children's texts, female masculinity in young adult fantasy novels, and depictions of motherhood in various works.

KaaVonia Hinton is a professor in the Teaching and Learning Department at Old Dominion University and the author of several articles and books, including *Angela Johnson: Poetic Prose* (2006), *Integrating Multicultural Literature in Libraries and Classrooms in Secondary Schools* (2007), with Gail K. Dickinson, *Sharon M. Draper: Embracing Literacy* (2009), and *Young Adult Literature: Exploration, Evaluation and Appreciation,* 3rd ed. (2013), with Katherine T. Bucher. She is also the coeditor, with Lucy E. Bailey, of the book series Research in Life Writing and Education (Information Age Publishing).

Holly Blackford Humes is professor of English at Rutgers University-Camden, where she teaches and publishes literary criticism on American and children's literature. Her books include *Out of This World: Why Literature Matters to Girls* (2004), *Mockingbird Passing: Closeted Traditions and Sexual Curiosities in Harper*

Lee's Novel (2011), *The Myth of Persephone in Girls' Fantasy Literature* (2011), *Alice to Algernon: The Evolution of Child Consciousness in the Novel* (2018), and the edited volumes *100 Years of Anne with an 'e': The Centennial Study of Anne of Green Gables* (2009) and *Something Great and Complete: The Centennial Study of My Ántonia* (2018). Her next project is *The Animation Mystique: Sentient Toys, Puppets, and Automata in Literature and Film*.

Melanie Hurley is a PhD candidate in the Department of English at Memorial University of Newfoundland. In her dissertation, tentatively entitled "Cinderella: Disney's Foremost Postfeminine Icon," she analyzes how the Disney Princess™ brand evolved out of girl-power discourses of the 1990s. She uses Cinderella as a case study of how the significations of these popular icons shift and multiply through Disney's various princess-themed texts (e.g., animated and live-action films, picture books, and television series). Through her work on princesses, she has developed research interests in fairy tales, picture books, and girl-centered animation, both films and cartoon series. She has published in the journal *Artifact & Apparatus* and has two articles forthcoming in edited collections, *The 1980s Resurrected* and *Mythological Equines in Children's Literature*.

Kara K. Keeling serves as professor of English at Christopher Newport University in Newport News, Virginia, where she teaches courses on children's and young adult literature. She and Scott T. Pollard are the coauthors of *Table Lands: Food in Children's Literature* (2020) as well as a number of articles on food in the works of children's authors, such as Pamela Muñoz Ryan, Polly Horvath, Neil Gaiman, Beatrix Potter, and Maurice Sendak. They also coedited *Critical Approaches to Food in Children's Literature* (2009). With Marsha Sprague, she has also coauthored *Discovering a Voice: Engaging Adolescent Girls with Young Adult Literature* (2007).

Maleeha Malik teaches second grade at Friends School of Baltimore. As a veteran teacher, she is passionate about diversity, equity, and inclusion in literature for children. She has written on diversity and teaching for the Good Men Project. In 2019, she led a workshop at the People of Color Conference on South Asian characters in literature for children. Her upcoming picture book on vitiligo, *At Home in My Skin*, will be published by Lee & Low Publishing. Malik is pursuing her MFA in Children's Literature at Hollins University.

Claudia Mills is associate professor emerita of philosophy at the University of Colorado at Boulder and teaches regularly in the graduate programs in children's literature at Hollins University. The author of over sixty books for young readers, most recently *The Lost Language* (2021), she has also published scholarly articles on Laura Ingalls Wilder, Louisa May Alcott, Maud Hart Lovelace, Betty

MacDonald, Rosamond du Jardin, and Eleanor Estes, as well as an award-winning edited collection, *Ethics and Children's Literature* (2014).

Elena Paruolo, formerly affiliated with the University of Salerno–Italy, has contributed several essays on Joseph Conrad to specialist journals, among them *Joseph Conrad: Critical Assessments* (1992). In 2003, she was elected as a member of the scientific committee of the network Littératures d'enfance (LDE) of the AUF (Agence Universitaire de la Francophonie) and worked with them until December 2007. She is the author of a great number of essays on children's literature. She has published the volumes *Brave New Worlds: Old and New Classics of Children's Literatures* (2011), *Le Letterature per l'Infanzia: Ne parlano Peter Hunt, Jean Perrot, Dieter Richter, Jean Foucault, Anne Fine, Sandra Beckett* (2014), and *Il Pinocchio di Carlo Collodi e le sue riscritture in Italia e Inghilterra* (2017).

Scott T. Pollard is professor of English at Christopher Newport University. He and Kara K. Keeling cowrote *Table Lands: Food in Children's Literature* (2020) as well as numerous articles on food in the works of children's authors, such as Pamela Muñoz Ryan, Polly Horvath, Neil Gaiman, Beatrix Potter, and Maurice Sendak. They coedited *Critical Approaches to Food in Children's Literature* (2009). Pollard also coedited, with Margarita Marinova, Marinova's translation from the Russian of Mikhail Bulgakov's dramatic adaptation of *Don Quixote* (2014), and he edited a special volume of *Children's Literature Association Quarterly* on disability in 2013.

Jiwon Rim is a lecturer in the English Department at Seoul National University. Her PhD dissertation focused on the ethical, epistemological, and aesthetic construction of the "cute" stuffed animal in picture books for children. Her project aims to explain the puzzling coexistence of the heightened sensibility about individual animal suffering and the systematic exploitation of animal bodies en masse in our cultural present. Her areas of interest include animal studies, ethics of animal consumption, early twentieth-century Anglo-American culture, and children's picture books.

Paige Sammartino is an MA/MAT candidate in English at Salem State University. A former publishing professional, she also teaches children's literature and writing courses in the greater Boston area. Her research interests are the political underpinnings of children's fantasy novels, visual literacy, the multimodal reading experience of illustrated and graphic texts, and writing craft and technique. She has presented on the writings of Diana Wynne Jones, Antoine de Saint-Exupéry, and Jamaica Kincaid.

About the Contributors

Adrianna Zabrzewska is a Fulbright Scholar and feminist interdisciplinary researcher affiliated with the Institute of Philosophy and Sociology of the Polish Academy of Sciences (IFiS PAN). She has published on gender in American and Polish children's literature publishing (*International Research in Children's Literature*), feminist methodologies of children's literature research (*Avant*), and Adriana Cavarero's philosophy of voice (*Teksty Drugie*). Dr. Zabrzewska is also the coeditor of two sourcebooks: *Gender Quotas in the Post-Communist World: Voice of the Parliamentarians* (2020) and *Gender, Voice, and Violence in Poland: Women's Protests during the Pandemic* (2021), both from IFiS PAN Publishers. She has translated over two hundred children's books from English to Polish.

Wenduo Zhang received her MA in children's literature from Simmons University. Her recent publication is "Understanding Multi-World Metafiction through Place-Attachment: Base World, New World, and (In)Complete World in the Inkheart Trilogy" in *Places of Childhood Fancy: Essays on Space and Speculation in Children's Book Series* (2022), edited by Michael G. Cornelius and Marybeth Ragsdale-Richards. Her research interests include animal stories and anthropomorphized creatures in children's fiction and picture books, in particular from an eco-critical perspective.

Index

ableism, 197, 202–7
adaptations, 4; Enchantment Theatre of Philadelphia, 9; illustrations in, 41, 50–59; Italian versions, 130–52; Japanese version (Sakai), 114–28; Whiteness in, 112–13, 219–25
Adventures of Pinocchio, The (Collodi), 24, 69; *Le avventure di Pinocchio*, 131, 147–48, 150, 152
allegory, 7, 11, 64, 65, 66, 67, 68, 76n7, 172–73
Animal Land (Blount), 3, 7, 20n6
animation: film, 72; puppetry, 25–26, 28, 34; stop-motion, 27–28, 36; of toys, 66, 157, 162, 164, 199
anthropocene, 103, 108
anthropomorphism: and conceptual metaphor, 12; of Edward Tulane, 167, 174; in illustrations, 55, 57, 106, 117; and self-awareness, 158; of stuffed animals, 112n4; in *Toy Story*, 63, 72
anxiety, 23, 29, 30, 40, 45, 64–65, 93; existential, 69, 140; parental, 58; separation, 40, 50
Aristotle, 44, 82
authenticity, 24, 27, 29, 91, 97, 103–5, 108, 109–10
authority, 156–60, 163
avatar, 24, 32, 34–36
awards: in Japan, 114; Lewis Carroll Shelf Award, 4; Newbery Honor (Williams for *Winterbound*), 5

Balint, Michael, 169, 178
Bang, Molly, 41, 42, 43, 44, 118, 122, 124
Barad, Karen, 91–101
Baudrillard, Jean, 24, 25

Bechtel, Louise Seaman, 6, 7
becoming Real, 3, 23, 31, 44, 65–66, 150, 160, 162, 170; by mattering, 98; through moral status, 79–81; as narrative prosthesis, 202; ontologically, 64, 68–69, 90–96; through play, 9, 25, 30; through redemption, 167, 194–95. *See also* love: made Real by; REAL; Realness; virtual reality
Befana's Toyshop, The (Rodari, *La freccia azzurra*), 147, 150–52
Bentham, Jeremy, 80
Bernstein, Robin, 213, 214, 215, 218, 219, 220, 221, 222, 224
betrayal, 4, 5, 9, 30, 40, 44, 100, 205
Bianco, Pamela, 6–7
Bianco, Margery. *See* Williams, Margery
Blackford, Holly, 12, 157–58, 189, 190, 192
Blount, Margaret, 3, 7, 20n6
Boy (character), 4, 5, 7, 9, 10, 12, 40–41
— caretaking, 157–64
— illness, 191–93, 205
— normative, 199, 214
— parental, 64, 158
— privileged Victorian, 185–87
— puppetmaster, 24, 26–27
— relationship with Rabbit, 29–36, 91, 168–70, 202–4, 206, 207; love, 82, 83, 84, 85, 87, 110; play, 96–97, 121, 124; queer performativity, 187–90; sleeping together, 69, 79, 95, 120
— representation in illustrations: absence (Nicholson), 39–41, 45, 212; presence in adaptations, 50–58, 213, 220–25; Sakai, 120–22, 124–27
— rewritten as a girl, 135–39
— White, 216–25

Brownies' Book, The, 211, 215, 216, 225
Buell, Lawrence, 115–16, 119, 124
Butler, Francelia, 9–10
Butler, Judith, 33

Camus, Albert, 63, 70, 71–73
capitalism, 27, 103–4, 108, 212
caretaking, 156–58, 160–62
caring, 81, 82
child development, 4, 10, 12, 24, 58, 64, 65, 140, 150, 178, 189, 192
Christianity, 11, 91, 172–76, 194–95, 223. *See also* love: Christian
Christmas, 108, 167, 173, 186; illustrated scene (Massini), 56; in Italian versions, 134, 136, 138, 144–45; in *The Skin Horse*, 207–8; stocking illustrations, 39, 43, 45, 51–52
class, 28, 51, 167, 212, 217, 209; lower, 29; middle, 26, 53, 56, 181, 182, 216; upper, 166, 214; working, 25
Collodi, Carlo, 24, 69, 131, 147, 150
colorblindness, 214–16, 220, 225
commodified animals, 34, 103–4, 105–6, 109–11
commodity, 24, 26, 29, 30, 36, 107, 109
counterpoint, 116–17, 119, 127–28

Daniels, Steven V.: anxiety, 29, 30, 65; guilt of abandonment, 33; Kleinian psychoanalytic reading, 10, 40–41, 44, 64, 98, 201; parental absence, 56, 158; passivity, 27
death, 5, 35, 68, 69, 91, 98, 193, 206, 224; of Christ, 99; dying, 11, 81; in *Edward Tulane*, 171, 175, 176; love and, 10, 40, 177; in *Pinocchio*, 150; reality of, 25, 27, 64; in *The Skin Horse*, 208; in *Toy Story*, 70, 71, 72; trash as, 73, 75
de la Mare, Walter, 6
DeLuca, Geraldine, 9
denaturalization, 103–7, 109
deus ex machina, 12, 23, 24, 30, 111
DiCamillo, Kate, 166–78
dignity, 78–79, 85, 193
disability, 81, 131, 139, 197–208
doctor (character), 5, 69, 98; as authority, 159, 214, 216, 224–25; in illustrations, 53, 58, 122, 222; and medicalization of narrative, 205; queer reading of, 192
dolls. *See* toys

domestic: caregiving, 158, 159; sphere, 181, 184; stories, 52, 185
domestication: of animals, 23, 35; of toys, 28, 29, 34, 36, 161; as translation modality, 132, 136, 138, 145
Du Bois, W. E. B., 215

ecosystem, 115–20, 127–28
Edward Tulane (character), 166–78
Eiss, Harry E., 6, 8, 182, 216, 217
empathy, 58, 134, 167, 168, 170, 172
environmentally oriented text, 115–16
ethics, 80, 82, 85, 104, 105, 111, 116, 128
existentialism, 24, 62, 63, 69–75, 96, 140

Fairy (character), 27, 30, 35, 81, 83, 99, 204; in illustrations, 39, 43, 52, 53, 56, 125, 136, 222–23; magic, 85, 111, 150, 151, 164, 177, 194, 214; as "pity Fairy," 206–7; in translation to Italian, 142, 145; as White, 212, 213, 219
fairy tale(s), 156–58, 159, 160, 164; in *The Brownies' Book*, 211; metamorphosis, 150, 152; as metaphor in *Edward Tulane*, 174; popularity in Italy, 131, 135, 136, 138, 139–40
Fancher, Lou, 212–13, 219, 222–24
Flavia and the Velveteen Rabbit (Weedn and Weedn), 131–32, 135–36, 138, 142
Flora (Bianco and de la Mare), 6
Frankfurt, Harry, 84, 85
Freud, Sigmund, 10, 25, 27, 39, 40, 50
full moral standing. *See* moral status
foreignization, 132, 136, 142, 145

Galbraith, Mary, 11, 200
game, 24, 34, 36, 124, 185; in bed, 170, 189, 192
Garland-Thomson, Rosemarie, 197, 208n2
Gates, Henry Louis, Jr., 211
gender, 51, 52, 157, 161, 162, 182–87; appropriateness, 55, 191; fluidity, 58, 171; identity, 192; performativity, 33; role reversal, 56, 158; socialization, 217; transformation, 138
Goffman, Erving, 198–99, 203, 207
Green, Michael, 53
Guroian, Vigen, 11, 173

Hague, Michael, 52–53, 212, 213, 219–23
Hannah's Night (Sakai), 120–21

Haraway, Donna, 97
Harris, Violet, 211, 212, 214, 215, 216, 225
hierarchy, 25, 28, 90, 92, 122, 198, 201, 213, 214
Hoffmann, E. T. A., 25, 27
Honeyman, Susan, 11
hope, 83, 87, 111, 174–75, 177; in *Toy Story* films, 63, 70, 72, 73; in *WALL-E*, 74

Ibatoulline, Bagram, 166, 172
illustrations: in *Edward Tulane* (Ibatoulline), 167, 172, 174, 176; Italian versions, 132, 134, 136, 138, 140, 145, 147; Nicholson's originals, 38–50, 111, 123, 186, 212; in *Peter Rabbit* (Potter), 103, 105–7; Sakai's version, 114–28; subsequent adaptations, 41, 50–59
immortality, 11, 69, 81, 164, 173
innocence, 208, 220, 221, 222, 223; innocent play, 105, 188, 203, 218; racial, 213, 214, 215; sexual, 181, 183, 189

Jacobson, Kirsten, 12, 29, 40, 41, 158, 177, 201, 204, 205
Jaworska, Agnieszka, 80, 81
Johnson, Steve, 212–13, 219, 222–24
Jorgensen, David, 53, 56

Kant, Immanuel, 78–80, 85
Kellehear, Allan, 10, 40, 41, 58, 101, 177, 178
Kincaid, James R., 184
Klein, Melanie, 10, 40, 64, 98
knowing in being, 93
Kory, Fern, 211
Kuznets, Lois Rostow, 10–11, 28, 35, 75n4, 150, 183, 189, 193, 206, 216, 218; anxiety, 65; deus ex machina, 23; gender modeling, 161, 167; guilt of abandonment, 35; magic metamorphosis, 64, 66, 69, 172, 194

Lewis, David, 115–16, 118
Little Prince, The (Saint-Exupéry), 156–59, 162–64
love
— Christian, 99, 167, 172–76, 194–95
— made Real by, 23, 66, 90, 98, 158, 160, 163, 170, 201, 214; and abandonment, 4, 5, 111, 206–7; personhood, 78–87

Mad at Mommy (Sakai), 120, 122
Mascot, The (Starewicz), 26, 28
Massini, Sarah, 56–58
materiality, 91, 92, 98, 100–101, 213, 219, 220
mattering, 98
McNulty, Faith, 4–5, 10, 40, 50, 100, 205
media, 24, 27, 28, 29, 33, 145–47
metamorphic tradition, 11, 64, 69, 151, 152
metamorphosis, 66, 69, 150, 152, 172, 190, 194, 197, 207
Miller, Bertha Mahony, 8, 38
Miller's Antiques Encyclopedia, 186
Miraculous Journey of Edward Tulane, The (DiCamillo), 166–78
Misner, Jared, 3, 7
Mitchell, David T., 198, 200, 201, 207
mobility, 26, 32, 35, 81, 199, 203–5, 208
Moebius, William, 38, 41, 42, 45, 58
Moore, Anne Carroll, 4, 5, 6, 7, 8, 38, 39
moral status, 78–81
Mukerji, Dhan Gopal, 8
Myers, Mitzi, 11

Nana (character), 31, 79, 84, 168, 206; feminine influence, 184, 187–88; hierarchical authority, 214; in illustrations, 55–56, 57–58, 122, 212, 222; in Italian translation, 142; signifier of White privilege, 218, 223–25
narrative prosthesis, 198, 200, 201–3, 207, 208
Natov, Roni, 168, 169, 171
natural: animal, 11, 24, 44, 103–11, 189; instinct, 35; as real, 85; scientist, 95; sexuality, 192–93; Whiteness, 213, 215–16, 225
nature: and commodification of animal bodies, 104, 107, 108; illustrated by Nicholson, 45; illustrated by Sakai, 115–16, 119–22, 124–25, 127–28; as play space, 157, 162–63; in Rabbit-land, 111; Rabbit's detachment from, 34; and Realness, 23, 110, 214; Whiteness in, 221, 222
Nelson, Victoria, 25
Nicholson, William: criticism, 40–41; Fairy depiction, 111, 219, 223, 225; historical background, 38–39, 41; and race, 212; subsequent illustrators compared to,

51–52, 53, 58, 123, 220; visual storytelling focus on Rabbit, 42–50
Nikolajeva, Maria, 90, 116–17, 122, 127
Nodelman, Perry: picture-book theory, 42, 44, 50–51, 52, 53, 58, 122, 123; Reader's Choice Survey, 10
normativity: ableist, 197–98, 205, 206; gender/sexual, 182–83, 186, 187, 192–93, 195; Whiteness, 213–15
nursery
— bed, 188–89, 192
— magic, 177, 186, 190, 202; as Christian metaphor, 173; Fairy, 7, 85, 194; Italian translation of, 142; as narrative prosthesis, 207; and Realness, 34, 206
— queer reading of, 187–95
— setting, 92–93, 161, 168, 193, 195, 203–4, 224
— social hierarchy, 92, 201, 214
— toys, 27, 90, 91, 109, 158, 186; in illustrations, 117, 223; and stigma, 198–201; as trash, 69; as Williams's inspiration, 9
— Victorian, 181–87, 190–92, 217

obsolescence, 63, 64, 69, 70, 73
Oittinen, Riitta, 132, 41, 44, 50, 119
ontology, 63–65, 68–69, 92–96, 199
op de Beeck, Nathalie, 41, 44, 50, 119
otherness, 11, 92, 98, 115, 128, 132, 168, 191, 204

performativity: Baradian, 92–96; queer, 187–90
personhood, 78–82, 86, 87
Peter Rabbit, 103, 106–7, 166, 172
philosophy: new materialist, 91–93, 100; of personhood, 78–88; Platonic, 12, 62–75
Pinocchio (Collodi), 24, 26, 32–33, 69, 131, 147–50, 152
pity, 50, 99, 206–7
Pixar, 62–64, 69, 70, 73, 75
Plato, 62–69, 75; Platonic ideal, 27, 63, 64, 68, 69, 99; *Republic*, 63, 64, 65, 66, 67, 68; *Symposium*, 63, 68
play, 9, 29–30, 96, 98, 99, 105, 111, 134, 182, 201; bed-play, 187–89, 192, 193–95; caretaking, 160–64; as game, 36; in illustrations, 51, 52, 54, 57, 220–21, 222; in Italian translation, 142; mobility and, 203; in nature, 120, 121–22, 124, 127, 157; performative, 33, 34; puppet, 25; social hierarchy of, 90; with toys, 69, 73, 92, 93; Victorian, 184, 185, 186–87; White privileged, 217, 218
postwar context, 7, 200
Potter, Beatrix, 103–8, 110
Potter, Walter, 103–5, 107–8, 110
puppets, 24–32, 34–35, 150, 152, 176

queer reading, 181–95

Rabbit (character)
— object: under capitalism, 27; of child caretaking, 157, 163; love, 29–30, 84–85, 169; material, 93; medical, 205; performing, 28, 32; position, 12; puppetry, 26, 31; replaceable, 5, 69, 110; transitional, 11, 40, 151; waste, 63
— subject, 11, 12, 26, 80, 93, 158, 197, 204
Rabbit-land, 11, 99, 108, 111, 164, 177
"Rabbits' Village School, The," 104–5, 106, 107, 111
race, 51, 211–12, 214–17, 221
Raiten-D'Antonio, Toni, 132, 142, 145
rationality, 79–80, 101n1
REAL, 31, 66, 79, 81, 160. *See also* becoming Real; love: made Real by; Realness; virtual reality
Realness, 67, 68, 75, 82–83, 85–86. *See also* becoming Real; love: made Real by; REAL; virtual reality
redemption, 91, 100, 167, 171, 173–77, 193–95
Reimer, Mavis, 122
representationalism, 92, 97
Rodari, Gianni, 131, 139, 140, 151–52
romanticism, 25, 26, 111, 221

Saint-Exupéry, Antoine de, 156–58
Sakai, Komoko, 114–28
Santore, Charles, 56, 212, 213, 219–20, 222–24
scarlet fever, 12, 35, 110, 163, 225; and disability, 205; and doctor's orders, 5, 69, 98, 192, 225; in illustrations, 221, 222; in Italian translation, 138, 142, 152
Schindler, S. D., 53
Scott, Carole, 116–17, 127
Sedgwick, Eve Kosofsky, 183, 188, 189
selective tradition, 211–25

self-help books, 4
Sendak, Maurice, 44, 50, 51–52
sentience, 24, 26, 27, 62, 94, 96; in illustrations, 117; and moral standing, 80; in *Toy Story*, 63, 72, 74
sentimentality, 4–5, 8–9, 12, 29, 44, 191, 207
Shershow, Scott Cutler, 25, 28, 29
signifying, 211
simulacra, 24–25, 27–28, 30, 31–32, 33–34, 35–36, 199, 202
simulation. *See* simulacra
Sisyphus, 63, 70–72
Skin Horse (character), 3, 9, 26, 27, 92, 93–94, 160, 169, 170, 182; disabled, 201–3, 204, 206; in illustrations by Nicholson, 43; in illustrations by Sakai, 117–20, 124; as influencer, 29; manufactured from horse skin, 128n3, 186–87; and personhood, 80, 81–82, 85, 86, 87; prophetic, 172; in *The Skin Horse*, 207–8; Socratic, 66–68; Williams's inspiration, 6
Skin Horse, The (Williams and Bianco), 7, 207–8
Smuts, Aaron, 82, 84
Snyder, Sharon L., 198, 200, 201, 207
Socrates, 63, 65–68
Spielberg, Steven, 24, 27
Spirin, Gennady, 212–13, 219–24
Spitz, Ellen Handler, 9
Starewicz, Ladislas, 26, 28
stigma: of disability, 198–204, 207; of otherness, 92

Tale of Peter Rabbit, The (Potter), 10, 103, 105–7, 111, 112n5
taxidermy, 104–5, 112n2
tear (Rabbit's real), 7, 26, 32, 99, 111, 177; precursor in *The Mascot* (Starewicz), 26, 28; queer, 193–94; of self-pity, 34, 206–7
technology: art reproduction, 50, 56; and domination of animal bodies, 105, 106, 108, 109, 110; Italian app, 147; stop-motion animation, 27–28
Thompson, Pat, 56
Timothy (character), 91, 200, 214, 187
toys
— china dog, 69, 79, 84, 109, 138, 166, 168, 187, 190, 218
— china rabbit, 166, 167, 168, 179, 171, 173, 176; Edward Tulane, 166–78
— doll(s): and class distinctions, 167; and gender modeling, 161, 171; mender (in *Edward Tulane*), 176–77; as simulacra, 25; in *Toy Story*, 70–71
— gender-coded, 29, 161, 186–87, 217
— stand-ins for children, 12, 94, 142, 150, 157–58, 178, 189, 214, 224
— *See also* nursery: toys
toy stories, 9, 11, 24, 28, 32, 34, 69; philosophical, 62–64, 73–75; *When Toys Come Alive* (Kuznets), 10, 23, 75n4, 167; as Williams's inspiration, 6, 7
Toy Story, 28, 29, 62–64, 69–75
transformation, 69, 151, 157, 160; Christian, 172; criticism, 5, 40, 64–65, 99; through disability, 207; Edward Tulane's, 177; gender, 138; hierarchical, 214; in illustrations, 39, 42, 44, 45, 50, 58, 126; metamorphic, 152; to Real, 23, 35, 63, 85, 164
transitional object, 11, 29–30, 40, 151
translation, 114, 125, 130–50
trash, 53, 62–64, 68–69, 71, 73–75, 171, 176

value (importance), 27, 72, 78, 92, 140; commodity/market, 27, 107, 109; hierarchical, 198; inherent, 80; love and, 82–85, 157; and personhood, 79, 193
values (standards), 32, 36, 142, 146, 200, 212, 215, 217
Velveteen Principles, The (Raiten-D'Antonio), 4, 130, 132, 142, 143, 145
Velveteen Rabbit, The
— author biography. *See* Williams, Margery
— characters. *See* Boy; doctor; Fairy; Nana; Rabbit; Skin Horse; Timothy
— history, 3–5, 38–40; subsequent editions, 50–59, 219–25
— scholarship, 8–12, 40
virtual reality, 23, 24, 25, 29, 34–35, 36
visual storytelling
— narrative moments, 39, 41
— "picture sentence," 42
— plot sequencing through images: Boy's story (subsequent adaptations), 50–59; Rabbit's story (Nicholson), 43–50

— Sakai: characterization through color and light, 116–22; distance and framing perspectives, 125–28
von Kleist, Heinrich, 25, 26

WALL-E, 63, 70, 73–75
Warner, Marina, 9, 152
Weales, Gerald, 52, 99
Weedn, Flavia, 131–32, 135–35
Weedn, Lisa, 131–32, 135–35
Whiteness, 211–25; Critical Whiteness studies, 213
Williams, Margery: biography, 5–8, 147, 182; family, 5–6; professional reputation, 8; writing philosophy, 8
Williams, Raymond, 211–12
Wilson, Katherine, 55–56
Winterbound (Williams), 5, 7
World War I, 6, 8, 215

www.ingramcontent.com/pod-product-compliance
Lightning Source LLC
Chambersburg PA
CBHW022006220426
43663CB00007B/977